T0360736

Strong Security Governance through Integration and Automation

Strong Security Governance through Integration and Automation

A Practical Guide to Building an Integrated GRC Framework for Your Organization

Priti Sikdar

CRC Press
Taylor & Francis Group
Boca Raton London

CRC Press is an imprint of the
Taylor & Francis Group, an **informa** business

First edition published 2022
by CRC Press
6000 Broken Sound Parkway NW, Suite 300, Boca Raton, FL 33487–2742

and by CRC Press
2 Park Square, Milton Park, Abingdon, Oxon, OX14 4RN

© 2022 Taylor & Francis Group, LLC

CRC Press is an imprint of Taylor & Francis Group, LLC

Reasonable efforts have been made to publish reliable data and information, but the author and publisher cannot assume responsibility for the validity of all materials or the consequences of their use. The authors and publishers have attempted to trace the copyright holders of all material reproduced in this publication and apologize to copyright holders if permission to publish in this form has not been obtained. If any copyright material has not been acknowledged please write and let us know so we may rectify in any future reprint.

Except as permitted under US Copyright Law, no part of this book may be reprinted, reproduced, transmitted, or utilized in any form by any electronic, mechanical, or other means, now known or hereafter invented, including photocopying, microfilming, and recording, or in any information storage or retrieval system, without written permission from the publishers.

For permission to photocopy or use material electronically from this work, access www.copyright.com or contact the Copyright Clearance Center, Inc. (CCC), 222 Rosewood Drive, Danvers, MA 01923, 978–750–8400. For works that are not available on CCC please contact mpkbookspermissions@tandf.co.uk

Trademark notice: Product or corporate names may be trademarks or registered trademarks and are used only for identification and explanation without intent to infringe.

Library of Congress Cataloging-in-Publication Data

Names: Sikdar, Priti, author.
Title: General strong security governance through integration and automation : a practical
    guide to building an integrated GRC framework for your organization / Priti Sikdar.
Description: First edition. | Boca Raton : CRC Press, 2022. | Includes bibliographical
    references and index.
Identifiers: LCCN 2021050181 | ISBN 9780367862770 (hardback) | ISBN 9781032139012
    (paperback) | ISBN 9781003018100 (ebook)
Subjects: LCSH: Information technology—Management | Knowledge management. |
    Information resources. | Strategic planning.
Classification: LCC HD30.2 .S569 2022 | DDC 658.4/038—dc23/eng/20211015
LC record available at https://lccn.loc.gov/2021050181

ISBN: 978-0-367-86277-0 (hbk)
ISBN: 978-1-032-13901-2 (pbk)
ISBN: 978-1-003-01810-0 (ebk)

DOI: 10.1201/9781003018100

Typeset in Times
by Apex CoVantage, LLC

Love of elder sisters knows no words; it is not memories or memento or any written proof. It runs as one blood and beats with our pulse.

I dedicate this book to my three sisters Smita, Chaula, and Chetna,

Contents

Preface

My inspiration for this book, *A Strong Security Governance Through Automation and Integration*, has been the word 'fatigue', which is attached to GRC audits nowadays. Take the instance of an organization that has ISO 27001, Payment Card Industry Data Security Standard (PCI DSS), General Data Protection Regulations (GDPR), and ISO 22301 compliances for certification. Not only the pain of meeting compliances is there but the pain of attending to multiple assessments/audits can consume a lot of time and efforts. Over the years of consulting for these companies, I realized that these compliances or standards have a lot of controls that are common. After all, global best practices in common areas cannot differ much – hence the idea of having organizations build up an integrated framework as a 'baseline' of controls can be implemented by the risk and compliance team and monitored with the help of automated dashboards.

Security has become a buzzword of the 21st century. With business moving the global way, legal and regulatory norms of each country need to be considered by the compliance team. The European Union came up with the GDPR; California Privacy Act was imposed; and there were a number of financial and regulatory compliances that made way for security standards like NIST, ISO 27001, and ISO 31000. Again, Service Organization Controls (SOC 2 Type 1 and 2) replaced the original SAS 70 provisions. This covers the third- and fourth-party involvement of service providers to the organizations. Organizations have to choose the Trust Service Criteria from:

- Confidentiality
- Processing integrity
- Availability
- Security
- Privacy

A certified public accountant (CPA) can test the controls at the service organization and certify the report of compliance for SOC2 Type 1 for design of controls and Type 2 for efficiency of controls implemented for a minimum period of six months.

Building a proprietary compliance infrastructure with a baseline to cover controls from all standards, laws, and regulatory requirements applicable to the organization will ensure that compliance is assured. Monitoring and tying up with an application for monitoring via visual aids such as dashboards will facilitate prompt identification of deviations, and this approach will definitely take away audit fatigue by encouraging integrated audits. This increases the speed of compliance and reduces redundant processes, hence leading to cost economy to some extent. The book is lucid, and at different places, professionals will get a hint to integrate compliances and integrate the audit process.

Finally, I want to thank my friends Swati Phadke and Preeti Sharma for helping me with edit and validation and my son Kunal and daughter Saloni for their everlasting support throughout my writing and helping make the diagrams for the book.

Business Impact of Emerging Technologies and Trends

1

INTRODUCTION

Rapid advance of technology is here to stay. More and more businesses that fail to adapt will find themselves left behind, while the savvy ones that learn to keep up to date will reap the rewards. It is not necessary to rebuild from scratch. Businesses just have to understand how they can leverage technology to align their business processes to it in a more optimized way so that they reap benefits of cost and efficiency. Success of a business model depends on the linkage of business strategy and objectives, aligned with information technology strategy and organizational infrastructure.

There has been a revolutionary change in the use of technology and its manifold applications in making business smooth and transgressing global boundaries. There is a phenomenal growth in both the digitized and digital environment. Markets have now expanded from local to international, customers do online purchases, and logistics have grown exponentially to meet the delivery needs of online businesses.

Technology has invaded every nook and corner of modern living. Devices such 'Alexa' given by Amazon and Google 'Home' have been unique examples of artificial intelligence–based entertainment and information. It would be good to look at some of the emerging technologies that are a driving force for businesses today. Warren Tucker, PwC Partner (UK), has identified emerging technologies in his publication www.pwc.co.uk/services/consulting/technology/insights/eight-emerging-technologies-learn-to-love.html) as under-

Artificial Intelligence

Artificial intelligence (AI) is a set of software services that provide solutions to learn and store knowledge, undertake analysis, identify patterns and make recommendations, sense and interpret the external world, and interact using natural language. A unique example is that of neural networks used to identify patterns and report unusual behavior in systems to detect errors and frauds faced by the banking sector. The financial sector uses real-time reporting and processing of large volume of data to make important decisions. AI-enabled systems are used to get accurate and efficient results. This has helped financial companies to implement machine learning, algorithmic trading, chatbots, automation of processes, etc.

Technologies such as voice recognition and facial recognition effectively use AI for authenticating users. AI is also used in smart homes to bring in home surveillance from office and hence secure one's loved ones. Other examples include face recognition at passport control, financial fraud detection, virtual assistants on your smartphone, etc.

Augmented Reality

Augmented reality (AR) is a multisensory interactive experience of the real-world environment. The experience is woven with the physical environment in such a way that it seems to be a part of the real world. A common example would be looking at a building with an AR device and seeing its historical information superimposed via computer-generated graphics. Content in multimedia format is integrated into a real-time learning environment, popularly with scannable markers embedded in flashcards (Figure 1.1).

It is a visual or audio 'overlay' on the physical world that uses contextualized digital information to augment the user's real-world view. AR-enabled smart glasses help warehouse workers fulfill orders with precision, airline manufacturers assemble planes, and electrical workers make repairs. The power of bringing information to the point of action in a seamless, unobtrusive manner is undeniable. This blending of the

FIGURE 1.1 Augmented reality example.

physical and virtual worlds is cracking open a new realm for businesses across the board to explore.

AR is likely to change the way we work. It has been used in theme park planning, magazines, toy products, and military. AR application can be witnessed by retail business wanting to improve customer experience by using AR. This serves to bridge the gap between customer preferences and provide improved ways to shop. For instance, AR in digital clothing stores could enable users to see the product in a 3D format. A manufacturing company could introduce AR for its product designers, who will be able to quickly iterate on designs and model them in a 3D space

Blockchain Technology

A blockchain is a type of database – a collection of information that is stored electronically on a computer system (Figure 1.2). Information, or data, in databases is typically structured in table format to allow for easier searching and filtering for specific information. What is the difference between someone using a spreadsheet to store information rather than a database?

A key difference between a typical database and a blockchain is the way the data is structured. A blockchain collects information together in groups, also known as blocks, which hold sets of information. Blocks have certain storage capacities and, when filled, are chained onto the previously filled block, forming a chain of data known as the

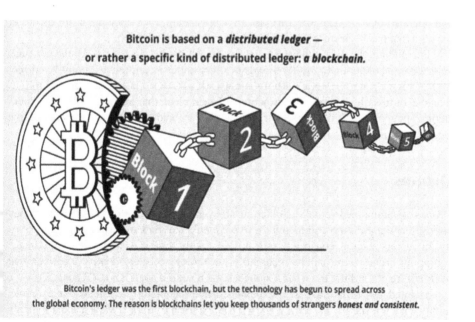

FIGURE 1.2 Blockchain technology.

'blockchain'. All new information that follows the freshly added block is compiled into a newly formed block that will then also be added to the chain once filled.

A database structures its data into tables, whereas a blockchain, like its name implies, structures its data into chunks (blocks) that are chained together. This makes it appear so that all blockchains are databases but not all databases are blockchains. This system also inherently makes an irreversible timeline of data when implemented in a decentralized nature. When a block is filled, it is set in stone and becomes a part of this timeline. Each block in the chain is given an exact time stamp when it is added to the chain.

For the purpose of understanding blockchain, it is instructive to view it in the context of how it has been implemented by Bitcoin. Like a database, Bitcoin needs a collection of computers to store its blockchain. For Bitcoin, this blockchain is just a specific type of database that stores every Bitcoin transaction ever made. In Bitcoin's case, and unlike most databases, these computers are not all under one roof, and each computer or group of computers is operated by a unique individual or group of individuals.

Imagine that a company owns a server comprising 10,000 computers with a database holding all of its client's account information. This company has a warehouse containing all of these computers under one roof and has full control of each of these computers and all the information contained within them. Similarly, Bitcoin consists of thousands of computers, but each computer or group of computers that hold its blockchain is in a different geographic location, and they are all operated by separate individuals or groups of people. These computers that make up Bitcoin's network are called nodes.

In this model, Bitcoin's blockchain is used in a decentralized way. However, private, centralized blockchains, where the computers that make up its network are owned and operated by a single entity, do exist. In a blockchain, each node has a full record of the data that has been stored on the blockchain since its inception.

For Bitcoin, the data is the entire history of all Bitcoin transactions. If one node has an error in its data, it can use thousands of other nodes as a reference point to correct itself. This way, no one node within the network can alter information held within it. Because of this, the history of transactions in each block that make up Bitcoin's blockchain is irreversible. It is possible for a blockchain to hold a variety of information like legal contracts, state identifications, or a company's product inventory.

Drones

Drones are unmanned vehicles. Sometimes they are described as miniature robots, they are used in the military, commercial, and personal areas and are increasing in popularity. In sectors such as construction or utilities, with large sites and assets to manage, equipping drones with pattern recognition technology to help identify locations that may require closer human inspection is just one potential application (Figure 1.3).

Oil and gas firms have also exploited drone technology to check, for example, remote pipeline networks. In the COVID-19 pandemic, drones were used to supply medicines to some remote locations in a speedy manner. Drones have reduced the need for manual intervention, especially in surveillance and monitoring applications.

FIGURE 1.3 Drones technology.

Use of drones for commercial purposes: 'Commercial use' means that there is money consideration involved with the use of drones.

Some examples:

- taking aerial photos for a video production company;
- making a promotional video for your business;
- companies that need to view sites that are difficult to access;
- using drones for site inspection.

Applying for a Drone License for Commercial Use

If you use a drone commercially, you need to take some permissions/licenses. Drone owners have to procure a driver's license even if it is a personal drone and even for a single use of the drone. The user shall have to follow the same rules as applicable to recreational uses of drones.

In sectors such as construction or utilities, with large sites and assets to manage, equipping drones with pattern recognition technology to help identify locations that may require closer human inspection is just one potential application. Oil and gas firms have also exploited drone technology to check, for example, remote pipeline networks. This reduces the need for engineers to manually check these locations and can increase the frequency of checking.

Internet of Things

There is potential to link not only consumer appliances to the web but also a larger number of industries connected under the Internet of Things (IoT). Connecting physical assets to digital networks generates large volumes of data, enabling the potential for unprecedented levels of insight, prediction, and real-time control over production processes. The ability to track, measure, and monitor in real time opens up the scope for companies offering involving such aspects as part of the service.

Robotics

Robots have been used in car assembly for a long time. But its increased application in cruise ships, in care homes, and at tourist attractions is growing. Software robots are being used at help desks for query resolution (called 'chatbots' in many businesses) and for automating back-office operations, especially in banks. In financial services, robotic process automation (RPA) has helped banks and credit unions accelerate growth by executing pre-programmed rules across a range of structured and unstructured data. This intelligent automation gives processes the power to learn from prior decisions and data patterns to make decisions by themselves – reducing the cost of administrative and regulatory processes by at least 50% while improving quality and speed (Figure 1.4).

FIGURE 1.4 Robotics used in business.

RPA in banking also simplifies compliance by keeping detailed logs of automated processes, automatically generating the reports an auditor needs to see, and eliminating human error. Since it is intuitive and easy to reconfigure software robots at any time, tweaking processes to fit new or updated regulations are never difficult. A point to note is that robots, drones and autonomous cars/vehicles use artificial intelligence to perform automatic functions.

3D Printing

It is being used as a prototyping tool and to support the manufacture of certain precision components and in some cases to develop finished products – for example, hearing aids and dental braces. The intern application within an organization is to assist with design virtualization. For example, a consumer goods firm can test new packaging design in multiple locations. Challenges remain around printing methods, the software for product design, and whether different materials can be combined for use in printing more complex organic and metallic and combined components.

Virtual Reality

Virtual reality (VR) is a computer-generated environment with scenes and objects that appear to be real, making the user feel they are immersed in their surroundings. VR is commonly used in the entertainment and gaming industry and partly in the sports industry also. But the advantages and applicability of VR in industries has increased since the cost of development has decreased. Hence, VR is now opening huge possibilities in retail, healthcare, education, tourism, and journalism. This environment is perceived through a device known as a VR handset or helmet. VR allows one to immerse in video games as if they were one of the characters, assists in performing heart surgeries, or improves the quality of sports training to maximize performance.

Although this may seem extremely futuristic, it would be interesting to note that the first VR device was called 'Sensorama', a machine with a built-in seat that played 3D movies, gave off odors, and generated vibrations to make the experience as vivid as possible. Subsequent technological and software developments over the years brought with them a progressive evolution both in devices and in interface design.

Change in the Way Business Is Done

All the aforementioned emerging technologies have changed the way we do business. Technology has opened global doors, and seamless integration of organizations with common objectives and line of business is emerging at a fast rate. Information technology has served as an enabler in resolving business, economic, and social issues.

Products have become accessible over a wider geographical area, a digital culture, and sophisticated technology with many emerging technologies. This has transformed the way to do business. Outsourcing and connectivity have driven down costs and made technology affordable to all sizes of businesses. This is the reason that start-ups are adopting a digital business strategy.

Effective Communication Channels to Connect and to Share Information   In widely distributed business locations, technology makes connecting over different time zones and connecting over diversified range of products and services faster, easier, and more efficient. For communication, with applications like Slack, Zoom, Microsoft Teams, social media platforms, chatbots, and more being leveraged daily, there are choices for us to choose. Sales enablement provides the ability to track buyer–seller conversations and receive analytics based on user behaviors.

Deeper intelligence makes it easy to obtain customer information and use it to enhance customer experience. While messaging apps that make real-time communication possible were already mentioned as a negative, the truth is they also have an extremely high upside. Real-time communication lets employers and executives stay plugged in to everything that is going on with their team.

Technology enables businesses to mine into the customer information and create personalized messaging available. Automated communication means providing support to business and enhancing productivity through a better reach to customers. Using a variety of channels helps businesses boost marketing productivity and reach customers, as well. But one must use these formal and informal channels of communication carefully; otherwise, there is an exposure of losing the personal touch in customer relationships.

Use of Smart Devices Loaded with Appropriate Applications   Today, top executives run their business operations by the click of their fingers. Operations such as shipping, invoicing, sales promotion and content marketing are all enabled by smart devices. Mobiles have become universal. Customers use it for their personal purposes like grocery shopping and other retail purchases, to seek information, to sell their goods, to share their experiences about various products, and to provide real-time information. Technology helps us to be connected on a 24/7 basis and has blended with communication software to give alerts, set reminders of meetings, and many more things.

The Establishment of Paperless Office   A paperless system allows employees to instantly access the data they require and informs anyone who opens the document of any changes. By tracking changes and allowing multiple users to access workflow documents, the process is vastly improved – it is faster, more agile, and fewer mistakes are made. Paperless technology is even making headway into industries that rely heavily on paperwork, from healthcare to legal services; going paperless is one of the fastest and easiest ways to integrate technology into your workspace without making a huge investment.

Facilitating Remote Working   In the recent situation of the COVID-19 crisis, the business operations' continuity itself was at stake. People were not able to travel to their place of work, and due to the pandemic, lockdown was imposed in several countries for a prolonged stretch of time. Those organizations that did not view remote working favorably were also forced to make the transition; the concept of work from home was also accepted.

Companies had to quickly ensure that their teams had access to the right technology and infrastructure to support remote log-ins, the bandwidth to handle video conferencing, and project management tools so that teams could continue to work on projects and update status together as a team instead of working in silos. Empirical study has proved that remote working increases employee productivity, it saves costs in having elaborate offices and paying high rent, and it has cut carbon emissions, with less vehicles plying to and fro. Work from home culture employed with proper security policies have led to more agile, scalable organizations working seamlessly over global boundaries.

Cost of Acquiring and Running Software Has Decreased   The technology market has become affordable, cost of hardware and software is comparatively lower, and it is a buyer's market. The number of fresh professionals interested in technology development has increased manifold. Proliferation of user-friendly solutions at affordable rates and sometimes obtained free to use is the hallmark of this century. Software has multiplied human capabilities exponentially and facilitated the modern executive to do multitasking. Client-relationship management software is used by most businesses, and it allows them to keep track of an unlimited number of customer records.

Increased Collaboration   The inability to chat in the break room, walk down the hall to a coworker's office, or even gather together in a meeting room in front of a whiteboard has drastically increased the need for collaboration. Collaboration tools that companies have adopted are Google Drive/Docs, Slack, Microsoft SharePoint, and OneDrive, Monday.com, and many, many more. These simplify how we can work together for team discussions, file sharing, project collaboration, tasks, and storage. Alignment of people and goals is the primary responsibility for these tools, and they are here to help provide real-time insight into projects and help us become more efficient.

Some Prevalent Types of Computing

Cloud Computing   Cloud computing is defined as the utilization of computing services, i.e. software as well as hardware as a service, over a network. Typically, this network is the internet. Cloud computing offers three types of services:

    i. Infrastructure as a Service (IaaS),
   ii. Platform as a Service (PaaS), and
  iii. Software as a Service (SaaS).

Cloud technologies provide the foundation for becoming more agile, collaborative, and customer-focused. Cloud computing allows businesses to move some of their operations to third-party servers accessible via internet connectivity. Cloud technology makes it easier to store and retrieve data. Organizations can access everything, from SaaS to manage their workflow and processes to statistics and research data from their workstations. Cloud transition has allowed small- to medium-sized businesses access to resources that would have been cost-prohibitive for them in the past and cloud service providers take full responsibility for the security of the data on the cloud.

Cloud computing eases maintenance of systems since installation is not required on every end user machine. It reduces IT infrastructure costs and supports the concept of virtualization that enables server and storage devices to be used across the organization. But cloud computing has some security concerns related to privacy, compliance, legal, governance in security, etc. Use of cloud should be controlled to safeguard these concerns.

Cloud is becoming increasingly popular, with Dropbox, OneDrive, Facebook, Airbnb, Twitter, Uber, and many other on-demand computing and storage services. The use of cloud-based service providers is now common.

Mobile Computing   People and executives are always on the go. Business is so dynamic that senior executives like to control the business on their fingertips. Mobile applications loaded on smartphones, tablets, or other mobile devices enable this feature and functionality. They can be downloaded from various mobile operating systems like Apple, Blackberry, and Nokia, either as a free download or at a cost.

Touchscreens for User Interfaces   User interface has undergone a revolution since touchscreen capability has been introduced. Users interact with applications with a click without having to use any other handheld device like mouse with the introduction of touchscreen. Touchscreen feature is applied in smartphones, tablet, information kiosks, etc.

Offshoring Processing Work   Increased connectivity and reduction in the cost of communication like video conferencing and webinars has now made it possible for organizations to offshore their workforce and reap some economy as well as source people who do not live on the same continent and pay them online. Both large- and medium-sized organizations find the offshoring option advantageous because they have a wider talent pool to choose from and because they do not have to pay tax returns for the people who work in a different country.

Business Process Outsourcing   Business process outsourcing (BPO) involves contracting one or many front-end (customer-related) or back-end (finance, HR, accounting, etc.) activities within a company to a third-party service provider. The number of jobs within the BPO industry has increased exponentially in the last decade. BPO is one of the new faces in business environment.

Outsourcing has helped companies reduce their overhead expenses, improve productivity, shorten innovation cycles, encourage new market penetration, and improve customer experience. India has seen tremendous growth in the BPO industry within functions like customer care, finance/accounts, payroll, high-end financial services, and human resources.

Use of Analytics in Operations, Programming, and Related Disciplines   The field of analytics comprises a combination of programming, statistics, operations research, and related disciplines. Data analytics helps in analyzing data and finding data trends and patterns. Another analytics type is predictive analysis used to predict future events based on current and historic data. Data on social media is analyzed to understand customer feedback and preferences.

In the global competitive environment, innovation and process improvement are desired characteristics. Demand and supply are governed by customer needs, and there is always scope for fine-tuning and customization to keep the customer happy. A common example is during Christmas, the Barbie doll had many customized versions based on requirements from the children all across the globe.

Exports and imports form an integral part of international business. Some countries like the United States and the United Kingdom are heavily dependent for food grains, fruits, and vegetables on other countries. For software industry having global customers, licensing arrangements form a significant part; for the purpose of doing business strategic alliances, acquisitions and mergers are emerging as the new basis for business relationships.

Organizations nowadays spread their processing facilities according to the availability of raw materials. For example, Walmart sources its produce for its food sections from local farms that are near its warehouses. It saves transportation costs. Proximity to location is also preferred due to advantages in logistics as well as convenience experienced in geographic neighbors in terms of accepted practices and culture.

Along with ease of licenses for trade, small businesses can enter global markets through strategic alliances. Business models tend to be more flexible, and entities have complex organizational structures. This brings in the legislative complexities, and compliance with legal and regulatory provisions pertaining to all geographical locations where business is spread; this becomes challenging. With a rise in cross-border acquisitions, cross-border laws also become important.

The former dean of Harvard University, Mr. Joseph Nye has impressed the power of soft skills to influence other people based on culture. It is the capability to attract and influence customers, employees, and stakeholders to fulfill objectives. Every company wants to build a unique brand. Samsung has been able to live to that image in the cell phones market. Japanese companies such as Toyota emphasize their strong management controls. Some organizations such as General Electric pull the trump card for being environmentally friendly. Apple has projected itself to cater to the high-end segment and hold their products as status symbols: For example, iPhone and iPod. Globalization has enabled free movement of goods and services over a wide geographic area and use of e-commerce and mobile commerce tools to enhance capabilities and provide more customization for products. From applications for Amazon's Alexa to bank-developed virtual assistants like Bank of America's Erica, the future of smart machines acting as digital concierges on behalf of consumers is upon us.

The banks and credit unions that invest in better digital engagement will have more profitable relationships with customers. At the end of the day, customers will continue to self-select the bank that provides the least amount of friction and the most relevant support and guidance.

Risks Surrounding Business and Technology Connected to Them

Conduct of business and use of disruptive technologies are subject to manifold risks. Natural risks originate from climatic changes, global warming, storms, tornadoes, etc. Impact to business is also caused by frequent changes in legislation, stress due to migration, corporate social responsibility (CSR), contribution of industry in achieving social objectives, pandemics, etc. Technology-driven anomalies, technological obsolescence, logic bias, etc., also pose a threat to the continued availability and integrity of data.

AI is useful but is affected by poor training bias and bad data. Research has found that approximately 85% of AI projects will show erroneous results in 2020 due to bias in algorithms, data, or development teams.

Third-party risks arise because of reliance on external providers of products and services. Risk arises on account of nonavailability of core parts in production if they are not supplied on time. Dependency on one provider can lead to a single point of failure.

Cloud computing has many advantages and is becoming increasingly popular. But it brings in concerns in terms of:

- Regulatory risk
- Data security
- Operations risk
- Vendor risks
- Privacy risk
- Reputational risk

Internet-enabled applications have a full suite of cyber threats from malware to malicious attacks. Technology enables business, but the cyber risk incidence is lingering and lots of preventive, detective, and corrective measures need to be in place. Periodic vulnerability scans using appropriate tools to identify risk and plan incident response should be performed, and a plan for disaster recovery should be documented.

Need for Compliance

A highly complex environment leads to manifold concerns for an organization. New technologies from all over the globe are being introduced to ease business operations. With regulators serving like watchdogs, IT departments are increasingly finding it difficult to achieve compliance with multiple laws, policies, guidelines, and standards that the business is subject to. Organizations still prefer to work in silos and deal with compliance requirements in isolation; this leads to inefficiencies in effort or resources in achieving compliance.

Also, many redundant processes may result for lack of cohesiveness to list and map total compliance needs. Cross-border business brings considerations for diverse regulatory controls and different criteria for compliance. This has led to the proliferation of different standards, guidelines, and frameworks that enable organizations to do business in a secure and compliant way. The first rule here is that every organization has to plan for their information governance. This means the proper alignment of business and IT should be implemented. The storage, custody, and transfer of data should be securely carried out.

The basic tenets of security, risk, and governance are the same, and there is a lot of commonalities between various compliances that are prescribed for industries. With the growing need for compliance, various auditees have observed audit fatigue when separate auditors demand to audit the implementation of the same control repeatedly, thus obstructing business operations.

An integrated approach and holistic view of an organization's governance, risk, and compliance (GRC) are the need of the hour and can help the development of common controls, thereby reducing regulatory uncertainty. Management monitoring of GRC controls can be facilitated in a central repository that can lead to economy of cost and time.

The span of a GRC process includes three elements:

- *Governance* is the oversight role and the process by which companies manage and mitigate business risks.
- *Risk management* enables an organization to evaluate all relevant business and regulatory risks and controls and monitor mitigation actions in a structured manner.
- *Compliance* ensures that an organization has the processes and internal controls to meet the requirements imposed by governmental bodies, regulators, industry mandates, or internal policies.

Use of Tools to Ease the Compliance Process

Smartsheet is a documentation tool for tracking the status of a project and evaluating the work done. Data loss prevention (DLP) software is a set of tools and processes used to ensure sensitive data is not lost, misused, or accessed by unauthorized users. It classifies regulated, confidential, and business critical data and identifies violations of policies defined by organizations or within a predefined policy pack, typically driven by regulatory compliances such as Health Insurance Portability and Accountability Act of 1996 (HIPAA), PCI-DSS, or GDPR. DLP tools fulfill three objectives:

i. Personal information protection/compliance
ii. Protection of intellectual property (IP)
iii. Providing data visibility

Building a Compliance Framework

Organizations face panic, frustration, and despair over the increasing compliance obligations that must be fulfilled by them. To name a few:

1. Compliance with internal policies and procedures
2. Compliance with legal and regulatory provisions

3. Compliance with industry-specific regulations: HITRUST, HIPAA, PCI DSS, etc.

4. Compliance with security frameworks such as COBIT, risk standards such as ISO 31000, etc.

5. Compliance with cybersecurity laws and guidelines

6. Compliance with security standards such as ISO 27001 and business continuity standards such as ISO 22301

7. Trigger-based compliance needs due to industry frauds or severe hacks leading to high business losses

Complying with a compliance framework can be a powerful business driver that will give businesses a competitive edge. However, compliance can come with a set of complications and challenges that may be operational or legal.

Many organizations find themselves managing their GRC initiatives in silos – each initiative including common controls treated separately even if reporting needs overlap. Even though each of these initiatives individually follows the GRC process outlined here, when they deployed software solutions to enable these processes, the selections were made in a very tactical manner, without a thought for a broader set of requirements.

As a result, organizations have ended up with multiple instances of such systems to manage individual GRC initiatives, each operating in their own silos.

By taking an integrated approach, issues can be addressed by creating a clear, unambiguous process and a single reference point for compliance. Organizations need to have a single compliance infrastructure or a compliance stack, which will include legal and regulatory provisions, industry-specific compliances including technical- and process-related controls, and other specified compliance (Figure 1.5).

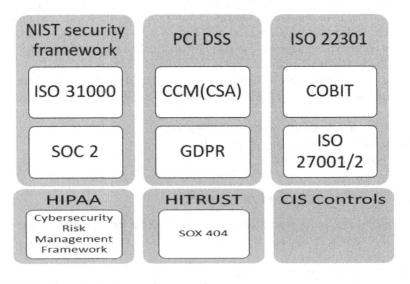

FIGURE 1.5 Organization's compliance stack.

It is critical that a GRC solution must be able to address a wide range of standards, guidelines and legal/regulatory requirements and must be receptive to accommodate new compliance or rule.

Within the purview of this book, we shall cover the following compliances and touch base similar compliances in different geographic locations (Table 1.1).

Different organizations have different national and international compliances in respect of financial compliance, legal compliance, third-party assurance, regulatory compliance, and many more. Generally, the Risk and Compliance department has been

TABLE 1.1   A List of Compliance Standards, Regulations, and Guidelines

SN	CATEGORY	NAME OF COMPLIANCE	INITIATOR OF COMPLIANCE	BRIEF DESCRIPTION
1.	Standard	ISO 27001/2	International Organization for Standardization (ISO)	It is an information security compliance standard that helps companies manage the security of assets, such as employee or third-party data, financial information, and IP.
2.	Standard	ISO 22301	International Organization for Standardization (ISO)	Standard issued by BSI that specifies requirements to plan, establish, implement, operate, monitor, review, maintain, and continually improve a documented management system to protect against, reduce the likelihood of occurrence, prepare for, respond to, and recover from disruptive incidents when they arise. It is organization wide and applies to all parts of the organization.
3.	Framework	COBIT	Information Systems Audit and Control Association (ISACA)	COBIT is a framework for the management and IT governance, created by ISACA. The framework defines a set of generic processes for the management of IT, with each process defined together with process inputs and outputs, key process activities, process objectives, performance measures, and a basic maturity model.

(Continued)

TABLE 1.1   (Continued)

SN	CATEGORY	NAME OF COMPLIANCE	INITIATOR OF COMPLIANCE	BRIEF DESCRIPTION
4.	Guidelines	ISO 31000	International Organization for Standardization (ISO)	ISO 31000-2018, for risk management, provides principles and a framework for organizations universally irrespective of their size to manage risks. The standard provides a guideline for identifying threats and opportunities, allocating proper resources for risk treatment, and helping businesses achieve their objectives by overseeing risks and treating them in time to avoid or reduce losses from incidents.
5.	Technical Standard	Cloud Security Alliance Cloud Controls Matrix (CCM)	Cloud Security Alliance (CSA)	CCM is designed to provide fundamental security principles to guide cloud vendors and to help prospective cloud customers in assessing overall risk of cloud provider. CSA CCM provides a control framework that provides a detailed understanding of security concepts and principles that are aligned to the CSA guidance in 13 domains. The foundation of CCM is based on the customized relationship with other industry-accepted security standards, regulations and controls, and frameworks such as ISO 27001/ISO 27002, COBIT, and PCI DSS and covers relevant controls for cloud infrastructure.
6.	Regulation	GDPR	The *General Data Protection Regulation* (EU) May 15, 2018)	GDPR is a legal framework that sets guidelines for the collection and processing of personal information and rules regarding the storage and use of such information.

SN	CATEGORY	NAME OF COMPLIANCE	INITIATOR OF COMPLIANCE	BRIEF DESCRIPTION
7.	Standard	PCI DSS	The Payment Card Industry Security Standards Council (PCI SSC)	The PCI Security Standards Council maintains, evolves, and promotes standards for the Payment Card Industry for the safety of cardholder data across the world. It sets the technical and operational requirements for organizations accepting or processing payment transactions and for software developers and manufacturers of applications and devices used in these transactions. The PCI Security Standards Council provides illustrative mapping of PCI DSS framework with the NIST Cybersecurity Framework.
8.	Law	HIPAA (Health Insurance Portability and Accountability Act of 1996	The US Department of Health and Human Services 'HHS')	HIPAA is designed to protect patient information and, with the increase in electronic medical records, ensure that this highly personal data doesn't get into the wrong hands.
9.	Standard	HITRUST CSF	HITRUST Alliance	HITRUST undertakes programs for safeguarding sensitive information and manage information risk for global businesses across the third-party supply chain. In collaboration with privacy, information security, and risk management, HITRUST has developed and maintained a widely followed risk and compliance framework and related assessment and assurance methodologies.
10.	Framework	NIST security framework	NIST	The NIST Cybersecurity Framework is a voluntary framework consisting of security guidelines, standards, and best practices designed for individual businesses and other organizations to assess and manage cyber risks.

(Continued)

TABLE 1.1   (Continued)

SN	CATEGORY	NAME OF COMPLIANCE	INITIATOR OF COMPLIANCE	BRIEF DESCRIPTION
11.	Standard	CIS Controls (Version 7.1)	Center for Internet Security (formerly sponsored by SANS)	CIS controls have been globally adopted to ensure cybersecurity. CIS Controls v 7.1 introduces CIS implementation groups called IGs, and these groups help organizations to classify themselves and focus on allocation of resources and leveraging the value for CIS controls.
12.	Attestation Standard	SOC 2	AICPA (The American Institute of Certified Public Accountants)	A SOC 2 report provides assurance about a service organization's security, availability, processing integrity, confidentiality, and/or privacy controls, based on their compliance with the AICPA's (American Institute of Certified Public Accountants) Trust Services Criteria.
13.	Framework	Cybersecurity Risk Management Reporting Framework	AICPA (The American Institute of Certified Public Accountants)	AICPA has developed a security framework for reporting for organizations in relation to their risk and cybersecurity reporting. This framework is a key component of a new System and Organization Controls (SOC) for cybersecurity engagement in which a CPA reports on organization's enterprise-wide cybersecurity risk management program. Such report helps senior management and other stakeholders gain insight into the organizational efforts and controls for security.

SN	CATEGORY	NAME OF COMPLIANCE	INITIATOR OF COMPLIANCE	BRIEF DESCRIPTION
14.	Law	SOX 404	Paul Sarbanes and Michael Oxley	Under Sarbanes–Oxley Section 404 (SOX 404) compliance, companies can design, assess, and improve internal controls under the COSO framework, monitor their compliance processes, and provide evidence to the external auditors that an internal control was tested to the satisfaction of the internal audit group. It has a document control capability that provides a central repository with comprehensive change control capabilities. The SOX compliance solution also provides greater control and clear visibility into issues, status, and plans to all stakeholders.
15.	Standard	ISO 27017	BSI	ISO 27017 generally focuses on the protection of the information in the cloud services, while ISO 27018 focuses on protecting the personal data,

provided by organizations, and the roles and responsibilities have been given to the department for the governance-related and the risk- and compliance-related compliances. For instance, the enforcement of GDPR made identification of privacy officer necessary. GRC standards and guidelines if systematically deployed can bring about a consistent compliance environment and will prevent fines and penalties on the organization.

An assurance for proper compliance is to enforce a flexible control infrastructure, monitoring, assessments, and remediation of audit points. Competition will be in the mainstay in 2021, and it will require businesses to flaunt new capabilities and perspectives to be there in the market. In a dynamic environment, new platforms and strategic partnerships will be commonplace.

More and more management professionals have acknowledged that with increased complexity and multiplicity of audits and compliance reporting, there is a need to automate some processes and build an integrated Compliance Management Framework that is aligned to the organizational size and nature of the business. The idea is that monitoring of controls becomes easier and the fatigue of repetitive tasks and repetitive audits gets reduced. The decision to optimize business opportunities and make the organization a 'next-generation learning' organization is required to be taken. Due to a concentration of industries and risk connected to business, any change organizations will make will have to be pre-empted and managed.

CONCLUSION

In an environment of ever-increasing uncertainty, risks, and economic pressures, new perspectives and capabilities will have to be developed to remain in competition. External orientation has become imperative with a variety of platforms and markets around the globe; approachability and ability to influence customers have become important. With risks from cyberspace, risks from natural disasters, and risks from social, political, and economic pressures, businesses find it difficult to survive. Developing inbuilt resilience to absorb untoward incidents and avoid unnecessary risks is of prime concern for organizations.

We live in a generation of big data and knowledge-based systems that are transforming business. Adequate levels of data classification, secure storage of data, proper coordination between processes and access control policy to grant access on a 'need to know' basis is necessary for the security and integrity of data. Also, factoring data retention and destruction policy and implementing it is important to keep data current and optimize storage space.

To keep the business environment conducive, involvement and coordination with the external environment for both sourcing resources and reaching out to remote markets are advisable. An open approach to new ideas and innovative practices will broaden perspectives and add value to the way business is carried out. Likewise, introducing diversity brings variety and a fresh approach to business strategy. Success is planning and developing insight into future obstacles and roadblocks and a defined strategy to build good market standing

In the next chapter we will discuss the pain areas in adhering to various compliances that business organizations are subject to. Regulators have set some compliances that are mandatory; there are some frameworks that are globally accepted and some function specific.

Challenges and Roadblocks to Compliance

2

THE PAIN POINTS IN GRC

There is a multiplicity of compliances applicable to different businesses, and these keep on increasing with growth, expansion to new territories, and customer demands (Figure 2.1). Aligning compliance activities in accordance with the laws, regulations, contracts, strategies, and policies of the business is important for effective running of business. Business contracts include 'right to audit' clause, and organizations are subject to audit anytime at a short notice. Regulators exert more pressure through increased regulations and compliance norms.

Compliances can be briefly classified as:

1. Legal and regulatory compliance
2. Industry-specific compliance (regulator-driven)
3. Compliance with security and risk standards (adopted and implemented by the organization, maybe dictated by clients)

There are data security laws such as HIPAA and GDPR, which also covers privacy issues, PCI DSS for online financial institutions, SOC 2 and ISO 27017/18 compliance for third-party and cloud providers, information security (ISO 27001), and business continuity (ISO 22301) standards and guidelines; hence, the development of a sound integrated compliance program that makes the best fit for each industry is necessary. In an ever-increasing business environment spanning global boundaries, organizations cannot escape legal, regulatory, and compliance requirements that will have to be integrated within the enterprise and regularly monitored so that resulting fines, penalties, and losses due to noncompliance can be contained.

It is generally observed that organizations address compliance requirements by creating silos and addressing each requirement separately rather than having

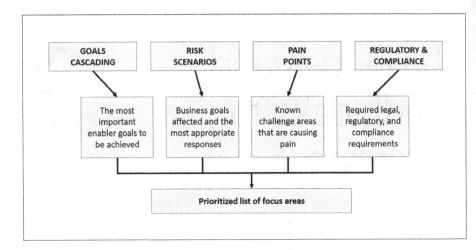

FIGURE 2.1 Identify pain points.

an integrated approach, thus wasting resources and time and increasing redundant efforts in meeting their compliance needs. Often, enterprises struggle to prioritize compliances, try to identify as to who should handle compliance, and also whether compliance should be handled exclusively in-house or it should be an outsourced function.

There are risks associated with noncompliance, and organizations assess the magnitude of such risks to consequences of noncompliance. Organizations must determine their risk appetite and their capacity to absorb loss or loss to reputation or goodwill, and then determine what controls must be enforced to lower risks arising out of compliance. The decision on risk reduction depends on the following criteria:

1. Nature of industry and regulator levy of security provisions – for instance, health and wellness industry governed by HIPAA, privacy and data security regulations such as GDPR, etc.
2. Legal and regulatory landscape
3. Internal policies and procedures
4. Industry best practices (Guidelines)
5. Industry standards in cybersecurity, enterprise security, data security, customer-triggered compliances, etc.

We shall restrict our study to governance, risk, and security to give a detailed caricature of building an integrated framework. Before organizations initiate the building up of a compliance framework, it will be good to know what is it that needs to be covered. The following frameworks are broadly defined:

1. Risk framework
2. Cybersecurity framework
3. Security governance framework

Let us see what the suite of compliances that organizations deal with is.

Before we start planning, let us take conceptual clarity and differentiate between frameworks, security standards, and guidelines. Besides that, legal and regulatory and industry-specific regulatory provisions get added to the stack of our compliance needs.

1. **Policies**: They are formal high-level statements signed by the Board or the highest level of management portraying an organization's intent on issue-specific or system-/security-specific objectives. It represents a mandatory pressure on the entire organization to comply with the provisions set and serves as a guide in case of dispute.
2. **Procedures**: They are a description of the steps to be followed in order to comply with policies and standards. For instance, the Board will come up with the policy to implement security standards, and the CISO will develop the procedures to implement a chosen standard like ISO 27001 and lay step-by-step procedures to be followed to achieve adoption, implementation, and maintenance of the standard.
3. **Guidelines**: They are a statement of industry best practices that are good to have, open to interpretation, and not mandatory unless a policy mandates the adoption of such policies.
4. **Standards**: They are the setting of rules and boundaries and actions to support policies and give directions for implementation.

NIST CYBERSECURITY FRAMEWORK

The National Institute of Standards and Technology (NIST) has published the cybersecurity framework. It provides guidance to organizations for their programs for protecting their cybersecurity. NIST portal offers a free reference tool that represents asset of industry standards, guidelines and best practices.

Policies serve as baseline since they are supported by the executive management. Having said that, it is really challenging to achieve an organization-wide consensus on policies, procedures, and guidelines. Policies must reflect the basis for compliance with standards, guidelines, and procedures and should be aligned to compliance requirements.

Business is facing ever-increasing demands from customers and clients. Organizations find it difficult to accommodate such demands; there is a need for an integrated and scalable compliance platform that would comprehensively cover all policies, procedures, guidelines, and future additions to the compliance suite.

COMPLIANCE CAN BE ATTESTED OR ASSURANCE FUNCTION

Different audits to check compliance with multiple laws, regulations, risk frameworks, cybersecurity standards, etc., are a strain on organizational time and resources. There is a part of the IT governance dedicated to attend to these compliance audits.

Compliance audits can be of the following types:

1. Internal audit (can be outsourced)
2. Regulator conducted audits
3. Surveillance audits by certifying bodies
4. CPA-led audits for SOC 2 and SOX
5. Third-party/vendor audits
6. Any other type of audit to test compliance

The challenge with compliance is that it is not enough to comply; organizations must prove that they comply by providing enough evidence during audits. Further audits are not a onetime affair; they are periodic and repetitive depending on the nature of compliance.

CHALLENGES TO ADDRESS SECURITY GOVERNANCE IN THE ORGANIZATION

Governance of enterprise IT involves adoption of a proactive approach toward threats and probable risks and enforcement of a continuous compliance environment responsive and resilient to incidents and disasters. Threat governance involves reduction and timely mitigation of risk exposures and detection, responding to threats, and yet containing costs of security operations.

Some of the roadblocks in this direction are:

To Combat Incidence of Security Breaches

Cybercrime continues to escalate in frequency, impact, and sophistication and threatens enterprises regardless of size and sector. A data breach or intrusion can cause an organization to lose customers, revenue, and reputational value; experience loss of operational continuity; and question the integrity of its data. For some businesses, those losses would range from costly to downright irreversible. Cost of cybercrime is high, it is all pervasive and of higher impact, and preparing to combat security breaches is one of the biggest challenges.

Existence of Skill Gaps

There is a big demand for Info-sec professionals, but there are not enough professionals available when required. There also exists a skill gap between security professionals and their ability to understand business processes. This problem poses a serious risk to an organization.

It is necessary for security practitioners to understand organizational processes and nature of business in order to secure relevant assets that go into the fulfillment of organizational goals and objectives. This gap forms a deterrent to the security compliance within the organization. Each business must address the hiring and training of appropriate skills to meet the security requirements and lead to a good security governance and compliance.

Challenge of Connected Devices

Technology has evolved such that everything is now, or shortly will be, connected, accessible, serviced, and controlled from the network. This set of connected devices brings in a scaling problem, and organizations need skilled professionals to safeguard this diverse array of endpoints as of present state or IT environment as well as predicted for the future. For organizations to provide compliance for every device as per industry standard is a bit of a challenge considering the cost of securing all devices.

Changing Face of Technology

The security priorities and needs are different for different organizations, and security is constantly evolving with changes in the sophistication of threats. Hence, a proactive approach to risks and security is important. Organizations need to develop threat intelligence and threat modeling and develop a rich, contextual picture outlining what they want in terms of security. This should involve identifying the critical assets that need the most protection as well as which technologies, people, and other resources are necessary to help get the job done.

Control process involves an accurate assessment of business needs with a risk-based approach and a customized framework befitting the nature of business or industry and as per compliance standards applicable. Planning the scope of security programs so that they encompass the entirety of their environment and include long-range plans designed to mitigate risks is a challenging job and needs prioritization as per significance.

DATA GOVERNANCE

An effective data governance program introduces reliability in data and preserves its quality and promotes its consistent usage throughout the enterprise. For example, imagine a board room presentation where five different employees of the organization belonging to different sections present the same statistics and it does not match (Figure 2.2).

FIGURE 2.2   Features of data governance.

DATA GOVERNANCE SERVES TO OVERCOME THE FOLLOWING OBSTACLES

Delay in Submission of Compliance Reports

Data-specific regulations such as privacy regulations, SOX, GDPR, place an emphasis on how organizations use, report, and manage data. Organizations need to understand what they must report, who owns the responsibility for the reports, and where they can find the information. A sound governance model for data management helps ensure regulatory compliance.

Avoids Breach of Data Integrity by Secure Access

Data is used for analysis, reporting, and meeting compliance requirements. The integrity of data is important for the appropriate use of data for business decision-making and for accurate reporting for compliance.

Removes the Fear of Wrong Comprehension of Data and Data Subjects

Introduction of data glossaries and data dictionaries provides a better understanding of data and a structured manner of accessing data. It increases ease of use of data.

Allows Better Centralized Control Over Compliance and Other Data

With data governance, much of data is structured and classified. It is easy to centralize data by building a data enterprise, a data warehouse, or a data mart.

Data Governance Brings Autonomy and Reduces the Dependence on Individual Employees

Organizations can document critical knowledge through data governance programs. Sometimes, there is heavy dependency on a single person, leading to a single point of failure in case of absence or quitting of that person. Apart from a good data governance framework, there are challenges in keeping data security in backup and storage. Some of the challenges in this area include:

• *Size of Data*

The first challenge is the tremendous increase in organizational data every year, which is becoming unmanageable, and despite extended networks, cloud, organizations do not have the capacity or the systems or the processes in place to ascertain how much they create every year. And that is a problem from a compliance and a storage perspective.

• *Existence of Legacy Data*

Legacy data may or may not be used, but for some regulatory reason, it may have to be preserved and hence backed up in order to maintain compliance. Strict adherence to data regulatory laws such as the GDPR and the Privacy laws of the United States has strict provisions for data breach notification and this makes compliance difficult and the cost of noncompliance unbearable. Having a dedicated data protection officer (DPO) and conducting privacy impact assessments and other things under GDPR have made data governance a 'strictly compliance' affair.

• *Regulatory Requirements of Business Continuity*

Regulatory requirements are for the preparation of the disaster recovery plan for the organization. Health Insurance Portability & Accountability Act (HIPAA) is a data-focused compliance that mandates an adequate security on stored data and their backups. Likewise, ISO 27001 also speaks of data security, proper backups, storage of backups, restoration and testing of backups, and presence of a disaster recovery plan and its testing. Even PCI DSS standard for card data requisitions the mapping of all data, defining of data flows, and security of stored data and data in transit.

CHALLENGES IN CLOUD COMPUTING

Sometimes, choice of technology poses risks and challenges. Cloud computing is one such instance. It is the delivery of various hardware and software services over the internet through a network of remote servers.

Cloud computing is increasingly used to provide better data storage, data security, flexibility, increased collaboration between employees, and changes the workflow of small businesses and large enterprises to help them make better decisions while decreasing costs. Recent trends prove that more than 75% of organizations are using cloud services as a part of their computing infrastructure. Cloud services include:

1. **Software as a Service (SAAS)** – software is owned, delivered, and managed remotely by one or more providers.
2. **Infrastructure as a Service** (IaaS) – compute resources, complemented by storage and networking capabilities that are owned and hosted by providers and available to customers on demand.
3. **Platform as a Service** (PaaS) – the broad collection of application infrastructure (middleware) services; they include application platform, integration, business process management, and database services.
4. **Privacy as a Service** – the emerging privacy regulations on a global scale are shooting up the cost of compliance. Organizations find it difficult to interpret the legal provisions in relation to privacy and strive to meet the high costs of appointing privacy professionals to sort out the privacy compliance in the organization.

Also, the need for a DPO is warranted in some countries. Service providers have started consulting online as a helpdesk on privacy issues of their clients and advising them on legal recourse in case of breaches. The concept of a virtual DPO is also emerging where a contracted DPO can attend to the privacy concerns of several organizations through operating on demand at a fixed periodic fee.

CHALLENGES WITH CLOUD SERVICES

Security Issues

Security has been a main consideration in the adoption of cloud computing solutions. The cloud provider is responsible for data storage and processing, hence dependence on cloud provider is increasing. Many times, it is responsible for backups and continuity as well. Organizations may entrust their sensitive and proprietary data to third party security and compliance considerations are always at stake.

The following risks hover around cloud storage:

- Extensive troubleshooting
- Slow data migration
- Migration agents
- Cutover complexity
- Application downtime

Cost Management and Containment

While an organization can easily ramp up its processing capabilities without making large investments in new hardware, businesses can instead access extra processing through pay-as-you-go models from public cloud providers. However, the on-demand

and scalable nature of cloud computing services make it sometimes difficult to define and predict quantities and costs.

Lack of Resources or Expertise

One of the cloud challenges companies and enterprises are facing today is lack of resources or expertise. Organizations are increasingly placing more workloads in the cloud while cloud technologies continue to rapidly advance. Due to these factors, organizations are having a tough time keeping up with the tools. Also, the need for expertise continues to grow. These challenges can be minimized through additional training of IT and development staff.

Appointing cloud specialists in IT teams may be difficult for small- and medium-sized enterprises. Luckily, many common tasks performed by these specialists can be automated. To this end, companies are turning to DevOps tools, like Chef and Puppet, to perform tasks like monitoring usage patterns of resources and automated backups at predefined time periods. These tools also help optimize the cloud for cost, governance, and security.

Governance/Control

In cloud computing, it is not always possible to have full control over the provisioning, de-provisioning, and operations of infrastructure. This has increased the difficulty for IT to provide the governance, compliance, risks, and quality of data management needed. Organizations should also include governance support and best practices from their cloud service providers.

Compliance

Another risk of cloud computing is compliance. It is an issue for anyone using backup services or cloud storage. Every time a company moves data from the internal storage to a cloud, it is faced with being compliant with industry regulations and laws. For example, healthcare organizations in the United States have to comply with HIPAA and public retail companies have to comply with the Sarbanes–Oxley Act (SOX) of 2002 and Payment Card Industry Data Security Standard (PCI DSS).

Depending on the industry and requirements, every organization must ensure compliance is factored into when entering a contract with the cloud vendors. For instance, many cloud vendors need to be compliant with the SSAE 18 standard for third-party controls and regularly provide for such reports on their website as evidence for compliance.

Managing Multiple Clouds

Challenges facing cloud computing haven't just been concentrated in one single cloud. The state of multi-cloud has grown exponentially in recent years. Companies are shifting or combining public and private clouds, and, as mentioned earlier, tech giants like Alibaba and Amazon are leading the way. A large number of organizations have a multi-cloud strategy.

Performance

When a business moves to the cloud, it becomes dependent on the service providers. It is observed over the past couple of years that all the big cloud players have experienced outages. Real-time data is necessary to drive decision-making process in business. Being able to access data that is stored on the cloud in real time is one of the imperative solutions an organization must consider while selecting the right partner. With an inherent lack of control that comes with cloud computing, companies may run into real-time monitoring issues. Organizations to ensure real-time monitoring policies exist at the SaaS service provider.

Segmented Usage and Adoption

Most organizations did not have a robust cloud adoption strategy in place when they started to move to the cloud. Ad hoc strategies centered on speed of migration and full integration were prevalent. So, it has been observed that isolated cloud projects lack shared standards and security configurations are not adequate.

Migration

The process of moving applications to the cloud poses many challenges, especially when the applications are existing applications. Adopting industry standards that will help address regulatory, management, and technological matters is important.

COMPLIANCE ISSUES FOR SPECIFIC INDUSTRIES

Challenges in Healthcare Industry

HIPAA required the Secretary of Health and Human Services to enact privacy regulations to protect individually identifiable health information. The HIPAA Security Standards create a regulatory requirement that those businesses falling within its purview create administrative procedures to protect and manage protection of data, physical safeguards over computer systems and buildings preventing intrusion, technical

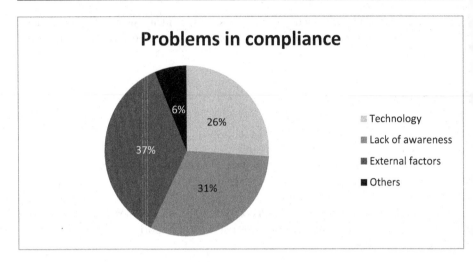

FIGURE 2.3   Some salient problems faced by healthcare industries.

security services that review access to information, and technical security mechanisms that prevent unauthorized transmission of information.

The healthcare industry is vast, complex, and widespread with a large amount of patient data lying in different places and sometimes very little means to protect the data. Threats like ransomware, employee negligence, a growing demand for medical records in the black market, and device-dependent healthcare lacking adequate security pose potential risks that can damage organizational reputation if they are not properly addressed (Figure 2.3).

Some problems related to security in the healthcare industry are listed here.

Healthcare's Attack Surface Is Growing

Use of latest technologies like machine learning and IoT is becoming a part of the health and wellness industry, with the advantage of quality outcome with reduced costs. It will be critical to ensure that information communication technology (ICT) infrastructure is secure, a task that has become exponentially more complicated due to the proliferation of mobile devices like smartphones and tablets, which are used by healthcare professionals in the field and in hospitals.

Existence of personal monitors and fully connected machines can enable access of data from anywhere on multiple devices. But from a compliance and legal point of view, these new technologies will affect their organization's ability to maintain security of data collected and stored in the organization. Healthcare underwent a digital transformation with the adoption of electronic health records (EHRs). Compared to paper documents, digital documents yield huge benefits in terms of efficiency and the quality of patient care.

Majority efforts went in the installation of hardware and software, but investment in cybersecurity did not take place at that pace. Some of the risks that surfaced were as follows:

i. **Ransomware** – It is a major information security threat to healthcare, and majority of ransomware is propagated through phishing, a user-based mechanism that tricks people into facilitating malicious network connections. Organizations need to identify entry points where an adversary can bring in malware. Healthcare information is extremely valuable on the black market; organizations need to step up security in order to identify patterns of ransomware.

ii. **IOT exploits** – IoT and connected healthcare bring some huge opportunities for healthcare organizations, but they also bring challenges, with security and data privacy at the top of list. Wearable and implantable IoT healthcare devices, such as pacemakers, insulin pumps, monitors, etc., are vulnerable to attack. Since existence of diverse platforms and volume of data running on IOT devices is significant, endpoint security is a huge challenge.

iii. **Mobile device exploits, cloud-based data breaches, ransomware** – these are just three of the major information security threats healthcare organizations will have to watch out for in 2021 and the years that follow.

Use of Old Hardware and Software

Medical equipment is expensive. Healthcare organizations must balance between purchase of advanced medical equipment and need for updated computers or firewall or new fittings. As a result, we find old machines and legacy applications running in many organizations, and there were several instances noted of malware entering through legacy systems. Research has found a multitude of backdoors and botnet connections installed using unsupported operating systems such as Windows XP.

Healthcare Gives Low Priority to Cybersecurity Risks

The level of awareness to cyber risks is low in the healthcare sector, and there exist severe consequences of breach. This has caused an increase in data breaches and data loss year after year. The United States experienced a large amount of social security numbers that got exposed in the year 2016 according to the Identity Theft Resource Center.

Healthcare Is Interconnected

The healthcare industry comprises many interconnected smaller units. While individually small units cannot sustain dedicated cybersecurity resources, these small units become the entry source through which bigger units are targeted and compromised. An extract from the HIPAA journal describes the case of Anthem. It iterates:

> OCR has announced that an Anthem HIPAA breach settlement has been reached to resolve potential HIPAA violations discovered during the investigation of its colossal 2015 data breach that saw the records of 78.8 million of its members stolen by cybercriminals.

Anthem failed in implementing proper security measures to prevent compromise of passwords and stealing of private information. In addition, victims had to be paid compensation and on behalf of 19.1 million customers, Anthem agreed to settle the lawsuit of $115 million.

Stolen Healthcare Data Is Valuable

Patients' medical history including their diagnoses, treatments, and personal data such as full name and social security number are easy targets for fraud, and this data is more valuable than stolen credit card numbers. Criminals steal patient data and sell the data in the black market; sometimes, they use it for blackmailing

Patients Are Given Access Rights to Medical Data

Health organizations provide patients with details regarding their medical records on demand and sometimes enable this feature on their websites for easy download. This is done in ignorance of cybersecurity norms. Consumers do not protect their medical records and credentials as meticulously as they protect the login credentials with their bank. Patient information on the website and patients logging in to take appointments before they visit the healthcare unit may serve to save on cost, but it increases exposure to patient data, which poses a big risk.

Limited Budget for Cybersecurity

- Healthcare organizations do not have budget to employ dedicated resources to protect their networks and other systems. Healthcare budgets always compete with other priorities like new medical technologies, medical staff, medicine stock, etc. The proliferation of connected devices like medical equipment and other web-connected elements like the IoT can be particularly weak security endpoints and need to be properly secured and updated at all times. Especially, it is impossible to have dedicated IT resources in places which are so small that only three to four people run it.

Lack of Cybersecurity Education

The healthcare industry treats cybersecurity as the responsibility of IT, and the operations team is not aware of the risk of data breaches and the need to safeguard data. This is due to failure on the part of management to educate their staff, including doctors and nurses, and conduct awareness campaigns within the organization against the nature of cyber threats and consequences of data breaches. Patient data is used for treatment, but it can be used for fraudulent purposes such as identity theft, blackmail, and misuse of information and cause disruption to patient care.

Healthcare Industry to Comply with GDPR

Compliance with the GDPR regulation in the context of healthcare providers protecting against the misuse or theft of patient information is a serious concern and requisitions an even higher standard of protection for sensitive healthcare, genetic, and biometric data.

Healthcare organizations' IT departments shall have to ensure that all patient data as well as healthcare organization data are compliant with current standards and regulations, while being prepared to up the ante as new GDPR-driven benchmarks make their way stateside.

Change in Legal and Regulatory Provisions

With looming uncertainties in healthcare laws, compliance officers, senior leadership, and legal teams must be prepared to update or overhaul existing policies and procedures at a moment's notice to capture new requirements, maintain compliance, and adapt to any fallout. Compliance to be attested by Assessment firm and all this has to be done without compromising patient care and safety.

There Is No Accountability for Cybersecurity

Responsibility for healthcare cybersecurity is not properly defined. Hence, accountability for security of systems and network against attacks is lacking. Empirical research has proved that around three-fourths of US hospitals do not have a designated IT security officer, and the situation with smaller organizations is that they do not have any dedicated IT professional onboard who can take care of security. Earmarked resource for IT must have the expertise as well as the authority to identify, prioritize, fulfill, and maintain cyber risks and enforce security

In the security processes, organizations are now adopting encryption to protect personal data. With increased use of mobile technology in the healthcare industry, mobile device management is included in security measures. Healthcare organizations implementing cloud storage and messaging applications have to give due priority to privacy and security.

HITRUST

HITRUST was started in 2007 to help protect patient information. The HITRUST model aims at creating a baseline across the health and wellness industry that is based on organizations' risk profile and maturity in understanding risk. Instead of starting with risk and creating controls in response to those risks, HITRUST identifies common risks pertaining to the industry and enables entities to tailor their compliance program through the Common Security Framework.

Compliance Challenges for Banking and Financial Services

The banking industry is transforming at a rapid pace, with an increase in competition, changing business models demands, new regulations, and compliances coupled with disruptive technologies. As data breaches become prevalent and privacy concerns intensify, regulatory and compliance requirements are becoming more restrictive. To add to that, customer expectations are always sky high, and round-the-clock personalized services are expected. Banks are going for digital transformation in the race to be more competitive and to survive in the global markets.

Maintaining manifold compliances poses a big challenge. Further cross-border regulations and policies will require a centralized approach and strategic assessment of regulatory risks. Surveillance audits are a common feature of compliance standards/ frameworks; it is a continuous process, and attending to these audits and providing evidences and documents for individual audit becomes stressful. The costs and people resources for meeting compliance requirements are also a burden, especially for small organizations (Figure 2.4).

The business environment in which banking business operates has many challenges that include:

Acute Competition

The banking industry is subject to acute competition from other banks and must be proactive to retain existing customers and build new customers. Customer analytics and compliance data maintenance are becoming important processes for the banking industry. Although customer satisfaction is difficult to measure, customer turnover is tangible and customer loyalty is becoming hard to maintain in the face of competition. Understanding customers and their expectations goes toward building good client relationships.

The compliance stack for banking may include:

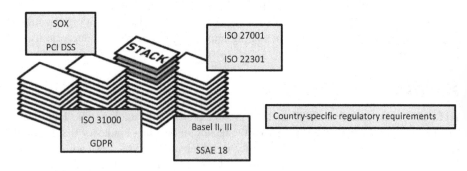

FIGURE 2.4   Compliance stack-banking.

Banks aim at restructuring business processes and lowering costs. Leveraging technology to meet customer expectations as well as focus on compliances is a challenge for the banking industry. Use of smart devices/tokens is fast becoming a medium for online payments.

Increase in Breaches

With a series of high-profile breaches over the past few years, security of online transactions has become high priority. Use of biometrics, multifactor authentication, and other techniques for security is becoming prevalent, but they have their own challenges. There is increased use of third-party service providers in areas such as:

- Customer authentication
- Fraud checking
- Know-your-customer (KYC) checking
- Processing of online payments

Challenges and risks involve third-party providers as well, with additional compliance requirements set in.

Changing Business Models

Banks have started adopting customer-centric models and competitive offerings to rationalize business lines and seek sustainable improvements in operational efficiencies to maintain profitability. Adapting to changes in demand is compulsory, but providing for agility and inculcating risk and compliance into each model is a challenge. Young-generation customers are techno-savvy and adapt to modern banking products, but older-generation customers still prefer traditional mode of banking, and hence a hybrid model is more acceptable that meets rising customer expectations.

Addressing Issues of Making a 'Global Footprint'

Anti-money laundering regulations are still localized, banks having a global presence have to decide whether they want to follow each country's regulations or to develop their own anti-money laundering policy based on best practices and global standards.

Adapting to Rapid Changes

Collaborative technologies bring in automated processes and systems that change the organizational culture. A culture that promotes a culture of innovation, in which technology is leveraged to optimize existing processes and procedures for maximum efficiency, is desirable. Organizational acceptance of change sometimes poses a challenge.

Technology Challenge

Leveraging technology such as artificial intelligence (AI) and 'big data', in anti-money laundering applications is a bit difficult. Employing and training highly specialized, capable, and skilled individuals in this sector and rewarding them for their skills are good ways of retaining the skill.

Supervisory Pressure

Sometimes, excessive pressure can discourage some activities that entail higher money laundering risks. This concept, also known as 'derisking', can have undesired side effects. For example, refraining from offering correspondent banking services in developing countries may have a negative impact on local businesses and groups.

Use of Mobile Banking Applications

All banks are using mobile applications as part of service offerings with features such as live chat, voice-enabled features, digital assistance, etc. Mobile applications must be maintained and regularly updated to accommodate new business products and features. Existence of outdated mobile applications is also one of the challenges that have to be dealt with.

SOME BANKING-RELATED COMPLIANCES

PCI DSS Compliance Challenges   One significant compliance standard is the PCI DSS standard. It was organized by American Express, Discover Financial Services, JCB International, Mastercard, and Visa to help promote information security over electronic payment systems. In order to comply with PCI DSS, vendors must review their systems to determine their risk. Mapping of networks to review the storage and transit of information PCI DSS is an industry-specific standard trying to scope all members, and it offers a lot of information, such as lists of approved assessors, devices, and applications. Banks and financial institutions find many challenges in meeting the PCI DSS requirements spreading through 12 requirements and over 200 controls. To list a few concerns:

1. Costs of implementing and maintaining the certification are high and so are penalties for noncompliance.
2. There is a risk of card data compromise, which means card data are lying at places where there is no need to keep that data. It results in an unnecessary increase in area of inspection as well as increases exposure of breaches.
3. Network segmentation is another area where segregating PCI DSS scope data vis-á-vis non-PCI DSS scope data poses a big challenge for many organizations.
4. Rigorous testing of networks is a requirement that is causing a strain on financial and people resources.

Sarbanes–Oxley Act   SOX Act 2002 is known in US Senate as the 'Public Company Accounting Reform and Investor Protection Act' and in the House of Representatives as the 'Corporate and Auditing Accountability and Responsibility Act'. Commonly referred to as Sarbanes Oxley, Sarbox or SOX is a major compliance need for all companies listed on the NASDAQ.

SOX was designed with the *goal* of implementing accounting and disclosure requirements that:

- Increase transparency in corporate governance and financial reporting
- Formalize a system of internal checks and balances

Penalties for noncompliance: Formal penalties for noncompliance with SOX can include fines, removal from listings on public stock exchanges, and invalidation of D&O insurance policies. Under the Act, CEOs and CFOs who willfully submit an incorrect certification to a SOX compliance audit can face fines of $5 million and up to 20 years in jail. The stated goal of SOX is 'to protect investors by improving the accuracy and reliability of corporate disclosures. Given that an organization's IT infrastructure is the backbone of how it communicates, it makes sense that compliance with SOX should require introducing broad information accountability measures.

SOX COMPLIANCE AND DATA SECURITY

For IT managers and executives setting out high-level data security goals, compliance with SOX is an ongoing process. SOX IT examines existing IT infrastructure, identifying inefficiencies, redundancies, and superfluous controls in business processes. Maintaining a tighter control over breaches in security and giving quick response and resolution in the event of incidents are part of SOX controls.

Implementing SOX Compliance

IT management should identify the provisions of SOX compliance that applies to data security and reporting. These are:

- **Section 302:** SOX Section 302 relates to a company's financial reporting. The act requires a company's CEO and CFO to personally certify that all records are complete and accurate. They must provide assurance and take personal responsibility for all internal controls prevalent over the past 90 days; such controls include a company's information security infrastructure in so much as it involves financial statements' accuracy and authenticity.

From the IT side of things, typical audit challenges involve four things:

   Access: Access over physical facilities and electronic controls that prevent unauthorized users from viewing sensitive information must be secured. This includes not only keeping servers and data centers in secure locations but also making sure effective password controls, lockout screens, and other measures are in place. Implementing the access philosophy of 'need to know' basis is a good way to impose organization-wide access control.

Security: Taking steps to manage risk is a good policy regardless of SOX compliance status. Investing in services or appliances that will monitor and protect your financial database is the best way to avoid compliance and security concerns.

Change management: Change management involves IT department's processes for adding new users or workstations, updating and installing new software, and making any changes to Active Directory databases or other information architecture components. Change controls and maintaining documentation of changes made pose another challenge for SOX compliance.

Backup procedures: These are procedures to be in place to protect sensitive data. Data centers containing backed-up data including those stored off site or by a third party are subject to the same SOX provisions as are applicable to the primary site.

Section 404: Section 404 stipulates further requirements for the monitoring and maintenance of internal controls related to the company's accounting and financial controls. It requires an annual audit of these controls performed by an outside firm. This audit assesses the effectiveness of all internal controls and reports its findings back directly to the SEC.

The challenge for auditing SOX controls is particularly affecting small and medium enterprises that are hit by additional cost for these audits. The Public Company Accounting Oversight Board (PCAOB) was created to develop auditing standards and train auditors on the best practices for assessing a company's internal controls. Adherence to the latest guidelines and rules is essential for accomplishing the audit.

Top Compliance Challenges Facing Logistics Industry

Logistics industry is at the backbone of eCommerce business since it takes care of delivery. Today, the problem with logistics is not of running full capacity but of cutting costs of transportation by leveraging greater innovations and technology. Amazon has initiated the idea of having drones deliver to remote sites to ease delivery problems.

With rising fuel costs and inflation, credit crisis is imperative and to top that compliance with regulations is proving to be a big challenge. To list a few:

1. **Government regulations**. Carriers face significant compliance regulations imposed by federal, state, and local authorities.
2. **Tracing the delivery status** by means of advanced technology tools and providing after-sales services such as:
   - Proof of Delivery (POD) images online that are downloadable
   - Up-to-date status updates on your shipments
   - Streamlined administrative operations

3. **Environmental issues**. Regulations in favor of emission reduction, pollution control, and anti-idling have brought about increased costs of compliance.
4. **Technology strategy** and **implementation**. While deployment of new technologies has become imperative, the means of meeting the costs and training of people in accurate use of technologies are a challenge.
5. **Ensuring compliance of supply chain and third parties**. Ensuring compliance among external parties so that the supply chain is consistently compliant too is a challenge. The organization is only as compliant and secure as its weakest link. The cause of many vulnerabilities is often directly or indirectly a result of a third-party participant.

Compliance risk is a threat to an organization's economic, reputational, or market standing. A well-defined compliance process prevents violation of compliance standards and avoids the resultant consequences. The compliance function involves management of all compliances within a time and cost boundary. Noncompliance gives rise to compliance risk.

Compliance is a separate work area in many organizations with a dedicated compliance team working on proactively managing the compliance program. The team identifies, monitors, and reduces the risks of noncompliance by adopting adequate strategies. The compliance team keeps abreast of regulatory alerts and updates and integrates them into the compliance program.

THIRD-PARTY SERVICE PROVIDERS

Organizations use a host of different third-party providers to support core business functions, and often many of these parties will have access to a company's internal systems and data. This interconnectivity poses a huge risk to an organization's security and compliance posture.

Organizations may have iron-clad security and defense systems in place, but hackers are only too aware that the easiest way to bypass these defenses is to exploit vulnerabilities in third-party systems. Typically, these suppliers won't have the same robust cybersecurity defenses in place and provide an easy weak point to attack. Majority of cyberattacks in the past have been caused through third-party breaches and could be caused by slack controls at third-party installations.

CHALLENGES IN IMPLEMENTATION OF GDPR

Accountability and good governance are the main objectives of the European Union's (EU') GDPR. GDPR establishes a single set of rules that apply to all member states. It extends to data controllers that collect information from EU residents or process information (whether it be directly or as cloud service providers) from EU residents, or if the person about whom the data is collected is an EU resident. GDPR aims to safeguard privacy and maintain the lawfulness, fairness, confidentiality, and transparency of data held.

Organizations must be able to demonstrate compliance with the legislation or face hefty fines of up to 4% of annual global turnover or 20 million euros. Fines will also depend on the severity of the breach and if organizations have taken steps to show they are compliant.

Under the GDPR, organizations are now legally bound to provide assurance to regulators that their third-party service providers are compliant with the new regulations by having good cybersecurity and privacy controls in place. Given here are some of the challenges that implementation of GDPR has brought forth.

Keeping Abreast of Changes

GDPR has been a major change for most organizations and requires a lot of thought and strategy to implement the requirements to comply. Because it is a legal requirement, there is no way out of it, and the penalties are significant for noncompliance. Compliance changes affect every aspect of a business, including the staff. It is challenging and time-consuming to get people motivated to take care of compliance. Regulations keep changing; existing regulations are developed upon and brand-new ones evolve to address growing issues to specific problems. It is challenging for organizations to keep abreast of the latest regulatory provisions and to adapt their security program to accommodate regulatory changes in order to remain in compliance.

Maintaining Accountability and Transparency in Operations

The key requirements for GDPR are that organizations should adopt clear processes and controls to build a secure foundation. Transparency can be established by having measures for monitoring, reporting, and observing employee behavior to check that compliance is taking place as documented. Proper coordination with all IT resources brings in accountability for assets.

Complex Technology That Is Constantly Being Added to the Suite

Technology additions in complex multifarious environments and different platforms add to the compliance challenge. Technologies such as BYOD, IOT, third-party applications for some purpose may bring in vulnerabilities and impact compliance. As new technologies are adopted, there is a trail of legacy systems that are maintained for some purpose.

IoT, interconnected devices, and the merging of the digital and physical are expanding the potential threat landscape too. All these systems need to be compliant, so practices must be in place to ensure their continued compliance for data as well as applications.

Lack of Awareness, Education, and Cultural Barriers

Compliance is heavily dependent on acceptability and buy-in by key players in the organization. Everyone, irrespective of their job function, must understand their role in security and compliance. The policies, procedures, and controls should be directed to achieve security and compliance. Organizational culture must be congenial to accept changes and continuously adapt to changing compliance needs.

Ensuring Third-Party Compliance

It is believed that an organization is as secure as the security of its weakest link. The origin of many vulnerabilities is often directly or indirectly related to third-party participation, but it can cause disruption in the organization's secure running. It is important to ensure third-party compliance.

Data Breaches and Cyberattacks

Organizations are processing large volumes of data and cyberattacks are on the rise. Therefore, they have a responsibility to protect the data that they process, not only for compliance reasons but to protect their customers, brand, reputation, and ultimately the success of their business. Identity theft, financial fraud, and loss of data or privacy of data are primary concerns for many businesses. GDPR compliance plan can be enhanced by adopting adequate countermeasures in the following direction.

Build Strong and Adaptable Foundations

Since organizations must go through many compliances, it is better to make a scalable platform for data security and compliance. Flexibility is the desired characteristic since regulations and requirements keep on changing, and when changes need to be made, new ones can be mapped to them more efficiently and noncompliance in the transition period can be kept at a minimum.

Conduct Due Diligence on Third-Party Service Providers

Due diligence and security processes around third-party providers and the supply chain should be exercised to mitigate risks arising from them. It is always advisable to work with organizations and people that have the same security culture as the original organization.

Embed a Security- and Compliance-Aware Business Culture

Security and compliance should be included as a top-down initiative and by matter of policies and involvement of top stakeholders and board in the compliance oversight so that compliance is taken more seriously. Organization-wide awareness of costs of non-compliance such as monetary penalties, loss of competitive edge, and loss of brand and reputation will add to the understanding of the need for compliance.

Obtaining Right Skill Sets for Technology

Technologies keep evolving and skills required to support technologies also change. It is essential to provide for the right skill set to support these changes to maintain compliance. This may require employing or contracting individuals with specific talents that your resources lack.

Make Security and Data Protection a Priority

Data-driven protection against cyberattacks is encouraged with a layered security approach to address as many potential concerns as possible. Knowledge of potential risks and the security environment and the security assets is essential to plan an effective strategy to minimize the cyber-threat risk. For instance, access control is fundamental; procedures should be in place to manage who accesses what, how, and when not only from the compliance point of view but also to counter cyber threats. An adequate security framework should cover business processes to ensure security and all compliances.

Monitoring and Reporting

Monitoring and reporting are fundamental to the compliance plan to determine if what you are doing is effective and can establish where improvements are needed to maintain compliance.

Improve effectiveness with automated processes and controls. Implement procedures that enable you to audit your infrastructure for compliance, scan for vulnerabilities, and continuously monitor to protect against internal and external threats to identify, assess, and remediate existing threats and monitor for new ones. Maintain accurate records for audits.

Need for a Well-Drafted Compliance Plan

Customers, public, and clients are all becoming more conscious about security. The compliance plan should be evolving continuously, and in case gaps are identified, compliance best practices embedded into processes and workflow should be able to resolve them effectively.

Under the GDPR, organizations are now legally bound to provide assurance to regulators that their third-party service providers are compliant with the new regulations by having good cybersecurity and privacy controls in place.

EPRIVACY REGULATION

The ePrivacy provision focuses on privacy relating to electronic communications, including data on websites, SMS, email, social networks, blogs, apps, VoIP, video, social media messaging, and IoT devices. There is overlap between the GDPR and the ePrivacy regulation; the key difference is that GDPR covers the handling of personal data in all forms, while the ePrivacy regulation covers electronic communications. Organizations have to plan for compliance with the legislation; otherwise, they will have to face fines akin to that imposed by GDPR. The ePrivacy regulation is globally applicable to everyone and any country that provisions electronic communication services to the EU.

SECURITY POLICY IMPLEMENTATION

Organizations plan, document, and implement a security policy that covers compliance with regulations and to provide security for the organization. According to the E&Y global information security survey, 57% of organizations consider their employees to be the most likely source of an attack, with 38% viewing careless or unaware employees as the most likely threat. Human factor is still the weakest link in the information security chain, causing an increase in the number of security threats. End users are still unaware of the importance of information security and the risks associated with breaches.

Despite the presence of an appropriate information security awareness program, there are many challenges to the successful implementation of security.

To illustrate a few:

1. Not communicating policy to employees
2. Lack of comprehension of policy and their implementation
3. Too much information making the security policy bulky
4. Adoption of a one-size-fits-all policy without study of business processes
5. Lack of management oversight
6. Failure to follow up

Shadow security – a challenge to compliance: Shadow security is defined as 'employees going around IT to get the IT services they want on their own'. This means that employees implement their own security solutions when they believe that compliance is beyond their capacity or will affect their productivity. For instance, if they must implement a strong password policy, then to ease matters they might write the password on sticky notes and keep them handy for use. They do not realize the repercussions of the password being compromised to breach information security.

EMPLOYEES ARE ASSETS BUT SOMETIMES POSE A CHALLENGE

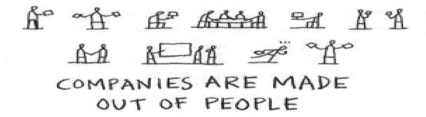

COMPANIES ARE MADE OUT OF PEOPLE

Employees are a very important asset for organizations, but they also pose challenges and prove to be a weak link. Cybercriminals often find employees as an easy way to break into organizational systems. Almost 88% of data breaches can be attributed to human error or gap in integrity, and hence organizations invest in skilled professionals and for their training on a continuous basis. These trainings must cover external risks, internal risks, risks due to remote working, and mobile applications. Enhancing awareness will educate the people, reduce occurrence of breaches, and inculcate a security culture within the organization.

CONCLUSION

The governance of enterprise IT to meet the needs for compliance has been covered in this chapter. There are some challenges faced by industry, and there are regulatory compliance provisions that have to be adhered to. There are many scenarios a multinational will face where each country in which they do business may require different controls for data privacy, data protection, data sovereignty, and data residency. To meet these challenges and succeed, multinationals must have enhanced visibility across their global key assets and comprehensive controls to meet the requirements of global, regional, and country-specific compliance regulations.

COMING NEXT . . .

As we browse through industries, pain areas and challenges faced by industry as well as regulatory compliance provisions, we find that there is a lot of commonalities in the problems as well as risks in the compliances with standards, guidelines, and practices adopted around the globe. In the next chapter, we will cover the consorted attempts organization are making to have an independent and business-specific framework that covers all compliances and provides the scalability and flexibility to establish, monitor, and adapt to changes.

In this chapter, we saw various obstructions and difficulties in carrying out the security governance function. In the next chapter, we shall introduce the concept of adopting an integrated approach to risk and compliance.

Adopting an Integrated Approach

3

Compliance can be regulatory compliance or other compliance enforced by industry or individual organization. Every organization is bound by certain legislations and regulations that are mandatory and may be subject to evaluation or scrutiny by regulators on a periodic basis. On the other hand, organizations are governed by internal controls, policies, and strategies. These are mandatory for an organization and all its employees. An organization has its own structure, lines of authority and responsibility, and processes/procedures to comply with policies. Policies are the first line of defense since it signifies management intent and sanction. It promotes a top-down approach that is more likely to be followed by employees, and if it is backed by a penal clause, it results in healthy compliance not only to internal controls and policies but also to external regulations and standards.

The organizational structure depicts the lines of reporting and different functional departments within the organization, functions they perform, processes they follow, and compliance with standard operating procedures laid down within the departments or functions. At the same time, all compliances and related controls must find place in documented policies and procedures. In this chapter, we discuss how management initiatives are directed to take stock on collective standards, regulations, and frameworks applicable to the organization considering the nature of business and its geographical spread and aiming to form an integrated compliance framework. This framework must be flexible and have the capability to adjust to changes in business, standards, or regulations and yet serve to be integrated to meet all requirements.

The governance of enterprise IT depends upon integration with business processes. For instance, business operations depend upon IT for maintaining IT infrastructure, on finance to manage the cash flows, on HR for providing resources, and so on. All sections work in unison to achieve common objectives of the organization (refer to Figure 3.1). An organization comprises its internal environment, values, culture, ethics, policies and people, process and technology, which help the organization to achieve organizational goals and objectives. Apart from that, an organization depends on its trading partners, stakeholders' suppliers, clients, regulators, and legislative bodies, and they are responsible for upstream and downstream exchanges, communication, and transactions. Hence, in modern day, it is considered to be an extended enterprise where internal and external people have a role to play.

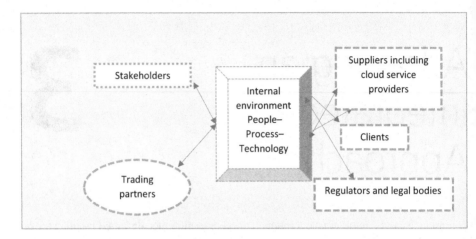

FIGURE 3.1   Extended enterprise of business.

FIGURE 3.2   Objectives of compliance.

Organizations have a global footprint and their interaction with external entities has increased manifold. They have to take care of internal governance as well as satisfy the requirement of outside entities that exist in the extended enterprise. This puts an additional strain on the GRC framework to be adopted by the enterprise. Organizations have compliance needs which have to be embedded within the organizational systems so that adherence to these compliance needs takes place. The internal environment comprises people–process–technology, and they drive risk and compliance function.

All regulatory provisions and all compliance standards and guidelines aim to establish best practices to help businesses achieve their business goals and to safeguard against threats and risks originating from within both the environment (insider threats) and external environment (like loss of data, phishing attack, etc.).

As seen in Figure 3.2, all objectives of compliance are interconnected, and security is a key word. In an organization-wide exercise, global factors, regulations, and standards must be adopted in order to fulfill the objectives and compliance requirements of the organization. The first step toward mapping the control environment is the identification of all standards, frameworks, and guidelines governing the organization.

PDCA APPROACH TO BUILDING ORGANIZATIONAL FRAMEWORK

The PDCA (Plan-Do-Check-Act) cycle is applicable to organizations planning to set up their own compliance framework. At any point, an organization is already fulfilling requirements of regulatory, industry best practices, and some known standards. But this may be taking place in silos in different parts of the organization, following the adoption of an overarching philosophy and a blueprint; hence, many redundant practices may be running in the name of compliance.

We observed in a financial institution where a multiplicity of organizational hierarchies working in silos were all indulged in the documentation of a standard operating procedure document, and it took them over three years to realize that this can be done only through a consultant. When final document was made, it was found it was a redundant exercise and the best part of the document already existed in different departments, but since they operated in silos, this full document could not be compiled. For this reason, performing an impact analysis for inventorying existing requirements and existing controls is a prerequisite for a comprehensive listing of compliance.

Keeping in line with regulatory compliance, new structures and new models are being introduced, and the legal and regulatory landscape is also undergoing constant change. Creating a comprehensive compliance program helps to reduce damage to an organization's reputation and adverse impact on business profits.

It is observed that regulatory compliances are more stringent in the banking and insurance industry. The regulatory landscape in respect of banks, insurance, and financial institutions globally have been stringent; this is due to the fact that the risk is high and stakes are big. The cost of noncompliance is high, and there is need for awareness on internal compliance for organizations. The main risks in banking industry include:

- Credit risk arising from lending made by the bank
- Market and counterparty risk from trading activities (especially derivatives trading)
- Liquidity risk arising from mismatched assets and liabilities
- Operational risk caused by error and omission in core systems and processes
- Risk associated with insurance contracts

To illustrate some of the compliances applicable to banks, the banking industry is bound by the following compliances:

1. PCI DSS (Payment Card Industry Data Security Standard)
2. Basel (Basel II is an international business standard that requires financial institutions to maintain enough cash reserves to cover risks incurred by operations. The Basel accords are a series of recommendations on banking laws and regulations issued by the Basel Committee on Banking Supervision (BSBS).
3. SOX (Sarbanes–Oxley Compliance)
4. GDPR (Global Data Protection Regulation)
5. SOC 2 (System and Organization Controls)
6. Other industry-specific/region-specific compliances

Every organization is subject to different types of standards which may be mandated by the regulators who regulate the industry. While considering the compliance requirements of different organizations, it is a necessary prerequisite to inventory all such mandatory regulations that have to be adhered to. The tone at top has to be reflected in the policies and procedures internal to the organization, which makes external compliances aligned to it. We cite here the typical case of a Knowledge Process Outsourcing organization. They have various compliances requirement that range from:

1. PCI DSS
2. GDPR
3. SOC2
4. SOX
5. ISO 27001(Information Systems Security Standard)

Each of these standards has some controls in common, and mapping all controls on a dashboard would mean compliance with the entire aforementioned standard. This is where integration is useful; it helps reduce redundancies and takes the fatigue out of audit and evaluation of individual standards to measure performance and compliance with standards.

CATEGORIES OF COMPLIANCE

The classification of different types of compliances is important for ensuring timely compliances.

- **Operational and financial compliance** that consists of internal policies and procedures aimed at minimizing organizational risks and promoting good governance.
- **Legal and regulatory compliance** that consists of all statutes, laws, regulations pertaining to all locations where the business is spread out.

- **Contractual compliance** that consists of service-level agreements (SLAs) with third-party providers, business partner agreements, nondisclosure agreements (NDAs), etc.
- **Compliance with business ethics values** and mission that drive strategies and business activities and influence decision-making process and preserve the integrity and goodwill of the enterprise.

WEAVING COMPLIANCE INTO THE ORGANIZATIONAL SETUP

The acquisition of compliance professionals well versed in all provisions of each category of compliance is important. Further, these professionals should be so placed in the hierarchy of the organization that they can act with independence. For instance, the reporting of compliance head should be directly to the audit committee or to the CEO. If it is to a level below that, the employees will not comply with his instructions and his independence to report on non-compliances may be hindered by his reporting position.

In many organizations dedicated compliance officers are appointed to take care of the overall compliance for the entire organization. Fitting compliance into the organizational chart is key to effective compliance. For instance, the financial and banking sector, operating in a dynamic and multinational environment, illustrates a blend of upcoming technology and market globalization. A threefold approach to compliance ensures a sound compliance environment.

A compliance management system is the primary responsibility of the top management (refer to Figure 3.3). The first part indicates a top-down approach to building a compliance management system. It includes Board policies and monitoring mechanisms to check compliance. Key actions that a board and management may take to demonstrate their commitment to maintain effective compliance and ensure a positive approach to compliance include:

i. Board's commitment toward compliance, which is demonstrated well to external parties as well as employees.
ii. Communicating compliance requirements to employees in a clear and concise form.
iii. Adopting a good compliance policy.
iv. Appointment of a responsible compliance officer with required authority to enforce compliance and show accountability for the overall compliance function.
v. Considering size and complexity of the business, allocating necessary resources to the program commensurate to the geographical spread of the organization.
vi. Combining reviews and management reporting in the form of periodic reports on the compliance status of the organization.

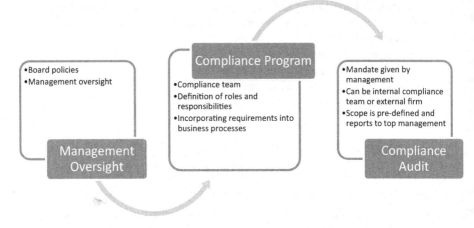

FIGURE 3.3   Compliance management system.

APPOINTMENT OF A COMPLIANCE OFFICER

The first step the board of directors and senior management should take in providing for the administration of the compliance program is the designation of a compliance officer. A compliance committee, as an alternative to or in addition to a full-time compliance officer, could be formed consisting of the compliance officer, representatives from various departments, and member(s) of senior management or the board. However, the ultimate responsibility of overall compliance with all statutes and regulations resides with the board.

The compliance officer must possess the requisite knowledge of all organizational compliances. He or she must also possess good communication skills to interact with all departments and branches to keep abreast of changes (e.g., new business lines, related compliances, employee turnover) that may require action to manage approaching new risks. Larger organizations may be able to afford and justify a dedicated compliance person, whereas in smaller organizations the function may be spread over a few persons earmarked to assume compliance responsibilities.

The functions of a compliance officer include:

- developing compliance policies and procedures;
- training management and employees in consumer protection laws and regulations;
- reviewing policies and procedures for compliance with applicable laws and regulations and the institution's stated policies and procedures;
- assessing emerging issues or potential liabilities;
- coordinating responses to consumer complaints;

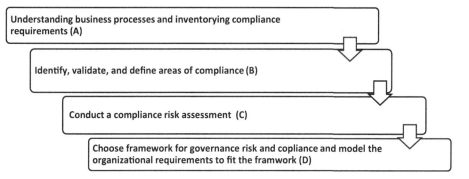

FIGURE 3.4   Steps in formulating a compliance program.

- reporting compliance activities and audit/review findings to the board; and
- ensuring corrective actions. When more than one individual is responsible for compliance, responsibility and accountability must be clearly defined.

In order to be effective, regular training, as well as adequate time and resources required to carry out compliance duties must be provided. In larger organizations, the compliance officer may use services of subject matter experts (SMEs) to assist him to maintain the compliance function. However, enough due diligence to verify competency of SMEs in specific compliance standards or regulations and signing of NDAs to maintain the privacy and confidentiality of organizational data must be performed.

Organizations need to put together a plan that brings together the people responsible for compliance (e.g., lines of business, HR, finance, physical security, legal, business continuity, IT, and of course information security) so that it covers their business comprehensively. Figure 3.4 gives steps to formulate a compliance program. Such program intersects with key government legislations and their compliance.

Understanding Organizational Processes and Structure

Defining the compliance function is important to planning and governance. Setting up steering committees with adequate representation from all concerned departments and which would be responsible for identifying compliance needs, putting in place processes and procedures, tracking progress and reporting on milestones is desirable.

An integrated compliance framework must include inputs from the following players. Key personnel to be included in the compliance program who are outside the compliance function are members of:

1. financial risk management;
2. internal audit management;

3. IT risk and compliance; and
4. operational risk management departments.

Depending on the size, complexity of business, and geographical spread of the organization, management will involve department heads and data owners; process owners may also be involved in compliance management. It has become increasingly necessary to have an expert, an external counsel, to guide the compliance team and to interpret regulations that are established to control threats and frauds.

Compliance Analytics for Identifying and Validating Compliance Requirements

Compliance analytics is being used to analyze the compliance-related information to ensure timely compliance and analysis of forthcoming regulations. It has been defined by Deloitte as 'a growing category of information analysis, involves gathering and storing relevant data and mining it for patterns, discrepancies, and anomalies'.

Conducting Compliance Risk Assessment

Management determines key stakeholders and other members to participate in the compliance analytics workshop. The purpose is to identify areas of high risk, especially those related to compliance. The workshop deals with the current state of compliances covered by the organization, some impending regulatory or legal compliances that may be levied in the near time period, and the processes that are existing to protect the organization from fines and penalties and loss of goodwill suffered from non-compliances.

It is worth organizing the compliance workshop since it helps perform a complete SWOT analysis in terms of listing down all technology assets that supplement the compliance function, gauging the level of awareness in the people involved with compliance and what are the gaps in processes that may lead to non-compliance with any of the compliances in the stack. It also helps in identifying information inconsistencies due to data lying in disparate systems and the risks surrounding all pain areas as well as examining the strength of internal controls that support compliance.

The compliance risk assessment lays down the baseline for covering slack controls and identifying priority areas for improvement. It also leads to the management oversight of priority areas and results in risk reduction.

'As-is' processes are reviewed during the compliance risk workshop as well as the recommended processes that cover gaps in controls having a scalable nature to accommodate changes and additions to the compliance stack in the next stage. Documentation is another tool where existing processes are documented from start to finish, mapping the workflow to provide clarity and comprehensibility for large and complex processes. Factoring large workflows/processes into smaller dataflow diagrams improves the understanding for new employees and makes compliance process simpler to follow.

Information gathering and collection of all relevant facts are key to compliance analytics process.

Compliance Analytics Is an Ongoing Program

The compliance risk assessment is to be carried out periodically. Information is dynamic, and it must be refreshed ideally every quarter; deployment of the compliance program must achieve sustainability. Recalibration in response to changes must go on continuously; the continued validity of the compliance analytics program in lieu of changes in compliance requirements is crucial to the effective functioning of the automated capability.

Choosing and Tailoring an Appropriate GRC Framework

After successfully completing the previous steps, after gathering data on types of regulations, compliances and risks, the compliance officer is ready to architect an appropriate GRC framework tailored to the organization. Figure 3.5 displays the three components of GRC to treat enterprise risk and meet compliance standards.

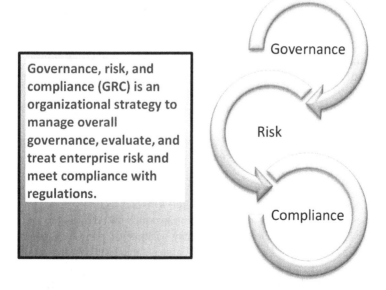

Governance, risk, and compliance (GRC) is an organizational strategy to manage overall governance, evaluate, and treat enterprise risk and meet compliance with regulations.

Governance

Risk

Compliance

FIGURE 3.5 GRC are interlinked.

Depending on the budget and cost considerations organizations can take decisions on adopting a unique GRC compliance model for their organization. Successful GRC programs must be closely aligned with the strategic objectives and values of business and must define the roles and responsibilities of every member of the team. Some advantages of a tailored GRC approach include improved decision-making, removing redundancies, optimal IT investments, elimination of silos, and avoidance of penalties and loss of reputation, to name a few.

STEPS IN BUILDING A GRC FRAMEWORK

The steps in building a GRC framework for the organization include:

1. Define a GRC charter.

The first step in this direction is to define a GRC charter that articulates the organization's GRC vision and mission, objectives and goals, success criteria, roles and responsibilities, types of solutions and technology that will be used, and critical milestones for success. Understanding how each of these parameters roll back to support the achievement of the organization's strategic objectives will enable each GRC function to deliver better value to the business.

It is also important to note that as strategic objectives change in response to internal or external events, GRC program charters need to be updated to avoid becoming redundant and to continue focusing on the risks that matter to business strategy and decision-making.

2. Define what information/assets have to be protected.
3. Classify information so that security levels can be set as per the significance or importance of the data/information.
4. Make a risk assessment to identify risks and to evaluate acceptability of those risks to the organization
5. Identify the risk treatment strategy; whether the organization wants to:
   i. avoid the risk by not carrying out a particular activity;
   ii. reduce risk by sharing with trade partners;
   iii. insure the risk;
   iv. accept the risk as mentioned in point '4' above.
6. Assess residual risk – the risk that remains once all controls for mitigation of risks is executed. Organizations may accept that portion of risk till the adverse effects from the risk rises above acceptable levels. At that time, organizations will choose to mitigate the risk by putting a control. For instance, organizations found one in 50 transactions caused delay in delivery. But

slowly the delay moved to one in seven transactions. Management immediately appointed a service delivery executive in that sector to deal with deliveries so that customers did not suffer. It became a goodwill issue and hence risk mitigation was necessary.

7. Document procedures for operating and also risks and controls existing in the organization. This can be done in the form of maintenance of a risk register where risks and controls would be documented and periodically reviewed.

8. Management oversight and reporting in the form of internal audit reports, performance measurement data, and any other source that helps to measure the state of GRC controls within the organization.

STAKEHOLDER PARTICIPATION IN GRC STRATEGY

A key to an integrated collaborative program for governance risk and compliance is involving stakeholders across the organization to participate and give their inputs in their area of operation. There is a need to align the benefits of the program to the needs of each stakeholder.

For instance, the objective of top management may be timely information about the top risks facing the organization and obtaining assurance that business processes operate within the defined risk appetite.

CEOs might want to know about data/information integrity and how they can make risk-informed decisions as well as identify opportunities quickly. By understanding these needs, and clearly outlining how they can be met with an effective GRC program, it becomes easier to gain the right level of support and collaboration for GRC investments.

Stakeholder's participation in GRC strategy enables safeguarding of stakeholder interest in the organization; it also enables their monitoring of controls relating to risk and compliance and having it discussed in audit committee meetings. Planning, strategizing, implementing, and maintaining GRC standards and controls will realize benefits for stakeholders. Hence, it is advisable that they participate throughout the GRC program.

In many organizations, GRC functions such as internal audit, risk management, and legal or third-party management follow different operating frameworks and standards. There is a lot of commonalities among these standards. There is a need to have an integrated approach toward GRC implementation in the organization. The different sections managing their tasks independently must be aware of GRC initiatives within the organization and work toward leveraging a common architecture and risk-control framework.

BUILDING A HYBRID SECURITY FRAMEWORK

Organizations can choose controls from industry standards and best practices and build a hybrid framework for GRC that covers mandatory regulations and standards as well as good-to-have controls that would enhance the security posture of the organization.

Figure 3.6 defines the elements of a hybrid GRC framework, which involves internal governance characterized by policies, procedures, and well-defined standard operating procedures – the risk of governance depending on accepted risk standards and external governance which revolves on security and cybersecurity.

Every organization has a suite of compliances, regulatory standards, law of the land, and standards on security, privacy, and third-party security that it must follow. A unique framework for the organization should aggregate all types of controls contained in all mandatory as well as 'good-to-have' controls decided by the management. For example, BPO organizations have a compliance requirement of SOC2, GDPR, ISO 27001, and regulations for IP rights. Many of these standards have redundant characteristics, enabling security teams to map certain controls to satisfy compliance with an array of regulatory standards.

FINDING A RIGHT FIT

Each individual standard has its own merits and demerits, and there cannot be a single fit for all organizations. This is because the culture, management philosophy and intent, risk acceptance capability of the organization, size of the organization and budget for

FIGURE 3.6   Elements of an effective hybrid GRC framework.

security, level of maturity, and the severity of the consequences of noncompliance differ between organizations.

Every organization is governed by the type of management, type of organization structure, and geographical dispersion that it has. For instance, in a multinational organization, the head office is in Tokyo and is having its presence in India, Hong Kong, New York, Australia, and New Zealand. Such a company may choose to have a centralized compliance department based in Tokyo and the compliance head will monitor the compliances at all other offices. Some compliance may be country specific, especially regulatory compliances. Hence, some organizations may allocate responsibility for compliance with individual country offices.

Another point is that in some countries like the Middle East, organizations prefer to implement COBIT as a governance framework, while in other countries commonly accepted standards are ISO 27001 for security, ISO 31000 for risk, and ISO 22000 for business continuity. So, when organizations plan non-mandatory standards or guidelines, it is entirely on their discretion to choose from commonly accepted standards. Sometimes, clients require compliance with some of the common standards, and hence management decides to implement these standards.

Governance is all about assessing and reducing internal and external risks. Risk applies to people, process, and technology – all three elements of business. Hence, one has to answer questions like:

1. What are risks to business?
2. What is it that we want to protect?
3. Who is responsible for protecting against risk?
4. How is the risk to be addressed or mitigated?
5. What would be the repercussions if risk is not addressed?

A hybrid framework can help organizations meet their unique business objectives and compliance requirements. This approach enables flexibility and ensures continued functionality as the technology and threat landscapes change. Aggregation of all controls from applicable compliance requirements, for combined and centralized monitoring of the compliance function looks like a better approach. But organizations that have generic requirements for security can go for established standards such as ISO 27001.

COMPONENTS OF GRC FRAMEWORK

It would be good to understand that the GRC framework would involve the aforementioned processes that have to be followed by organizations in order to achieve a healthy risk and compliance profile. Figure 3.7 lists down component processes in the GRC initiatives taken by an organization.

1. Inventory processes and classify assets

2. Identify, document and categorize risks

3. Provide for periodic risk assessments

4. Define and document controls

5. Assess effectiveness of controls over a period and report on risk containment

6. Fulfil requirements of disclosure and certification on standards and regulatory compliance

7. Remediate open issues and perfect the GRC model.

FIGURE 3.7   Component processes for GRC.

INFORMATION SECURITY GOVERNANCE FRAMEWORK

In Figure 3.6, we have seen that the building of a hybrid framework envisages the planning and implementation of a security governance framework as well. The underlying principles behind the risk framework would also be establishing a secure environment within the organization. Further, most of the mandatory and regulatory standards such as PCI DSS, ISO 27001, GDPR, SOC2, etc., are defining security to be a part of the organizational governance program.

To illustrate, we had done a project in a developing country where controls in banks had been assessed. Since the level of controls was much below normal security standards, the Central Bank decided to adopt ISO 27001 as a security standard and wanted to develop a security framework based on those controls to be adopted by all other banks. By enforcing the principles of ISO 27001 in all the banks under its jurisdiction, the objective of setting a basic security culture could be achieved.

Therefore, sometimes existing standards help organizations to adopt them and enforce their GRC objectives. The existence of multiple standards makes choice of an IT security framework a bit difficult. But certain indicative factors drive this choice. For instance, an organization that processes credit card transactions will have to follow and implement the PCI/DSS controls. For the Health and Wellness industry, preservation and security of electronic Personal Health Information (ePHI) is to be ensured to meet the HIPAA regulations.

Likewise, for enterprises that deal with the federal government, NIST 800–53 is mandatory. Companies listed on the NASDAQ may probably select COBIT in order to more readily comply with SOX. A more generic security standard would be ISO 27001; it is applicable to any type of industry, although implementation is elaborate and requirements for certification are rigorous. A list of security frameworks is indicated here (which is an inclusive list):

- **NIST** (National Institute of Standards and Technology)
- **CIS Controls** (Centre for Internet Security Controls)
- **ISO** (International Organization for Standardization)
- **HIPAA** (Health Insurance Portability and Accountability Act)/**HITECH** Omnibus Rule
- **PCI-DSS** (The Payment Card Industry Data Security Standard)
- **GDPR** (General Data Protection Regulation)
- **SOC2** (System and Organization Controls)
- **CCPA** (California Consumer Privacy Act)
- **AICPA** (American Institute of Certified Public Accountants)
- **SOX** (Sarbanes–Oxley Act)
- **COBIT** (Control Objectives for Information and Related Technologies)
- **GLBA** (Gramm–Leach–Bliley Act)
- **FISMA** (Federal Information Security Modernization Act of 2014)
- **Fed RAMP** (The Federal Risk and Authorization Management Program)
- **FERPA** (The Family Educational Rights and Privacy Act of 1974)
- **ITAR** (International Traffic in Arms Regulations)
- **COPPA** (Children's Online Privacy Protection Rule)
- **NERC CIP Standards** (NERC Critical Infrastructure Protection Standards)

CYBERSECURITY FRAMEWORK, A PART OF SECURITY GOVERNANCE

More than 80% of organizations now depend on the internet for carrying on their day-to-day activities. Internet is an unsecure network, and cyberattacks are rising. Organizations are under tremendous pressure to safeguard their data and protect their systems from cyberattacks. The greatest challenge however is to comply with the numerous regulations and standards applicable to the organization.

Cybersecurity is one of the biggest global challenges for developing economies like India, where cyber laws and policies are neither stringent nor well implemented. In such a difficult scenario, business should develop a customized internet security framework.

Cyber security frameworks are a good way for IT security professionals to create a solid baseline for measuring security effectiveness and to meet compliance requirements, but it can be a challenge to do this without the tools, talent and support from executive leadership.

Although a detailed discussion and comparative analysis of various cybersecurity frameworks will be dealt with in subsequent chapters, it is worth mentioning the main frameworks that are available:

1. **NIST Cybersecurity Framework** is a voluntary framework to guide critical infrastructure organizations to increase their resilience and reduce cybersecurity risk. It comprises three components; the core that provides a set of cybersecurity activities and outcomes, the framework implementation that provides the context for organizational risk management, and framework profiles that are used to identify and prioritize risks/opportunities for improving the cybersecurity within the organization. NIST helps organizations prioritize from the objective of business continuity and security.

2. **International Standards Institute (ISO)** has formulated a general security framework for organizations in the form of ISO 27001, which prescribes the formulation of the information security management system (ISMS) to manage risks for people, processes, and IT systems. Implementation of ISO 27001 includes the following:

    i. Documenting security policy

    ii. Identify the scope of ISMS

    iii. Conduct a risk assessment

    iv. Manage and treat risks

    v. Choose control objectives and determine placement of these controls

    vi. Document SOA (statement of applicability) delineating areas in scope

3. **PCI DSS** is a global standard for the payment card industry. It was initiated for the security of card payments. It enforces tight controls around storage, transmission and processing of cardholder data, and is applicable to banks and all other enterprises that process card data.

The payment standard has 12 principal requirements, all of which are covered by these six categories:

- Build and maintain a secure network
- Protect card data
- Maintain a vulnerability program
- Implement strong access control measures
- Regularly monitor and test networks
- Maintain an Information security policy

As seen in the focus areas, network controls and vulnerability assessments are important from PCI DSS point of view. Hence, it has been included under the cybersecurity network category.

OTHER FRAMEWORKS

In addition, there are some other frameworks which take a general, risk-based approach to information security by prescribing controls that directly counteract an organization's defined security risks.

- **AICPA Trust Services Principles and Criteria (SOC)** is a set of controls that are utilized in SOC 2 and SOC 3 engagements. It is a set of five trust principles with focus on Security, Availability, Confidentiality, Processing Integrity and Privacy. SOC 2 focuses on a business's non-financial reporting controls as they relate to security, availability, processing integrity, confidentiality, and privacy of a system, as opposed to *SOC 1/SSAE 18* which is focused on the financial reporting controls.
- **COBIT (Control Objectives for Information and Related Technologies)** is an organizational security and integrity framework that utilizes processes, control objectives, management guidelines, and maturity modeling to ensure alignment of IT with business. It maps directly to standards required for regulatory compliance (ITIL, ISO 2700X, COSO).

Risk Governance/Framework

A risk management framework is a set of related components that support and sustain risk management throughout an organization. There are two types of components:

1. Foundations include risk management policy objectives, mandate, and commitment.
2. Organizational arrangements include plans, relationships, accountabilities, resources processes, and activities used to manage organizational risk.

While Foundations have been discussed earlier in the chapter, it is worth discussing the point 2 which includes the following:

- Risk identification
- Risk measurement and assessment
- Risk mitigation
- Risk reporting and monitoring
- Risk governance

RISK IDENTIFICATION

Identifying risks that pose a potential threat to successful business operations is a key component of business planning. A well-prepared business can minimize loss of time and productivity caused by security incidents. Under most business models, organizations face the following types of threats-

- **Physical risks** that cover premises and risks from fire or explosions.
- **Business risk.** Some risks have the potential to destroy a business or at least cause serious damage that can be costly to repair. Potential threats include location hazards such as fires and storm damage, alcohol and drug abuse among personnel, technology risks such as power outages, and strategic risks such as investment in research and development. Engaging a consultant can help in employees training, security checks, insurance and annual maintenance contracts.
- **Location risks.** Natural disasters generally fall under location risks and organizations use siting controls before choosing their business locations. Liability or property and casualty insurance are being used to transfer the financial burden of location risks to a third-party or a business insurance company.
- **Human risks.** Protecting against theft and fraud is a challenging task in the workplace. Background check before hiring personnel can uncover previous offenses in an applicant's past. This can prevent wrong hires into the organization.
- **Technology risks**. A power outage is the most common technology risk. Organizations have generators for backup to serve as a fall back. Telecommunications and communication failure can also be caused due to technology risks. Organizations may choose to provide emergency use only cell phones to be used during such emergency for official use.
- **Strategy risks** are inherent to business objectives of the organization. Banks correlate strategy to decisions on lending to customers while for a pharmaceutical company risk relate to the research/development of a new medicine.

Risk measurement provides information on the quantum of either a specific risk exposure or an aggregate risk exposure and the probability of a loss occurring due to those exposures. When measuring specific risk exposure, it is important to consider the effect of that risk on the overall risk profile of the organization.

Risk mitigation. Having categorized and measured its risks, a company can then decide on which risks they are eliminating or minimizing, and how much of its core risks they want to retain. Risk mitigation can be achieved through an outright sale of assets or liabilities, buying insurance, hedging with derivatives or diversification.

RISK MONITORING AND REPORTING

Reporting periodically on specific risks and aggregate risks helps to maintain risk levels at an minimal level. Risk reports must be submitted to appropriate authorities to reduce risk exposure.

RISK GOVERNANCE

Risk governance is the process that ensures that conduct of business and activities is in accordance to the risk framework adopted by the organization. Roles and responsibilities for risk management must be defined and segregation of duties should be made. The right level of authority should be assigned duties for approval of core risks, risk limits, exception to limits and for general oversight.

It is important to prioritize risks and give it proper treatment. Hence a formal approach to risk and adoption of a risk framework with defined responsibilities is necessary. The responsibility for risk may also be shared by a risk committee who will report to the audit committee on a periodic basis on the risks faced by the organization.

COMMON RISK FRAMEWORKS

The choice when available, to select the risk governance framework or a security governance framework is the responsibility of the management. Many a times, the organizations go for inappropriate or over optimistic frameworks and land up in fatigue in trying to implement and more importantly maintaining the framework. Where it involves certification by certifying authority it results in monitoring, surveillance and audit on a periodic basis. A good way to begin would be to keep the program simple, small and achievable and slowly building on the success of the initial program. Also, it leaves room for fine-tuning, troubleshooting and perfecting the GRC program. Given below are some of the risk frameworks commonly used.

Risk IT Framework (ISACA)

Risk IT is a framework based on a set of guiding principles for effective management of IT risk (refer to Figure 3.8). The framework complements COBIT, a comprehensive framework for the governance and control of business-driven, IT-based solutions and

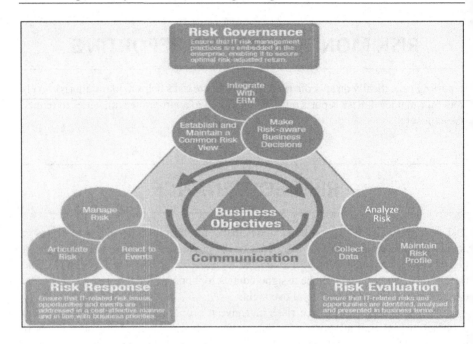

FIGURE 3.8   Risk IT framework.

services. While COBIT provides a set of controls to mitigate IT risk, risk IT provides a framework for enterprises to identify, govern, and manage IT risk

Enterprises who have adopted (or are planning to adopt) COBIT as their IT governance framework can use risk IT to enhance risk management

IRGC Risk Framework

IRGC's risk governance framework is a comprehensive approach to help understand, analyze and manage important risk issues for which there are gaps in the risk infrastructure and processes (refer to Figure 3.9). The framework comprises five linked phases including pre-assessment, appraisal, characterization and evaluation, management, and communication. These interlinked phases provide a means to gain a thorough understanding of a risk and to develop options for dealing with it. IRGC risk framework can contribute to the development of more inclusive and effective risk *governance* strategies. The report calls for improved governance to clarify, classify and confront emerging systemic risks.

A truly robust and integrated GRC program rolls up risk and regulatory intelligence from across the enterprise to help stakeholders make faster, better business decisions. It enables companies to take smarter risks, build a culture of ethics and integrity, and keep pace with constant regulatory changes – all of which are strong competitive differentiators and performance drivers in today's global business environment.

FIGURE 3.9   IRGC framework.

FORMULATING AN INTEGRATED COMPLIANCE FRAMEWORK

An integrated framework will allow organizations manage their GRC intelligently and cover the risks faced by their organizations. Within the framework would be policies, procedures, and processes approved by management and applicable on an organization wide basis.

Choosing the right framework among multiple frameworks available across geographies, industries and technologies requires many considerations and the head of compliance function must use discretion and an eye on mandatory regulations and include all essentials.

COMPLIANCE PROGRAMS

Compliance programs are offspring of their respective compliance frameworks; whether it is general security framework, risk framework or cybersecurity framework. A well-planned, well implemented, and well maintained compliance program will prevent or reduce regulatory violations, provide cost efficiencies, and is sound business strategy.

It is expected that no two compliance programs will be the same, and that the formality of a program will be dictated by numerous considerations, including: institution's size, number of branches, organizational structure and business strategy adopted. The objective or formal adoption of the compliance program is not as important as its effectiveness. Generally, the degree of detail or specificity of procedures will vary in accordance with the complexity of the issue or transactions addressed.

AUTOMATION FOR BETTER COMPLIANCE

With an increase in the scale of business, application of tools for compliance and automating processes for improving compliance is recommended. At the implementation stage, management must commit resources to automate the GRC. Considerations for this allocation of resources include:

1. **Cost:** All organizations cannot afford high-end tools for governance; cost must be justifying the benefits from automation.
2. **Desired features:** Tracking remediation measures and risk mitigation capabilities in the proposed application.
3. **Capability for third-party risk evaluations:** The tool should provide for evaluation of risks at vendors' installation.
4. **Dynamic updates to policy library:** A library update to ease the pain of manual updates for governance of applicable standards, regulations, and other industry should be organized.
5. **Requirement mapping:** Correlating requirements between different applicable standards such as COBIT, GDPR, ISO standards applicable, should be performed.
6. **Multiple compliances for group companies:** The application should provide visibility and compliance for each company within the group and allow collective monitoring for compliance.

The automated GRC tool must possess the following features:

1. Capability to import data from multiple sources/locations
2. Capability to detect suspicious activity by use of rules-based analytics, network linking, or predictive analysis
3. Presence of dashboard with a risk profile/risk score based on screening transactions, and relationships
4. Contain specific and concise guidance for remediating risk areas and action to be taken in risk situations.

Data has become a very significant asset for all organizations, and a majority of compliances are linked with the safeguarding of data. Data governance is an emerging term;

it defines guidelines for metadata management and data issue resolution to measure quality of data and initiate improvements. Without proper data governance, compliance with standards, rules, and regulations cannot be fulfilled.

GRC automation should move your organization toward a proactive approach, instead of relying on reactive models. Prevention of breach using GRC tool makes sense rather than giving reactive support for breach. Constant automated vigilance is a lower price to pay than fines, damaged reputation, and lost customers.

Metrics for performance must be pre-defined in order to provide compliance team to make decisions for effectively managing the compliance function. In a dynamic business environment, risks are volatile and a continuous watch over the risk landscape is necessary. It is rightly said that what cannot be measured cannot be improved. Regular assessment and adoption of appropriate metrics to measure the compliance program is required to gain a level of confidence in the compliance program and aim at improvising it when needed. The key criteria to look at include:

- Are appropriate metrics to drive compliance performance identified?
- Are the goals comprehensive and achievable?
- Are the time spans to measure performance and report to management defined and
- Are they enough to identify risks?
- Are issues and problems encountered documented and are corrective plans for recurring issues made available for the compliance team as guidance?

COMPLIANCE REQUIREMENTS OF PARTNER ORGANIZATION AND DUE DILIGENCE DURING CONTRACT SIGNING

Service providers, suppliers, trading partners are supposed to be aware of the compliance requirements of the organization and take steps to fall in line with the requirements. In many cases, the contractual agreements with partner organization mention the frequency and objectives of compliance training. Examples of effective training program include regulatory development monitoring, day-to-day guidance and compliance support available to operating locations or periodic company-wide functional area conferences.

A good compliance program must have a thorough planning and reporting system in-built to steer effective compliance. Primary organization must check performance and insist on audit reports. Business partners must evaluate compliance, provide support to ensure compliance and carry out corrective actions to address open points. At the time of extension of scrutiny and risk management to third-party suppliers and subcontractors, GRC processes must include stringent screening for all potential vendors, robust programs to enforce compliance and continual monitoring and auditing to identify noncompliant activities and prescribe corrective actions.

Penal clause for non-compliance must be mentioned within the contract. It must be made apparent that compliance is an ongoing process and is the responsibility of everyone in the organization including the enterprise and persons associated with the enterprise.

COMPLIANCE TRAINING

The compliance officer should be responsible for compliance training and establish a regular training schedule for directors, management, and staff, as well as for third-party service providers. Training can be conducted in-house or through external training programs or seminars. Once personnel have been trained on a subject, a compliance officer should periodically assess employees on their knowledge and comprehension of the subject matter.

Monitoring is a proactive approach by the institution to identify procedural or training weaknesses to preclude regulatory violations. Institutions that include a compliance officer in the planning, development, and implementation of business propositions increase the likelihood of success of its compliance monitoring function. Compliance officers should monitor employee performance to ensure that they are following an institution's established internal compliance policies and procedures.

An effective monitoring system includes regularly scheduled reviews of disclosures and reports to be made to appropriate authorities. Complaints may be indicative of a compliance weakness in a function or department. Therefore, a compliance officer should be aware of the complaints received and act to ensure a timely resolution. A compliance officer should determine the cause of the complaint and take action to improve the institution's business practices, as required.

Document filing and retention procedures; posted notices, adherence to laws and regulations; third-party service provider operations; and internal compliance communication systems that provide updates and revisions of the applicable laws and regulations to management and staff should all be a part of the monitoring process.

Changes to regulations or changes in an institution's business operations, products, or services should trigger a review of established compliance procedures. Modifications that are necessary should be made expeditiously to minimize compliance risk, and all affected personnel must be informed of the change.

COMPLIANCE AUDIT

A compliance audit is an independent review of an institution's compliance with consumer protection laws and regulations and adherence to internal policies and procedures. The audit helps management ensure ongoing compliance and identify compliance risk conditions. It complements the institution's internal monitoring system. The board of directors of the institution should determine the scope of an audit, and the frequency with which audits are conducted. The scope and frequency of an audit should consider the following factors:

- Size of organization
- Organization structure and number of branches
- Volume of transactions
- Expertise and experience of compliance personnel
- Outsourcing to third-party vendors
- Number and type of consumer complaints received
- Degree to which policies and procedures are defined and detailed in writing
- Magnitude/frequency of changes to any of the above.

An audit may be conducted once a year, or it may be ongoing where all products and services, all applicable operations, and all departments and branches are addressed on a staggered basis. An audit may be performed 'in-house' or may be contracted to an outside firm or individual, such as a consultant or accountant.

Enterprises may outsource the audit function, care to be taken that the auditor is well-versed in compliance, and that the audit program is based on current laws and regulation, as well as is comprehensive in scope. Generally, a strong compliance audit will incorporate vigorous transaction testing. Audit findings should be reported directly to the board of directors or the audit committee.

A written compliance audit report should include-

- scope of the audit (including departments, branches, and product types reviewed);
- deficiencies or modifications identified;
- number of transactions sampled by category of product type; and
- Descriptions of or suggestions for, corrective actions and time frames for correction.

FOLLOW-UP ACTION BY MANAGEMENT

Board and senior management response to the audit report should be prompt. The compliance officer should receive a copy of all compliance audit reports, and act to address noted deficiencies and required changes to ensure full compliance with consumer protection laws and regulations.

Management should also establish follow-up procedures to verify, subsequently that the corrective actions were lasting and effective. With new compliances becoming applicable, training the compliance team is necessary since it will increase understanding and give guidance for compliance with the employees. Considering constant amendments to regulations a process of periodic review of compliance environment is to be performed especially for changes in regulatory environment. This is needed to prevent breaches in compliance.

CONCLUSION

Compliance is an active, ongoing process that is the responsibility of everyone in the organization. The base of internal compliance lies with the policies, procedures and processes; mapping of risks by management and aligning these risks to controls, risk metrics, testing of controls and documenting results is relevant for monitoring and continuous improvement of the compliance programs.

The objective is to have a well-knit comprehensive GRC framework that provides assurance to stakeholders on the security, risk awareness and risk mitigation and strategies to combat risks arising out of external risk impact on business. A BIA (business impact analysis) approach is useful to evaluate current processes and its impact on all compliances that the organization must comply with. A scalable framework accords a visibility for an organization's capability to respond swiftly to risks/opportunities and accommodate business changes occurring within the enterprise is desirable.

The IT Security Policy of an organization lays down the various controls that must be in place in order to cover IT risk. IT can be deployed to develop tools that can automate compliance monitoring and tracing at the same time optimize costs in the long run. Organizations would therefore be able to reduce regulatory uncertainty and develop common controls applicable to a wide variety of their regulations.

GOING FURTHER . . .

In the next chapter, we will have a physical walkthrough of building an integrated compliance framework by considering mandatory regulations and nature of industry discuss the available frameworks and retrofit compliance requirements with existing frameworks and to point out commonalities between frameworks.

Compliance Frameworks – Possible Solutions

4

In the context of an increase in legal and regulatory landscape and stakeholder interest in the operations of an organization, it has become utmost necessary to adopt good governance. Corporate boards and executive teams are more focused on governance related issues than ever before

As seen in Figure 4.1, the governance function in an organization consists of IT Governance, IT Security, Information Security and Security Governance and all domains are interconnected.

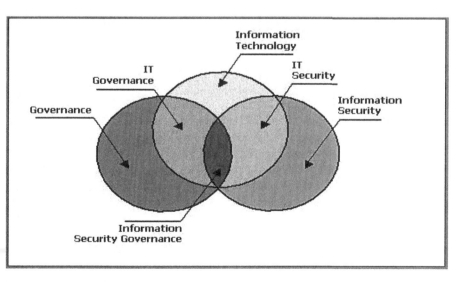

FIGURE 4.1 Governance process.

IT GOVERNANCE

GRC has become a significant function within the organization and adopting a framework of best fit is sometimes difficult to achieve. In this chapter we shall obtain a glimpse of all favorable frameworks in order to select the most appropriate one for the organization.

COMPLIANCE STANDARDS AND GUIDELINES

Standards are a means for identifying, developing, acquiring, evaluating disseminating, and providing access to applicable standards, codes, regulations, and laws. The standards system includes both internal and external standards; national and international standards and local, state and central regulations and laws as well as rules set by regulators of industry.

Responsibility for identification of standards and frameworks for the organization is done by someone with a technical background who is knowledgeable of the legal and regulatory environment; such person works closely with the legal department or consultant to ensure accurate interpretations of standards and regulations.

IT GOVERNANCE FRAMEWORKS

The governance process within an organization includes elements such as definition and communication of corporate controls, key policies, risk management, regulatory and compliance management and oversight over compliance activities

The initiation of IT Governance generally begins with an examination of available frameworks created by industry experts and widely accepted by organizations across the globe. IT governance frameworks help set the key metrics to measure the effectiveness of the IT function and the ROI (return on investment) in IT to the business. A few of the standards on governance are as under-

COSO (Committee of Sponsoring Organizations)

COSO was developed by the Committee of Sponsoring Organizations of the Treadway Commission to evaluate internal controls in an organization. It focuses on business aspects like enterprise risk management (ERM) and fraud deterrence.

The Committee of Sponsoring Organizations of the Treadway Commission (COSO) updated its *Internal Control – Integrated Framework*. The revised COSO framework's 17 principles of effective internal control are provided in Table 4.1.

TABLE 4.1 stated below, depicts the revised COSO framework's 17 principles of effective internal control

S. NO.	INTERNAL CONTROL COMPONENT	PRINCIPLES
1.	Control environment	1. Demonstrate commitment to integrity and ethical values 2. Ensure that board exercises oversight responsibility 3. Establish structures, reporting lines, authorities and responsibilities 4. Demonstrate commitment to a competent workforce 5. Hold people accountable
2.	Risk assessment	1. Specify appropriate objectives 2. Identify and analyze risks 3. Evaluate fraud risks 4. Identify and analyze changes that could significantly affect internal controls
3.	Control activities	1. Select and develop control activities that mitigate risks 2. Select and develop technology controls 3. Deploy control activities through policies and procedures
4.	Information and communication	1. Use relevant, quality information to support the internal control function 2. Communicate internal control information internally 3. Communicate internal control information Externally
5.	Monitoring	1. Perform ongoing or periodic evaluations of internal controls (or a combination of the two) 2. Communicate internal control deficiencies

Depending on a company's facts and circumstances, making the transition to the updated framework can take time, so it's a good idea to begin the process as soon as possible. Companies may familiarize themselves with the aforementioned 17 principles and other COSO guidelines and upgrade their internal control systems in line with the principles as shown earlier.

1. **Control Environment**: How has management put into place policies and procedures that guide the organization? The following activities should be performed:

I Demonstrate commitment to integrity and ethical values
   i. Ensure that board exercises oversight responsibility
   ii. Establish structures, reporting lines, authorities, and responsibilities
   iii. Demonstrate commitment to a competent workforce
   iv. Hold people accountable for actions
2. **Risk Assessment**: How does your organization assess risk in order to identify the things that threaten the achievement of their objectives?
   i. Specify appropriate objectives
   ii. Identify and analyze risks
   iii. Evaluate fraud risks
   iv. Identify and analyze changes that could significantly affect internal controls
3. **Information and Communication**: How does management communicate to their internal and external users what is expected of them? How do you make sure that you receive acknowledgment from those people that they understand what you're asking them to do?
   i. Use relevant, quality information to support the internal control function
   ii. Communicate internal control information internally
   iii. Communicate internal control information externally
4. **Monitoring Activities**: How does management oversee the functioning of the entire organization? How do you identify when things aren't working correctly and correct those deficiencies as quickly as you possibly can?
   i. Perform ongoing or periodic evaluations of internal controls (or a combination of the two)
   ii. internal control deficiencies
5. **Existing Control Activities**: What are the controls that you currently have in place?
   i. Select and develop control activities that mitigate risks
   ii. Select and develop technology controls
   iii. Deploy control activities through policies and procedures

COBIT and COSO are widely accepted IT governance frameworks. The implementation of the Sarbanes Oxley regulation, (SOX) has made it compulsory for organizations to adopt the COSO or COBIT framework.

COBIT (Control Objectives for Information Technology)

The Information Security Audit and Control Association (ISACA) produced the Control Objectives for Information Related Technology (COBIT) framework in 1996 to focus on risk reduction in financial organizations. It is also commonly used to comply with the Sarbanes–Oxley Act (SOX). With the latest revision, in 2019, COBIT has evolved to address best practices for aligning information technology functions and processes, and linking them to business strategy.

There are five principles that enable an organization to build a holistic framework for the governance and management of IT.

Principle 1: Meeting stakeholder needs
Principle 2: Covering the enterprise end to end
Principle 3: Applying a single integrated framework
Principle 4: Enabling a holistic approach
Principle 5: Separating governance from management

COBIT mentions seven enablers for building a holistic framework.

1. People, policies and frameworks
2. Processes
3. Organizational structures
4. Culture, ethics and behavior
5. Information
6. Services, infrastructure and applications
7. People, skills and competencies

Aligning business with the principles and enablers, organizations can optimize their risk and compliance framework to give benefit realization and adding to business value. Organizations perceive the following benefits from COBIT-

- Leverage information technology to achieve business goals and objectives.
- Manage high-quality information to support business decision-making and continuous improvisation and maintenance of such information.
- Achieve operational excellence through the use of technology.
- Ensure identification and management of IT risks
- Ensure organizations realize the proper Return on Investment (ROI) on their investments in IT.
- Compliance with laws, regulations and contractual agreements.

COBIT classifies management objectives as under-

i. **Align, Plan** and **Organize (APO)**: It addresses the overall strategy and support activities for information technology
ii. **Build, Acquire** and **Implement (BAI)**: It addresses the definition, acquisition and implementation of IT and integration of IT with business processes.
iii. **Deliver Service** and **Support (DSS):** It addresses delivery and support of IT services including security.
iv. **Monitor, Evaluate** and **Assess (MEA)**: It addresses performance monitoring with Internal set targets control objectives and external requirements.

COBIT 5 is based on the following principles for governance of IT:

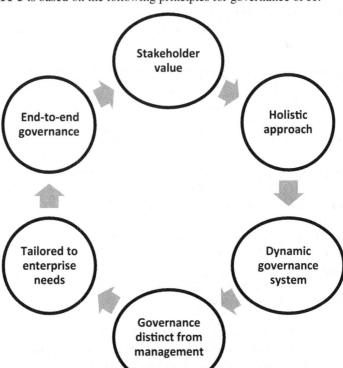

FIGURE 4.2   COBIT 2019 governance principles.

Aligning business with the principles and control objectives shall enable organizations to optimize their risk and compliance framework and reap benefit realization while adding business value.

COBIT 2019 is designed to integrate processes; it can be aligned with other best practice frameworks such as ITIL, ISO 20000, and ISO 27001. It also introduces 'focus area' concepts that describe specific governance topics and issues, which can be addressed by management or governance objectives (Figure 4.2).

Some examples of these focus areas include small and medium enterprises, cybersecurity, digital transformation, and cloud computing. Focus areas will be added and changed as needed based on trends, research, and feedback – there is no limit for the number of focus areas that can be included in COBIT 2019.

ITIL

ITIL advocates that it facilitates the alignment of IT and digital services to the needs of the business and in support of core activities and goals. ITIL is fundamental to businesses, enables transformation and helps organizations realize value. The 'Information Technology Infrastructure Library' is a set of best practices for creating and improving an ITSM process. It is designed to help businesses manage risks, strengthen customer relations, establish cost-effective practices and build stable IT environments for growth, scale and change. An **ITIL Practitioner** is an expert in continually shaping IT service development processes

ITIL Principles and **Core Components are as under-**

- Delivering maximum value to customers
- Optimizing resources and capabilities
- Offering services that are useful and reliable
- Planning processes with specific goals in mind
- Defining roles clearly for each task.

ITIL operates in five stages-

1. Service Strategy
2. Service Design
3. Service Transition
4. Service Operations
5. Continual Service Improvement.

Each of these stages has subcategories of processes. All of the ITIL processes and stages work together to maximize efficiency and reliability of services and to ensure continual improvement of services.

Sarbanes–Oxley Compliance

Sarbanes–Oxley Act (SOX) mandates a stricter governance model and tighter internal controls for public companies. The transfer of responsibility, the entire process of scheduling, testing and remediation needs to be automated, so the internal audit manager can ensure repeatability over time and across business units. In addition, strict change control needs to be implemented for processes and controls and associated documentation to stay in sync (once it becomes integrated with daily operational processes), so that the investments in year 1 in documentation can continue to be leveraged.

IT to ensure that spread sheets, emails, IMs, recorded phone calls and financial transactions will all be preserved for at least five years in case auditors require them, so it's essential the right management systems are in place. Tools to automate workflows, manage and monitor data flow and archive and retrieve information quickly will all have to be enabled.

While companies in the past spent a lot of money on SOX compliance initially they have now settled toward a project-oriented approach and streamlined their governance process in line with SOX provisions.

Organizations now hold process owners responsible for testing and documenting SOX requirements while retaining the overall ownership of Sarbanes–Oxley compliance with the internal audit group. The entire process of scheduling, testing and remediation needs to be automated, so the internal audit manager can ensure repeatability over time and across business units. In addition, strict change control needs to be implemented for processes and controls and associated documentation to stay in sync (once it becomes integrated with daily operational processes), so that the investments in year 1 in documentation can continue to be leveraged. SOX are a governance process that concentrates on controls around financial reporting.

Effective timely backups of key information and document management systems are essential in remaining compliant with these regulations. However, they must also ensure they have full visibility into every part of their firm's digital estate in order for this to be effective. IT teams also need to ensure all records are being properly retained. The role of IT when complying with SOX is to ensure recordkeeping and to facilitate the audit process. Tools to automate workflows manage and monitor data flow and archive and retrieve information quickly will be significant.

ISO/IEC 38500

ISO/IEC 38500:2008 provides guiding principles for directors of organizations (including owners, board members, directors, partners, senior executives, or similar) on the effective, efficient, and acceptable use of IT within their organizations. ISO/IEC 38500:2008 is owned by the International Standards Organization (ISO) and the International Electro technical

Commission (IEC). The standard helps to clarify IT governance from the top down by describing it as the means of directors demonstrating to all stakeholders and compliance bodies their effective stewardship over IT resources by ensuring that an appropriate governance and security framework exists for all IT activities by covering the following principles-

- **Responsibility** – Employees know their responsibilities in terms of both demand and supply of IT and have the authority to meet them.
- **Strategy** – Business strategies should be aligned with IT possibilities, and all IT within an organization should support the business strategies.
- **Acquisition** – all IT investments must be made on the basis of a business case with regular monitoring in place to assess whether the assumptions still hold.
- **Performance** – the performance of IT systems should lead to business benefits and therefore it is necessary that IT supports the business properly.
- **Conformance** – IT systems should help to ensure that business processes comply with legislation and regulations; IT itself must also comply with legal requirements and agreed internal rules.
- **Human behavior** – IT policies, practices and decisions respect human behavior and acknowledges the needs of all the people in the process.

The standard consists of three parts: **Scope, Framework and Guidance**.

ISO/IEC 38500:2008 applies to the governance of management processes (and decisions) relating to the information and communication services used by an organization. These processes could be controlled by IT specialists within the organization or external service providers, or by business units within the organization. The standard is universally applicable for all types and size of organizations.

Strengths

To ensure that accountability is clearly assigned for all IT risks and activities. This specifically includes assigning and monitoring IT security responsibilities, strategies and behaviors so that appropriate measures and mechanisms are established for reporting and responding on the current and planned use of IT.

Constraints

- Outsourcing of IT processes shall have to be bound for secure contracts that safeguard the information security objectives of the organization.

It also provides guidance to consultants who advise organizations and assist governing bodies. They include the following:

- executive managers;
- members of groups monitoring the resources within the organization;
- external business or technical specialists, such as legal or accounting specialists, retail or industrial associations, or professional bodies;
- internal and external service providers (including consultants);
- Auditors.

This International Standard applies to the governance of the organization's current and future use of IT including management processes and decisions related to the current and future use of IT. These processes can be controlled by IT specialists within the organization, external service providers, or business units within the organization. This International Standard is applicable to all organizations, including public and private companies, government entities, and not-for-profit organizations. This International Standard is applicable to organizations of all sizes irrespective of the extent of their use of IT.

The purpose of this International Standard is to promote effective, efficient, and acceptable use of IT in all organizations to:

- Assure stakeholders that, if the principles and practices proposed by the standard are followed, they can have confidence in the organization's governance of IT.
- Governing use of IT in the organization for meeting business objectives.
- Establishing concepts, definitions and processes for good governance of IT in the organization.

The primary advantage of the ISO/IEC 38500:2008 IT governance framework is to ensure that accountability is clearly assigned for all IT risks and activities. This leads to appropriate measures and mechanisms being established for reporting and responding on the current and planned use of IT – for example, meeting the data protection regulation under GDPR for EU residents if applicable.

ISO 38500 lays down three main tasks for implementation:

1. **Evaluate:** Management should continuously assess and examine the current and future use of IT and issues relating to sourcing, proposals and strategies attached thereto. In this context external factors such as economic or social trends and the development of business needs must be considered.

2. **Direct:** Management must assign responsibilities for and direct the preparation of implementation policies and plans. Policies indicate the way employees should use IT and make plans to regulate IT investments in the organization. Risks in projects and their impact on business practices must be considered while directing IT efforts and ensure they are consistent with desired outcomes.

3. **Monitor:** It becomes necessary to monitor performance and map it against IT objectives additionally, managers must make sure that IT conforms to external regulations and internal policies The six guiding principles listed in ISO 38500, and the proper execution of these tasks together make the standard effective. It is instrumental to aligning IT with business objectives.

ADVANTAGES OF ISO/IEC 38500 – IT GOVERNANCE

- Manage the IT investments optimally.
- Improve project governance for IT projects.
- Improve the competitive position of the organization
- Minimize IT risks
- Assure greater project success rates

Choice of standard has to be made by the appropriate authority having knowledge of available standards. COBIT is a good candidate when an organization wishes to create an organization-wide framework for management that is scoped outside of information security only. While not providing direct accreditation, certification can be achieved through closely aligned paths.

ITIL points to ISO standards as a framework in which to implement a solution. This applies well for organizations wishing to use ISO standards with global recognition without necessarily achieving an ISO 27001 certification. ISO 38500 on the other hand, does not replace COBIT, ITIL, or other standards or frameworks, but it complements them by providing a demand-side-of-IT-use focus.

Risk Frameworks

ISO 31000:2009, Risk Management

1. Principles and Guidelines were released in November of 2009. The authors designed the standard to be applicable for any organization and any risk type, but this standard is not certifiable. Standard was revised in 2018 and it supports risk management in the organization. Refer to Figure 4.3.

    Guidance for the implementation of ISO 31000, and International Standard ISO/IEC 31010, Risk management – Risk assessment techniques, developed jointly with the International Electrotechnical Commission. This standard is quite similar to the ANZ/NZS 4360:2004 on risk management. Further ISO/IEC 31010 is the document that supports ISO 31000 standard.

    Likewise, the auxiliary document Risk Management Guidelines and Companion to AS/NZS 4360:2004 provides guidance on the design and implementation of the risk management techniques.

2. There are three components of the ISO 31000 risk management process:

    The Framework, which guides the overall structure and operation of risk management across an organization; it mirrors the PDCA (Plan, Do, Check,

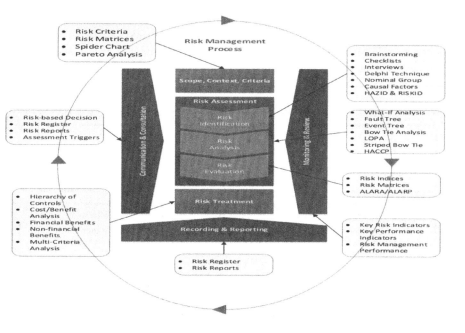

FIGURE 4.3 Risk management process.

Act) cycle. The Framework aims at helping organizations integrate risk management into the governance framework and consists of:

    i. Policy and management indicating intent and commitment toward the risk program

    ii. Program design that works within the organization, its culture, and environment, including:

- Understanding industry trends, regulatory requirements, and expectations of key external stakeholders
- Understanding the existing governance, organizational structure, culture, and organizational capabilities

    iii. Implementation of risk program

    iv. Continuous improvement of program.

3. **The Process,** which describes the actual method of identifying, analyzing, and treating risks. The Process, as defined by ISO 31000, is 'multi-step and iterative; designed to identify and analyze risks in the organizational context'.

In Figure 4.4, the first and third activities should happen continuously. Regular communication is critical to understanding stakeholders' interests and concerns, thus validating the focus of the risk process. In later stages also communication helps convey the rationale behind decisions and why the organization needs certain risk treatments. In addition, regular oversight ensures that the organization addresses changes in the risk environment and processes and that controls operate effectively. It is important that all stakeholders clearly understand expectations and the organization is able to address change in a proactive way.

ISO 31000 defines context of organization. The context is a combination of the external and internal environments, both viewed in relation to organizational objectives and strategies. The context is set during framework stage with the examination of internal and external environments in which the business operates. However, examining organizational context at the time of making risk assessments is equally important for new risks and changes.

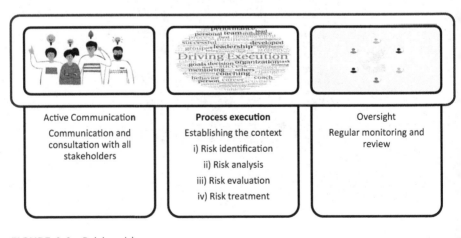

Active Communication	Process execution	Oversight
Communication and consultation with all stakeholders	Establishing the context i) Risk identification ii) Risk analysis iii) Risk evaluation iv) Risk treatment	Regular monitoring and review

FIGURE 4.4   Driving risk process.

The risk assessment steps involve developing techniques to identify, analyze, and evaluate specific risks. The following key elements must be considered-

1. **Risk Identification**
   - Identification of the sources of a particular risk, areas of impacts, and potential events including their causes and consequences
   - Classification of the source as internal or external
2. **Risk Analysis**
   - Identification of potential consequences and factors that affect the consequences
   - Assessment of the likelihood
   - Identification and evaluation of the controls currently in place
3. **Risk Evaluation**
   - Comparison of the identified risks to the established rick criteria
   - Decisions made to treat or accept risks with consideration of internal, legal, regulatory and external party requirements

Overall, the risk management principles and processes described in ISO 31000 and supported by the guidance of ISO/IEC 31010 provide a robust system that allows an organization to design and implement a repeatable, proactive and strategic program. The design of specific program elements is highly dependent on the goals, resource, and circumstances of the individual organization. Regardless of the level of implementation, management involvement in setting direction and regularly reviewing results should be a part of every program, which will not only elevate the management of risk but also ensure an appropriate treatment of risk based on organizational objectives and long-term strategies.

IEC 31010, Risk Management

It comprises risk assessment techniques to identify and lays down the risk assessment process in support of ISO 31000. It introduces a wide range of techniques for identifying and understanding risk in a business or technical context. When the only certainty is uncertainty, the IEC and ISO 'risk management toolbox' helps organizations to keep ahead of threats that could be detrimental to their success.

FAIR (Factor Analysis of Information Risk)

A new model based on risk quantification. It focuses on cybersecurity and operational risk and aims at guiding more informed decisions. It is a new framework but it has already gained acceptance among a lot of Fortune 500 companies.

The International Risk Governance Council (IRGC)

IRGC has developed a Risk Governance Framework whose purpose is to help policy makers, regulators and risk managers both to understand the concept of risk governance and apply it to their handling of risks.

IRGC's risk governance framework is a comprehensive approach to help understand, analyze, and manage important risk issues for which there are deficits in risk governance structures and processes. The framework comprises five linked phases including pre-assessment, appraisal, characterization and evaluation, management, and communication. These interlinked phases provide a means to gain a thorough understanding of a risk and to develop options for dealing with it.

The framework comprises the following:

1. **Pre-assessment – Identification and framing**.
   - Leads to framing the risk, early warning, and preparations for handling it,
   - Involves relevant actors and stakeholder groups, to capture the various perspectives on the risk, its associated opportunities, and potential strategies for addressing it.
2. **Appraisal – Assessing the technical and perceived causes and consequences of the risk**.
   - Develops and synthesizes the knowledge base for the decision on whether a risk should be taken and/or managed and, if so,
   - Identifies and selects what options may be available for preventing, mitigating, adapting to or sharing the risk.
3. **Characterization and evaluation – Making a judgment about the risk and the need to manage it**.
   - Process of comparing the outcome of risk appraisal (risk and concern assessment) with specific criteria,
   - Determines the significance and acceptability of the risk, and
   - Prepares decisions.
4. **Management – Deciding on and implementing risk management options**.
   - Designs and implements the actions and remedies required to avoid, reduce (prevent, adapt, mitigate), transfer or retain the risks.
5. **Cross-cutting aspects – Communicating, engaging with stakeholders, considering context**.
   - Crucial role of open, transparent and inclusive communication,
   - Importance of engaging stakeholders to both assess and manage risks, and
   - Need to deal with risk in a way that fully accounts for the societal context of both the risk and the decision that will be taken.

Enterprise Risk Management (ERM)

Risk within an enterprise can come from various sources including mergers/acquisitions requiring extensive integration in a business unit, new regulations that may be subject to varying interpretation or entry of a company into a new market with substantial exposure and return. By implementing an enterprise risk management (ERM) framework, organizations can reduce the likelihood of unexpected disruptive business events in their environment. As a result, they can increase their operating margins, reduce earnings volatility, enhance process efficiency, improve regulatory compliance and optimize cash flow reserves.

Organizations to identify, assess, quantify, monitor and manage their enterprise risk in an integrated manner. It brings together all risk management related data – a reusable library of risks and their corresponding controls and assessments; results from individual assessments; key risk indicators; events such as losses and near-misses; issues and remediation plans – in a single solution. Its workflow capabilities streamline the risk assessment process. Once risk has been assessed, it enables organizations to prioritize using risk heat maps and make strategic decisions on risk response.

NIST Cybersecurity Framework

Compliance of 800–53 is a major component of *FISMA compliance*. It also helps to improve the security of organizational information systems by providing a fundamental baseline for developing a secure organizational infrastructure. While NIST SP 800–53 compliance is a great starting place, the NIST guidelines themselves recommend that you should assess all your data and rank them in order of sensitivity to further develop your security program.

This security framework helps elevate cybersecurity standards for many entities that are uncertain where they should start with their cyber protection. Security frameworks make it possible for organizations to speed up the adoption of strong cybersecurity measures. They don't need to start from scratch when working on their security practices within their company. Some of these frameworks are mandated by the industry that they operate in, while others are voluntary to offer a security foundation

NIST **SP 800–53**: The National Institute of Standards and Technology established the *NIST SP 800–53* requirements for most federal information systems. It is a voluntary framework primarily meant for critical infrastructure organizations to manage and mitigate cybersecurity risk, based on existing standards, guidelines, and practices. However, the cybersecurity framework has slowly been adopted across the globe and is frequently amended to accommodate changing industry needs.

It has a five-step process for addressing cybersecurity risks and maintaining a secure system: identify, protect, detect, respond, and recover. The primary components consist of the Core, Profiles, and Implementation Tiers.

The Core offers guidance to organizations wanting to get better protection for their information systems. It uses straightforward language so the business doesn't need a specialist to understand exactly what to do.

The Profiles cover the company's priorities when it comes to its cybersecurity measures. It brings together the requirements, level of risk, and security resources to evaluate the controls in place.

The Implementation Tier helps companies establish a risk appetite and determine a budget for any cybersecurity changes that are necessary.

800–12 provides a broad overview of computer security and control areas. It also emphasizes the importance of the security controls and ways to implement them.

800–37, updated in 2010, provides a new risk approach: 'Guide for Applying the Risk Management Framework to Federal Information Systems'.

800–53, 'Security and Privacy Controls for Federal Information Systems and Organizations', published in April 2013 and updated to include revisions as of January 15, 2014, specifically addresses the 194 security controls that are applied to a system to make it 'more secure'.

800–63–3, 'Digital Identity Guidelines', published in June 2017 and updated to include revisions as of December 1, 2017, provides guidelines for implementing digital identity services, including identity proofing, registration, and authentication of users.

Octave

OCTAVE is a risk assessment methodology to identify, manage, and evaluate information security risks. This methodology serves to help an organization to:

- develop qualitative risk evaluation criteria that describe the organization's operational risk tolerances
- identify mission critical assets of the organization
- identify vulnerabilities and threats to those assets
- determine and evaluate the potential consequences to the organization if threats are realized
- initiate continuous improvement actions to mitigate risks

OCTAVE methodology is primarily directed toward individuals who are responsible for managing an organization's operational risks. This can include personnel in an organization's business units, persons involved in information security or conformity within an organization, risk managers, information technology department, and all staff participating in the activities of risk assessment with the OCTAVE method. This standard was established in 1999 and has undergone several updates since then.

Table 4.2 lists some differences between NIST and OCTAVE.

CIS Critical Security Controls

The Center for Internet Security (CIS) is a non-profit organization, to 'identify, develop, validate, promote, and sustain best practice solutions for cyber defense and build and lead communities to enable an environment of trust in cyberspace'. Used by 32% of organizations, the CIS Critical Security Controls are a set of 20 actions designed to mitigate the threat of the majority of common cyberattacks. They are as under:

CIS Control 1: Inventory and Control of Hardware Assets – Making a comprehensive assessment of devices on the network is the first step toward securing the devices against attack. Use both active and passive asset discovery

TABLE 4.2   Comparison Between NIST and Octave

CRITERIA	NIST	OCTAVE
Methodology	**NIST** is primarily a management system and allows for third-party execution. NIST SP 800–30 is most suited for Technology related risk. NIST guidance explores more tactical, organizational issues.	**OCTAVE** Method is self-directed. Only organizational resources are allowed to implement the process. Evaluation is an actual process managed by conducting elicitation, consolidation and analysis workshops.
Assessment Team	**NIST** mentions roles in methodology but does not create an assessment team	**OCTAVE** details the creation on an analysis (assessment) team comprising representatives from both the business lines and the IT department of the organization
	NIST uses typical techniques for information gathering such as questionnaires, interviews and document reviews	**OCTAVE** uses a workshop-based approach to both gather information and make decisions
Technical Perspective	**NIST** does not address human resources as a possible organizational asset	**OCTAVE** Method seeks to identify human resources that may be a 'mission-critical' asset with respect to IT issues
	NIST relies on role definition to determine use for testing purposes	**OCTAVE** uses a workshop for process 5, whose participants are primarily the core team, to use software tools specifically for previously identified vulnerabilities.
Documentation	**NIST** develops Security Requirements Checklists for the security areas of management, operational and technical.	**OCTAVE** relies upon the creation of three catalog of information: catalog of practices, threat profile and catalog of vulnerabilities. These catalogs then create the baseline for the organization.

solutions on an ongoing basis to monitor your inventory and make sure all hardware is accounted for.

CIS Control 2: Inventory and Control of Software Assets – This also includes asset discovery, making network inventorying the single most critical step you can take to harden your system.

CIS Control 3: Continuous Vulnerability Management Scanning of the network for vulnerabilities at regular intervals will reveal security risks before they result in an actual compromise of your data. It is important to run automated and authenticated scans of your entire environment.

CIS Control 4: **Controlled Use of Administrative Privileges** – Administrative credentials are soft targets for cybercriminals. Keeping a detailed inventory of admin accounts and changing default passwords will help to ensure security against attack.

CIS Control 5: Secure Configurations for Hardware and Software on Mobile Devices, Laptops, Workstations, and Servers – Leverage *file integrity monitoring* (FIM) to keep track of configuration files, master images, and more. This control speaks to the need for automating of configuration monitoring systems so that departures from known baselines trigger security alerts.

CIS Control 6: Maintenance, Monitoring, and Analysis of Audit Logs – System logs are an authentic source to trace all activity on the network. Thus, in the event of a security incident, logs will give the data needed to ascertain the who, what, where, when, and how of the event in question.

CIS Control 7: Email and Web Browser Protections – There are more security threats in email and web browsers than phishing alone. Hence, web and email security have to be provided for.

CIS Control 8: Malware Defenses Organizations – These ensure that their antivirus tools integrate well with the rest of the security tool chain. Implementing this control completely also means keeping accurate logs of command-line audits and DNS queries.

CIS Control 12: Boundary Defense – This control relates to control communications across the network boundaries. Implementing it requires using network-based IDS sensors and intrusion prevention systems.

CIS Control 13: Data Protection – Data protection is one of the more complex and difficult-to-put into practice and ongoing processes like inventorying of sensitive information must be implemented to enforce data remains secure.

CIS Control 14: Controlled Access Based on the Need to Know – By encrypting information in transit and disabling communication between workstations, you can start to limit potential security incidents that can occur when data privileges are overly lax.

CIS Control 15: Wireless Access Control – A step toward this would be to inventory network's wireless access points. All types of wireless access risks should be assessed and mitigated.

CIS Control 16: Account Monitoring and Control – Proper authentication should be in place and control of authentication mechanisms should be ensured.

CIS Control 17: Implement a Security Awareness and Training Program Security – Training should be a bigger priority at most organizations, due in part to the widening cybersecurity *skills gap*.

CIS Control 18: Application Software Security – For in-house development the code needs security assessments through processes like static and dynamic security analysis to uncover hidden vulnerabilities.

CIS Control 19: Incident Response and Management – Organization should put incident management strategies in place to plan and be resilient to cyber-security incidents.

CIS Control 20: Penetration Tests and Red Team Exercises – Regular penetration testing helps to identify vulnerabilities and attack vectors that would otherwise go unknown until discovered by malicious actors.

Security controls help organizations to enforce a security framework to protect the organization and data from cyberattacks.

Regulatory Compliance

Regulatory compliance describes the organizational goal to ensure that they are aware of and are taking steps to comply with the relevant laws, policies, and regulations. Over the last decade, there has been an increase in the number of regulations. Operational transparency is the need of the hour. Hence, organizations have started adopting an integrated approach and associating with accrediting organizations for certification and audit. Some of the frequently used frameworks, regulations, or standards are included here.

Global Data Protection Regulation (GDPR)

GDPR is a privacy and security regulation drafted and passed by the European Union (EU). It imposes obligations on organizations anywhere across the globe, in respect of data related to people in the EU that they target or collect. The regulation was put into effect on May 25, 2018. It does not just apply to firms based in Europe either. If you do business with any individual subject to the EU's jurisdiction, you are required to abide by GDPR's provisions (Figure 4.5).

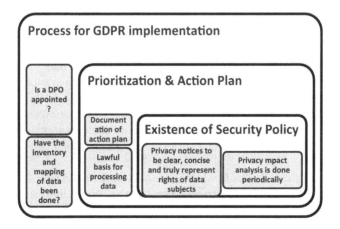

FIGURE 4.5   GDPR implementation process.

Some key terms under GDPR include:

i. **Personal data is any information that relates to an individual who can be directly or indirectly identified** – names and email addresses, location information, ethnicity, gender, biometric data, religious beliefs, web cookies, and political opinions can all be personal data

ii. **Pseudonymous data** – data such as pen names can also fall under the definition if it's relatively easy to ID someone from it.

iii. **Data processing** – any action performed on data, such as collecting, recording, organizing, structuring storing or erasing; whether it is through an automated or manual process

iv. **Data subject** – the person (customer or site visitor) whose data is being processed.

v. **Data controller** – one who handles the data and decides why and how personal data will be processed

vi. **Data processor** – a third party who processes personal data on behalf of a data controller. The GDPR has special rules for these individuals and organizations that include cloud service providers or email service providers.

Key Requirements under GDPR

- **Consent**: Organizations must get consent to collect personal data, with the level of consent varying according to the type of personal data being collected.
- **Data minimization**: GDPR stipulates that organizations can only collect personal data that is clearly related to a well-defined business objective. If an organization gathers personal data for one purpose but then decides it wants to use it for another purposes (such as consumer profiling), that could be considered noncompliance.
- **Individual rights**: Whether as a data controller or as a data processor, GDPR has set privacy rights for individuals or data subjects which aim at giving individuals better control over data in custody of other organization.

1. The right to be informed
2. The right to access: Customers have right to access their data
3. The right to rectification: Customers can update their data in your possession.
4. The right to erasure: Customers has right to get their data deleted
5. The right to restrict processing: Customers can request to stop processing of data
6. The right to data portability: Customers can receive their data in pre-agreed format
7. Right to object: Customers can object to processing of their data

Article 6 lists the instances in which it's legal to process personal data. Don't even think about touching somebody's personal data – don't collect it, don't store it, don't sell it to advertisers – unless you can justify it with one of the following:

1. The data subject gave specific, **unambiguous consent** to process the data (e.g., They've opted in to your marketing email list).

2. Processing is necessary to execute or to prepare **to enter into a contract** to which the data subject is a party (e.g., You need to do a background check before leasing property to a prospective tenant).

3. You need to process it **to comply with a legal obligation** of yours (e.g., You receive an order from the court in your jurisdiction).

4. You need to process the data **to save somebody's life** (e.g., Well, you'll probably know when this one applies).

5. Processing is necessary *to perform a task in the public interest* or to carry out some official function (e.g., You're a private garbage collection company).

6. You have a **legitimate interest** to process someone's personal data. This is the most flexible lawful basis, though the 'fundamental rights and freedoms of the data subject' always override your interests, especially if it's a child's data. (It is difficult to give an example here because there are a variety of factors you'll need to consider for your case. The UK Information Commissioner's Office provides helpful guidance *here*.)

Data Protection Officer (DPO): Organizations can choose to designate a DPO even though it may not be compulsory if you aren't required to. The role includes tasks involving understanding the GDPR and how it applies to the organization, advising people in the organization about their responsibilities, conducting data protection trainings, conducting audits and monitoring GDPR compliance, and serving as a liaison with regulators.

Consent is a significant process in GDPR. Rules are laid to specify what constitutes consent from data subject to process their information.

- Consent must be 'freely given, specific, informed and unambiguous'.
- Requests for consent must be 'clearly distinguishable from the other matters' and presented in 'clear and plain language'.
- Data subjects can withdraw previously given consent whenever they want, and you have to honor their decision. You can't simply change the legal basis of the processing to one of the other justifications.
- Children under 13 can only give consent with permission from their parents.
- You need to keep documentary evidence of consent.
- Organizations that have at least 250 employees or conduct higher-risk data processing are required to keep an up-to-date and detailed list of processing activities and should keep the list ready for audit or scrutiny by the regulator. The list must contain the purposes of the processing, what kind of data you process, who has access to it in your organization, any third parties (and where they are located) that have access, what you're doing to protect the data (e.g., encryption), and when you plan to erase it if possible.

Article 5.1.2 defines data protection principles. They include:

1. **Lawfulness, fairness, and transparency** – processing must be lawful, fair, and transparent to the data subject.

2. **Purpose limitation** – processing of data for legitimate purposes specified explicitly to the data subject when data was collected.

3. **Data minimization** – collecting only as much data as necessary for processing.
4. **Accuracy** – organization must keep personal data accurate and up to date.
5. **Storage limitation** – storage of personally identifiable information (PII) must be as long as necessary for the specified purpose.
6. **Integrity and confidentiality** – processing must be done in such a way as to ensure appropriate security, integrity, and confidentiality (e.g., by using encryption).
7. **Accountability** – lies on part of the data controller to be demonstrated in the following ways:
   - Designate data protection responsibilities to the team.
   - Maintain detailed documentation of data collected, how it is used, and where it is being stored.
   - Implement technical and organizational security measures and give training to staff.
   - Maintain data processing agreement contracts with third parties.
   - Appoint a DPO (where necessary).

A point of interest here is that ISO 27001 is complementary to the implementation of GDPR. Let us consider the following specific areas of parity:

1. GDPR's core focus is the management of personal data. ISO 27001 supports this by providing guidance on controls to identify personal data and manage how, where and for how long it is stored, who can access it, etc.
2. Both standards stress on the availability, integrity, and confidentiality of data processing systems.
3. A documented process for regularly evaluating the effectiveness of security controls is a key requirement of ISO 27001 and GDPR.
4. Risk assessment. GDPR mandates that businesses conduct risk assessments to ensure they have identified major risks to EU citizens' personal data. Similarly, ISO 27001 requires initial and ongoing risk assessment.
5. Data encryption. Identifying what data should be encrypted based on risk exposure is inherently part of risk assessment has been provided by both standards.
6. Breach notification. GDPR mandates that firms must notify authorities within 72 hours of when a breach involving personal data is discovered. This includes notification of impacted 'data subjects' if the risk to them is sufficient. ISO 27001 likewise mandates 'a consistent and effective approach' to handling information security incidents.
7. Third-party risk management (TPRM). GDPR stipulates those businesses that delegate processing or storage of personal data make a contractual agreement requiring GDPR compliance for those suppliers. ISO 27001 also mandates protection for data assets that are accessible to suppliers.

Penalties: GDPR comes with very stiff penalties for noncompliance (up to €10 million or 2% of worldwide annual turnover, whichever is higher) and breaches (up to €20 million or 4% of worldwide annual turnover, whichever is higher). Just as painful is the right of data protection authorities to prevent a company from collecting or processing personal data while a suspected noncompliance or breach is being investigated.

HITRUST

The HITRUST developed the Common Security Framework for healthcare organizations. These guidelines cover any information systems that work with protected health information, whether it's at rest or in transit. Many of the healthcare IT systems do not have proper cybersecurity measures; by providing correct guidance on how to protect information, organizations can protect themselves against the constant threat of ransomware and other malware. This framework provides another way for healthcare organizations to protect themselves against attackers.

HIPAA

The main objective of HIPAA is to improve healthcare efficiency and patient care outcomes by encouraging the free flow of health information in the United States. At the same time, these HIPAA compliance requirements mandated national standards to secure the privacy of personal health information HIPAA security rules have to be satisfied for HIPAA-compliant cloud storage.

HIPAA Privacy and Security Rules   The HIPAA rules and regulations apply to all 'covered entities' – health plans, healthcare providers, and healthcare clearinghouses that transmit health information in electronic, oral. or written form. It also applies to the business associates of covered entities, i.e., individuals or organizations that are contracted to provide services but are not part of the covered entity's workforce.

Privacy Rule has broader connotation than the Security Rule in that it protects all 'individually identifiable health information' that is either transmitted or held by a covered entity or its business associate, in any form or media – electronic, paper, or oral.

This protected health information (PHI) includes information related to the individual's physical or mental health or condition, healthcare provided to the individual or payment for the provision of healthcare to the individual. PHI also includes basic identifying information such as a patient's name, their date of birth, Social Security numbers (SSN) and home address.

Security Rule, on the other hand, focuses on PHI held or transmitted electronically, or e-PHI. Security rule mandates covered entities to implement appropriate administrative, physical, and technical measures to:

- Ensure the confidentiality, integrity, and availability of all e-PHI they create, receive, maintain, or transmit.
- Identify and protect against reasonably anticipated security threats.
- Protect against anticipated, impermissible uses or disclosures of PHI.
- Ensure compliance by their workforce and business associates.

HIPAA requisitions maintenance of full audit trails that detail every interaction with the data concerned. This means that by enabling event logs management software can ensure compliance with these regulations. This ensures that full records are automatically kept for changes made and can alert organizations of any potential security breaches when they occur.

Penalties for noncompliance. Since records organizations hold are sensitive records; the penalties for failing to protect this information can be severe. The Office for Civil Rights (OCR) oversees HIPAA compliance. It can impose civil monetary penalties (CMP) for non-compliance with the law that range from $100 to $50,000 per affected PHI record, up to a maximum of $1.5 million per incident. In 2018, for example, insurance provider Anthem agreed to pay a fine of $16 million after a hacking attack exposed the health information of almost 79 million people.

Industry-Specific Standards

PCI DSS (Payment Card Industry Data Security Standard)

The PCI DSS standard applies to any organization (regardless of size or number of transactions) that accepts stores, transmits or processes cardholder data The Standard PCI DSS is mandated by the Payment Card Industry Security Standard council. The council comprises major credit card bands and is an industry standard.

PCI DSS isn't a government-mandated set of rules, but an industry one. However, this doesn't make it less important, as any company found to be non-compliant with its rules, may face heavy fines or even have relationships with banks or payment processors terminated, making it very difficult for companies to accept card payments.

The Payment Card Industry's Data Security Standard framework covers companies that handle credit card information in one of four ways: accepting credit cards, processing the transactions, storing this data or transmitting credit card data. By putting this security framework in place, PCI has improved the security of the complete payment process.

Even if firms use third-party services for handling card payments, which is the case for many businesses, both large and small, it is still the merchant's responsibility to ensure the safety of any credit or debit card data it gathers, transmits or stores, is secure.

The exact steps firms will have to take vary depending on how many transactions they actually process – those with bigger customer bases will face much more stringent requirements – but ultimately, PCI DSS standards require businesses to ensure a certain level of security.

The PCI-DSS defines six categories of control objectives (refer to Figure 4.6).

These control objectives are to be achieved through the fulfillment of 12 requirements set by the PCI council. These are as follows:

Install and Maintain a Firewall Configuration to Protect Cardholder Data   Firewalls control the transmission of data between an organization's trusted internal networks and untrusted external networks, as well as traffic between sensitive areas of the internal networks themselves. This requirement mandates use of firewall to prevent unauthorized access.

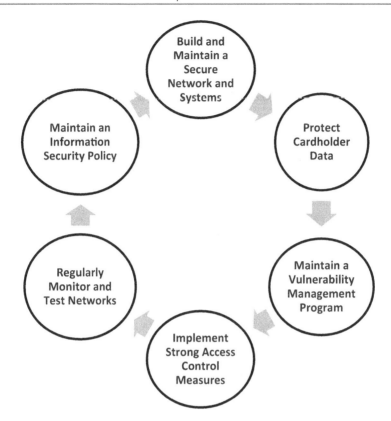

FIGURE 4.6 Six categories of control objectives of PCI DSS.

Do Not Use Vendor Supplied Defaults for System Passwords or Other Security Parameters The default settings of many commonly used systems are well known, easily exploitable and often used by criminal hackers to compromise those systems. Vendor-supplied default settings must, therefore, be changed, and unnecessary default accounts disabled or removed before any system is installed on a network. This can be achieved through:

    i. Procedural reviews on configuration standards
    ii. SNMP to be included as well as POS terminal setup guidelines are set
   iii. Firmware updates and support for strong encryption and authentication.
   iv. Developing system configuration standards
    v. SSL v3/TLS1.0 to be disabled
   vi. Remote admin tools to be used for better security

Protect Stored Card Data The storage of cardholder data should be kept to a minimum, and appropriate data retention and disposal policies, procedures and processes should be implemented.

Certain data – such as the full contents of the chip or magnetic strip, the CVV (card verification value) or the PIN – should never be stored.

There must be adequate safeguards in place when data storage is necessary. Encryption, truncation, masking and hashing are critical components of cardholder data protection.

Without access to the proper cryptographic keys, criminal hackers will be unable to read or access encrypted data, even if they manage to circumvent other security controls.

Cryptographic keys should therefore be stored securely, and access restricted to as few people as possible. Other data protection methods should also be considered.

Encrypt Transmission of Cardholder Data Across Open, Public Networks   Strong cryptography and security protocols should be used to protect sensitive cardholder data during transmission over open, public networks that could easily be accessed by malicious individuals.

Examples of such networks include the Internet, wireless technologies (e.g., Bluetooth), GPRS (general packet radio service), and satellite communications. Industry-best practices must be followed to implement strong encryption for authentication and transmission.

Security policies and procedures for encrypting the transmission of cardholder data must be documented and made known to all relevant parties.

Protect all Systems against Malware and Regularly Update Antivirus Software or Programs   Antivirus software capable of detecting, removing and protecting against all known types of malwares must be used on all commonly affected systems. For less vulnerable systems, evolving malware threats should be periodically evaluated to determine if antivirus software is needed. Antivirus mechanisms must be maintained, kept active and only be disabled if formally authorized for a specific purpose.

Develop and Maintain Secure Systems and Applications   Many security vulnerabilities are fixed by patches issued by software vendors. Organizations should establish a process to identify security vulnerabilities and rank them according to their level of risk.

Relevant security patches should be installed within a month of their release to protect against cardholder data compromise. All software applications, whether they're developed internally or externally, should be developed securely in accordance with the PCI DSS. They should also be based on industry standards and/or best practices, and incorporate information security throughout their entire development lifecycle.

Restrict Access to Cardholder Data by Business on 'Need to Know' Basis   Criminals find it convenient to access systems by exploiting authorized accounts and business user privileges. Documented systems and processes should therefore be put in place to limit access rights to critical data. Access control systems should deny all access by default, and authorization should be granted according to the clearly defined job responsibilities.

Identify and Authenticate Access to System Components   The ability to identify individual users ensures that system access is limited to those with the proper authorization and establishes an audit trail that can be analyzed following an incident. Documented policies and procedures must therefore be implemented to ensure proper user identification management for non-consumer users and administrators on all system components.

All users must be assigned a unique ID, which must be managed according to specific guidelines. Controlled user authentication management (e.g., the use of passwords, smart cards or biometrics) should also be implemented and 2FA (two-factor authentication) must be used for remote network access.

Restrict Physical Access to Cardholder Data   Electronic data breaches are not the only source of data loss; physical access to systems should also be limited and monitored using appropriate controls. Procedures should be implemented to distinguish between on-site personnel and visitors, and physical access to sensitive areas (e.g., server rooms and data centers) should be restricted accordingly.

All media should be physically secured, and its storage, access and distribution controlled.

Media should be destroyed in specific ways when no longer required. Devices that capture payment card data via direct physical interaction with the card must be protected from tampering and substitution, and periodically inspected. An up-to-date list of these devices should be maintained.

Track and Monitor All Access to Network Resources and Cardholder Data   The use of logging mechanisms is critical in preventing, detecting and minimizing the impact of data compromise. If system usage is not logged, potential breaches cannot be identified. Secure, controlled audit trails must therefore link all access to system components with individual users and log their actions. This includes:

- Access to cardholder data;
- Actions taken by individuals with root or administrative privileges;
- Access to audit trails;
- Invalid logical access attempts;
- Use of and changes to identification and authentication mechanisms;
- The initializing, stopping or pausing of audit logs; and
- The creation and deletion of system-level objects.

An audit trail history should be retained for at least a year, with a minimum of three months' logs immediately available for analysis. Logs and security events should be regularly reviewed to identify anomalous or suspicious activity.

Regularly Test Security Systems and Processes   New vulnerabilities are constantly found and exploited, so it's essential that system components, processes and custom software are regularly tested. Documented processes must be implemented to detect and identify all unauthorized wireless access points at least quarterly. Internal and external network vulnerability scans must be performed by qualified personnel at least quarterly and after any significant change in the network (e.g., new system component installations, changes in network topology, firewall rule modifications and product upgrades).

Intrusion detection/prevention techniques should be used to identify and/or prevent unauthorized network activity, and a change detection mechanism should be employed to perform weekly critical file comparisons, and to alert personnel to unauthorized system modifications.

Maintain Policy that Addresses Information Security for All Personnel To comply with the PCI DSS, organizations must establish, publish, maintain and disseminate a security policy, which must be reviewed at least annually and updated according to the changing risk environment. A risk assessment process must be implemented to identify threats and vulnerabilities, usage policies for critical technologies must be developed, security responsibilities for all personnel must be clearly defined and a formal awareness program must be implemented. Organizations must also implement an incident response plan so that they can respond immediately to any system breach

PCI DSS Annual Assessment: Merchants who process fewer than six million transactions per year must submit an annual Self-Assessment Questionnaire (SAQ) or a Report on Compliance (ROC). Merchants who process more than six million transactions per year must be audited on-site by a Qualified Security Assessor (QSA) certified by the PCI SCC.

It would be interesting to note some differences between the GDPR and the PCI DSS standard as listed below in Table 4.3:

TABLE 4.3 Points of Comparision Between the GDPR and the PCI DSS Standard.

GDPR	PCI DSS
Government mandate	Payment card industry self-regulation
Concerns the rights and freedoms of those in the EU	Concerns security and processing of payment card and cardholder data
Applies to ANY personally identifiable information of EU citizens	Applies to payment card and cardholder data
Covers ALL processing of personal data	Covers storage, transmission, and processing of cardholder data
Data controllers and data processors must demonstrate compliance	Merchants and service providers must demonstrate compliance
Certifying bodies in process of being defined	Certification authority: PCI Council
No formal method to demonstrate compliance	Compliance demonstrated through Attestation of Compliant (AOC)
Supervisory authorities from EU memberstates monitor compliance	Acquiring banks monitor compliance of merchants. Merchant monitors compliance for service providers

It is important that standards be understood, interpreted and implemented in the right essence. Compliance with standards can be done at individual facilities or in a cross-country culture in the office of residence since the staff are acquainted to local laws and regulations. Standards activities should begin early in the process life cycle to ensure that process designs meet applicable codes and standards from the outset, rather than having to make expensive changes later.

BUILDING A HYBRID SECURITY FRAMEWORK

Organizations can leverage a hybrid framework by choosing specific controls from other frameworks to meet their compliance requirements and business needs. Typically, hybrid models consist of cherry-picked controls from other standards that are driven by industry compliance requirements. For example, the Health Information Trust Alliance (HITRUST) framework and ISO 27799 are both used in the healthcare sector. The Cloud Security Alliance's Cloud Control Matrix (CCM) is another hybrid framework commonly used in cloud computing.

Many frameworks have redundant characteristics, enabling security teams to map certain controls to satisfy compliance with an array of regulatory standards. An organization could, for instance, use a combination of ISO 27001, NIST 800–53, and COBIT, selecting the controls that best help it meet its business objectives.

Other hybrid examples considered in earlier sections include:

- The Health Insurance Portability and Accountability Act (HIPAA);
- The Payment Card Industry Data Security Standard (PCI DSS);
- The Center for Internet Security (CIS) Top 20 Critical Security Controls.

Here we shall consider SOC2, which is the American Institute of Certified Public Accountants (AICPA) Service Organization Control (SOC).

SOC (System and Organization Controls) is an American standard that belongs to AICPA (the American CPA association). US public companies and companies that target the US market rely on SOC to help ensure that the services they use meet security and availability requirements.

While SOC 1 focuses on financial IT systems and is probably of lesser concern to you, SOC 2 is more relevant and is split into two types:

- **Type 1**: policies are defined and documented, and the audit is conducted at a single point in time.
- **Type 2**: policies are defined and documented and are then verified by a third party over a period of time.

TYPES OF SOC REPORTS

The Trust Services Criteria are in a SOC 2 report only. A SOC 1 report has a little more flexibility in what is tested and opined on by the auditor. In addition to reviewing security, a SOC 1 audit includes more of a focus on the service organization's controls that may be or are relevant to an audit of their client's financial statements. The service organization (with the help of the auditor) will figure out the key control objectives for the services they provide to clients, and that is what is included in the report. Control objectives in a SOC 1 always include objectives around IT general controls, but also include business processes at the service organization that impact their clients.

Trust principles are broken down as follows:

Security

- The security principle refers to protection of system resources against unauthorized access. *Access controls* help prevent potential system abuse, theft or unauthorized removal of data, misuse of software, and improper alteration or disclosure of information.
- IT security tools such as network and *web application firewalls* (WAFs) and two factors *authentication* and *intrusion detection* are useful in preventing security breaches that can lead to unauthorized access of systems and data.

Availability

- The availability principle refers to the accessibility of the system, products or services as stipulated by a contract or SLA. As such, the minimum acceptable performance level for system availability is set by both parties.
- This principle does not address system functionality and usability but does involve security-related criteria that may affect availability. Monitoring network performance and availability, *site failover* and security incident handling is critical in this context.

Processing Integrity

- The processing integrity principle addresses whether or not a system achieves its purpose (i.e., delivers the right data at the right price at the right time). Accordingly, data processing must be complete, valid, accurate, timely, and authorized.

- However, processing integrity does not necessarily imply data integrity. If data contains errors prior to being input into the system, detecting them is not usually the responsibility of the processing entity. Monitoring of data processing, coupled with quality assurance procedures, can help ensure processing integrity.

Confidentiality

- Data is considered confidential if its access and disclosure is restricted to a specified set of persons or organizations. Examples may include data intended only for company personnel, as well as business plans, IP, internal price lists, and other types of sensitive financial information.
- Encryption is an important control for protecting confidentiality during transmission. Network and application firewalls, together with rigorous access controls, can be used to safeguard information being processed or stored on computer systems.

Privacy

The privacy principle addresses the system's collection, use, retention, disclosure, and disposal of personal information in conformity with an organization's privacy notice, as well as with criteria set forth in the AICPA's generally accepted privacy principles (GAPP).

Personal identifiable information (PII) refers to details that can distinguish an individual (e.g., name, address, Social Security number). Some personal data related to health, race, sexuality, and religion is also considered sensitive and generally requires an extra level of protection. Controls must be put in place to protect all PII from unauthorized access.

Certification Readiness

Cyberattacks, unauthorized access, and the very portability of mobile devices place sensitive data at risk nearly every second. Increasingly, clients in every industry ask that their business partners meet or exceed the same regulatory requirements and guidance that they do.

SOC 2 Type 2 is the standard for indicating that the organization prioritizes security, privacy, confidentiality, availability, and processing integrity.

POINTS OF FOCUS IN AN SOC 2 AUDIT

There are around 200 points of focus associated with the *SOC2 common criteria* in the 2017 Trust Services Criteria. For all five categories (security, availability, processing integrity, confidentiality, and privacy) where the COSO principles map in, there are 61 criteria with almost 300 points of focus.

The knowledge and conformance to standards are necessary for organizations, and in so doing, it helps them in the following manner:

1. Organizations can build and maintain secure facilities
2. Can improvise processes on a continuous basis
3. Can avoid/minimize legal liabilities
4. Can adapt to changes in standards as and when it happens.

Annexure A
National Equivalent Standards

Countries	Equivalent Standard
Australia / New Zealand	AS/NZS ISO/IEC 27002:2006
Brazil	ISO/IEC NBR 17799/2007 – 27002
Indonesia	SNI ISO/IEC 27002:2014
Chile	NCH2777 ISO/IEC 17799/2000
China	GB/T 22081-2008
Czech Republic	ČSN ISO/IEC 27002:2006
Croatia	HRN ISO/IEC 27002:2013
Denmark	DS/ISO27002:2014 (DK)
Estonia	EVS-ISO/IEC 17799:2003, 2005 version in translation

Germany	DIN ISO/IEC 27002:2008
Japan	JIS Q 27002
Lithuania	LST ISO/IEC 27002:2009 (adopted ISO/IEC 27002:2005, ISO/IEC 17799:2005)
Mexico	NMX-I-27002-NYCE-2015
The Netherlands	NEN-ISO/IEC 27002:2013
Peru	NTP-ISO/IEC 17799:2007
Poland	PN-ISO/IEC 17799:2007, based on ISO/IEC 17799:2005

Russia	ГОСТ Р ИСО/МЭК 27002-2012, based on ISO/IEC 27002:2005
Slovakia	STN ISO/IEC 27002:2006
South Africa	SANS UNDERTALE 27002:2014/ISO/IEC 27002:2013[3]
Spain	UNE 71501
Sweden	SS-ISO/IEC 27002:2014
Turkey	TS ISO/IEC 27002
Thailand	UNIT/ISO
Ukraine	СОУ Н НБУ 65.1 СУІБ 2.0:2010
United Kingdom	BS ISO/IEC 27002:2005
Uruguay	UNIT/ISO 17799:2005

Annexure B

The following table shows the different cybersecurity frameworks and regulations, what they regulate, and which corporations would be subject to the scope of the Act:

S. NO.	STANDARD/ FRAMEWORK	DESCRIPTION	ORGANIZATIONS AFFECTED
1.	NIST (National Institute of Standards and Technology)	This framework was created to provide a customizable guide on how to manage and reduce cybersecurity-related risk by combining existing standards, guidelines, and best practices. It also helps foster communication between internal and external stakeholders by creating a common risk language between different industries.	This is a voluntary framework that can be implemented by any organization that wants to reduce their overall risk.
2.	CIS Controls (Center for Internet Security Controls)	Protect your organization assets and data from known cyberattack vectors.	Companies that are looking to strengthen security in the internet of things (IoT).
3.	ISO 27000 Family (International Organization for Standardization)	This *family of standards* provides security requirements around the maintenance of information security management systems (ISMS) through the implementation of security controls.	These regulations are broad and can fit a wide range of businesses. All businesses can use this family of regulations for assessment of their cybersecurity practices.
4.	ISO 31000 Family (International Organization for Standardization)	This set of regulations governs principles of implementation and risk management.	These regulations are broad and can fit a wide range of businesses. All businesses can use this family of regulations for assessment of their cybersecurity practices.

S. NO.	STANDARD/ FRAMEWORK	DESCRIPTION	ORGANIZATIONS AFFECTED
5.	**HIPAA (Health Insurance Portability and Accountability Act) / HITECH Omnibus Rule**	This act is a two-part bill. Title I protect the healthcare of people who are transitioning between jobs or are laid off. Title II is meant to simplify the healthcare process by shifting to electronic data. It also *protects the privacy of individual patients*. This was further expanded through the HITECH/ Omnibus Rule.	Any organization that handles healthcare data. This includes, but is not limited to, doctor's offices, hospitals, insurance companies, *business associates*, and employers.
6.	**PCI-DSS (Payment Card Industry Data Security Standard)**	A set of 12 regulations designed to reduce fraud and *protect customer credit card information*.	Companies handling credit card information.
7.	**GDPR (General Data Protection Act)**	This regulates the data protection and privacy of citizens of the European Union.	Any company doing business in the European Union or handling the data of a citizen of the European Union.
8.	**AICPA (American Institute of Certified Public Accountants) SOC2**	The security, availability, processing integrity, and privacy of systems processing user data and the confidentiality of these systems.	Service organizations that process user data.
9.	**SOX (Sarbanes–Oxley Act)**	This act requires companies to maintain financial records for up to seven years. It was implemented to prevent another Enron scandal.	US public company boards, management, and public accounting firms.
10	**COBIT (Control Objectives for Information and Related Technologies)**	This framework was developed to help organizations manage information and technology governance by linking business and IT goals.	Organizations that are responsible for business processes related to technology and quality control of information. This includes, but is not limited to, areas such as audit and assurance.

Annexure C
Points of comparison between NIST CSF & ISO 27001

S.NO.	NIST CSF	ISO 27001
1	NIST Cybersecurity Framework was created to help US Federal Agencies to organize and manage risk	ISO 27001 was enacted to help organizations build and maintain an ISM (information security management system) within the organization.
2	It is voluntary	It involves the auditors and certifying bodies
3	It consists of various control catalogues and 5 functions	It comprises of 10 management clauses and 14 control objectives with 114 controls contained in Annexure A
4	It is more technical	It is not that technical
5	It is suited to organizations who are in the initial stages of cyber risk program	It is implemented by organization who are required to be compliant ads part of their business dealings with clients
6	It is free for all to use	Audit and certification costs have to be borne

Annexure D

This table shows the different Cybersecurity frameworks and regulations, what they regulate, and which corporations would be subject to the scope of the act-

NAME OF REGULATION	WHAT IT REGULATES	COMPANY AFFECTED
NIST National **Institute of Standards and Technology)**	This framework was created to provide a customizable guide on how to manage and reduce Cybersecurity related risk by combining existing standards, guidelines, and best practices. It also helps foster communication between internal and external stakeholders by creating a common risk language between different industries.	This is a voluntary framework that can be implemented by any organization that wants to reduce their overall risk.
CIS Controls (Center for Internet Security Controls)	Protect your organization assets and data from known cyber-attack vectors.	Companies that are looking to strengthen security in the internet of things (IoT).
ISO 27000 Family (International Organization for Standardization)	This family of standards provide security requirements around the maintenance of information security management systems (ISMS) through the implementation of security controls.	These regulations are broad and can fit a wide range of businesses. All businesses can use this family of regulations for assessment of their Cybersecurity practices.
ISO 31000 Family (International Organization for Standardization)	Protect your organization assets and data from known cyber-attack vectors.	These regulations are broad and can fit a wide range of businesses. All businesses can use this family of regulations for assessment of their Cybersecurity practices.
HIPAA (Health Insurance Portability and Accountability Act) / HITECH Omnibus Rule	This act is a two part bill. Title I protects the healthcare of people who are transitioning between jobs or are laid off. Title II is meant to simplify the healthcare process by shifting to electronic data. It also protects the privacy of individual patients. This was further expanded through the HITECH / Omnibus Rule	Any organization that handles healthcare data. That includes, but is not limited to, doctor's offices, hospitals, insurance companies, business associates, and employers.
PCI DSS Standard	A set of 12 regulations designed to reduce fraud and protect customer credit card information.	Companies handling credit card information.
GDPR	This regulates the data protection and privacy of citizens of the European Union.	Any company doing business in the European Union or handling the data of a citizen of the European Union.
AICPA SOC2	The security, availability, processing integrity, and privacy of systems processing user data and the confidentiality of these systems.	Service organizations that process user data.
SOX	This act requires companies to maintain financial records for up to seven years. It was implemented to prevent another Enron scandal.	Service organizations that process user data.
COBIT (Control Objectives for Information and Related Technologies)	This framework was developed to help organizations manage information and technology governance by linking business and IT goals.	Organizations that are responsible for business processes related to technology and quality control of information. This includes, but is not limited to, areas such as audit and assurance.

Adoption of a Customized Approach to Compliance

5

Governance of risk and compliance has expanded in the light of increased level of legal and regulatory compliances and the involvement of internal and external entities in the running of business. Today, business may be spread across continents, and GRC has become an important business requirement, a critical component within the organization considering the rapid pace of globalization and ever-increasing compliances such as Sarbanes Oxley (SOX), GDPR, anti-money laundering provisions, etc. There is increased need for transparency of operations and reportability in various standards applicable to the organization.

OCEG defines governance as 'the culture, values, mission, structure, layers of policies, processes and measures by which organizations are being directed and controlled'. Governance includes the oversight over risk and compliance. Organizations strive to build their own customized model for GRC compliance so as to reap benefits of efficiency and economy as far as costs of compliance are concerned.

SETTING RIGHT BUSINESS IMPERATIVES

Every business has defined some business imperatives that become the input for their risk and compliance activities and drive their business. Business imperatives are specific to each business, based on the specific industry, company size, business strategies, and degree of IT dependency.

Business imperatives are objectives, selected at a strategic level, are critical to business, and act as business drivers which help businesses achieve their stated objectives and give them competitive advantage.

All business areas do not carry the same IT risk profile; therefore, the appropriate IT controls should be tailored to each company's specific and unique business imperatives,

DOI: 10.1201/9781003018100-5

specifically to address these areas. It is important to define business imperatives; some of them are listed below-

- **Productivity** to have a targeted level of productivity and to measure productivity by the formula – input/output.
- **Customer service** to give highest priority to customer services or customer facing applications to ensure its continued availability.
- **Replication** of repeatable compliance activities to ensure compliance and maintaining redundancies to prevent single point of failure.
- **Collaboration** appropriate collaboration with regulatory and legal entities to ensure compliance on a timely basis
- **Pro-active management** to adjust to changing economic and financial conditions and maintain compliance.
- **Mobility** in provision of services on a global basis
- **Reliability** which can be a hallmark of services/products provided by the organization.
- **Regulatory compliance** which can be a requirement that cannot be neglected.
- **Ease of use** of services/products can be a business imperative.
- **Diverse product lines** to develop diverse product lines that can hedge risk of failure or slow-down in one type of product.
- **Affordability** to maintain affordability considering the cost-benefit evaluation for all GRC compliance decisions.

No law or regulation can stop organizations to have their own business imperatives that are typical to the business and the management style of the organization; so long they are not unlawful. Business imperatives are directives that have to be followed and hence control areas related to business imperatives have to be identified.

NEED FOR AN INTEGRATED COMPLIANCE FRAMEWORK

Business imperatives shall form a foundation for building the integrated compliance framework of the organization. There are several pain areas associated with compliance; the multiplicity of standards, the existence or variance in country standards, the overlap in most of GRC standards and need to maintain elaborate documentation and testing of controls resulting in duplication of efforts and the presence of GRC auditors round the year to carry out different audits for checking compliance with applicable standards.

Business boundaries, styles, and methodologies are evolving at a fast pace. Complexities are increasing as business is faced with the task of doing business in varied economic environments having varied legal and regulatory implications. Good GRC is no longer a back-office operation but a business imperative and can include the imperatives mentioned in Figure 5.1.

FIGURE 5.1   Imperatives for good governance for a global business.

MAPPING OF KEY CONTROLS

Mapping key controls to address BI is easier than reviewing, following, and implementing multiple frameworks. In an integrated approach to GRC, a complete inventory of all the GRC standards and regulatory compliances to be made and a compliance stack to be prepared of all requirements related to these compliances. Refer to Figure 5.2. A lot of thought goes into gathering information from all business units, functional departments, so that a comprehensive collection of compliance needs takes place.

Frameworks that organization has to comply with may be rigorous only within the scope of their coverage. However, a HIPAA framework will not address cardholder data requirements. A COBIT framework, while perfectly effective for addressing the general computing controls needed for SOX compliance, does not provide a overreaching security program that addresses privacy needs. Frameworks are specific to the section of the business in which they operate and will never be generic.

Frameworks are, as stated before, typically high level, emphasizing controls to be implemented rather than the processes needed to achieve compliance. The gap between control and execution must be closed in order to address the framework requirements, but the means that organizations use to accomplish this vary greatly. Two like entities

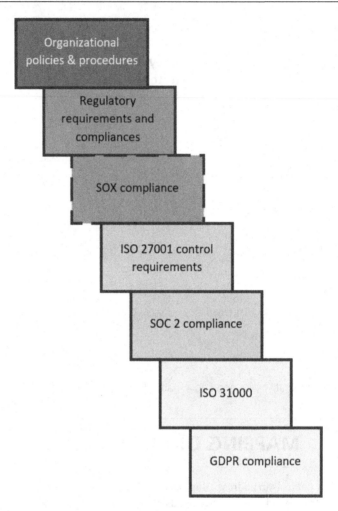

FIGURE 5.2 Compliance stack for the organization.

that carefully follow identical frameworks to protect the exact same data elements may have significantly different security postures.

Frameworks prevent unintended control gaps. Specific legal and regulatory standards provide finite requirements that must be addressed. What they do not necessarily address are the other elements that support either these requirements or areas that directly complement them, ensuring a more rapidly successful governance program. Frameworks assist in this, providing a set of goals, developed and vetted by the community, that define best practices that might be otherwise missed

It becomes critical for an organization to understand that their ideal framework may actually be a combination of several others. A company has only a single security practice, but they may be answerable to many differing laws and regulations. Ongoing review and audit requirements for entities that attempt to follow multiple distinct frameworks rapidly overwhelm and confuse even the most dedicated information security staff. Due to the limitations on budget, organizations need to prioritize efforts, but the need to address the overall threat landscape does not become any less critical. In the end, multiple frameworks are often needed, but the task of managing them becomes almost impossible to implement.

PLANNING AN INTEGRATED FRAMEWORK BEFITTING THE BUSINESS AND SCALE OF OPERATIONS

The process of planning for an integrated compliance model, the following considerations must be addressed:

1. **Context of organization:** The size of the organization, the number of employees, and the geographical spread of business across boundaries serve as key drivers in the design of the compliance structure. For smaller organizations with fewer than 50 employees and fewer than 2 offices, the cost of building an elaborate compliance framework would not be cost-effective.
2. **Type of products offered:** Where organizations offer a large range of products, regulatory compliance in respect of each of them will be extensive; hence the controls related to compliance will be extensive. It will require a wider range of skill sets across the compliance function will be required and compliance officers with appropriate knowledge and experience are deployed.
3. **Compliance as a control subsystem:** Compliance is an important control subsystem; OCEG defines compliance as a set of adhering to and ability to demonstrate adherence to mandated requirements defined by laws and regulations as well as voluntary requirements resulting from contractual obligations and internal policies.
4. **Maintaining the independence of a compliance function:** An effective control-based compliance function requires it to be independent. Compliance controls should also be allocated in a way that minimizes conflicts of interest and maintains independence. Let's take a look at examples of different compliance structures, to illustrate how unique structures can be in relation to their organization.

In Figure 5.3, the structure is designed to centralize the compliance function but clearly distinguishes between compliance activities and, importantly, retains independence and reduces conflicts of interest.

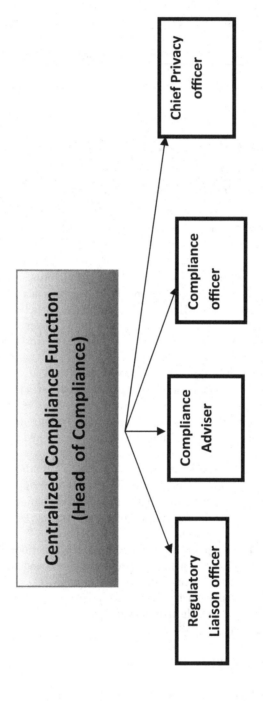

FIGURE 5.3   Compliance organization structure 1.

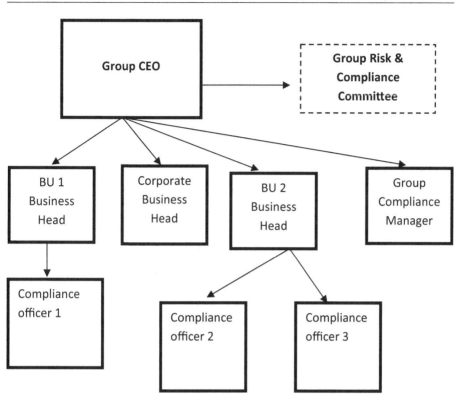

FIGURE 5.4   Compliance organization structure 2.

The approach in Figure 5.4 is typical in large banks where each business unit is representative of an organization in its own right. Note that the divisional Heads of Compliance report to their respective Business Heads but maintain a dotted reporting line to the Group Head of Compliance. This is to ensure that compliance risks are controlled for each business unit, whilst at the same time informing the Group Head of Compliance of delivery against the compliance program and any instance of noncompliance. The Group Head of Compliance will also support the Business Head in setting relevant objectives for the divisional compliance team and in carrying out appraisals of the divisional Head of Compliance. Often, in large organizations, each business unit has its own governance structures and risk management arrangements.

In Figure 5.4, an organizational structure that supports business-line segregation is shown.

To achieve the goal of independence, the following controls need to be exercised:

• Clear and concise definition of responsibilities within the compliance function.
• Appropriate provision of resources to the compliance function.

- An internal audit should oversee the compliance function.
- Compliance must participate in the identification of compliance risks and deciding about their mitigation.

5. **Customize the compliance framework:** Every organization has its own nuances and typical features, and there is no single fit for organizations having varying businesses, varying sizes, and different regulatory requirements. But in either case after defining business imperatives and the control areas corresponding to the same and after obtaining an inventory of GRC regulations and standards to be complied with, the information can be used to build a **Business Case**.

IN BUILDING THE BUSINESS CASE, THE FOLLOWING FACTORS HAVE TO BE CONSIDERED

The business case should be aligned with the overall governance structure of the organization and the integrated model proposed, has to be complementary to the governance structure.

1. Scope of the exercise should cover all compliances in the compliance stack built for the organization.
2. A benefit to be derived from program has to be delineated in the business case to get a sign off.
3. Best practices concerning the compliances and benchmarking with other organizations having similar legal and regulatory compliances must be performed.

It is found by empirical research that the biggest risk to the GRC model is improper alignment of business and compliance requirements with IT resulting in failure to deliver value for the organization. Integration is a top-down approach. First, after due analysis and review of the detailed business case for the program, senior management must be supportive of the GRC program. Second, management has to arrange for funding, staffing and technology resources to support the program. Lastly, goals and objectives of the organization must be fully defined and quantified.

WHY COMPLIANCE STANDARDS EXIST?

The function of compliance standards set forth by governing bodies is to ensure that participants in that industry have implemented *good enough* security practices to participate in the industry and keep the ecosystem secure. Often, we see standards in highly regulated industries, places where the failure of these functions is mandatory – for instance, energy and utilities, banking and finance, defense, and aerospace.

A **compliance framework** is a structured set of guidelines to ensure that the requirements of laws, regulations, industry codes, and organizational doctrines are met. This also applies to contractual arrangements to which the business process is subject. Most organizations fall under multiple authority documents (laws, regulations, standards, audit guides, etc.).

Multiple authority documents will contain multiple mandates in them; some of them can be overlapping. All these mandates need adequate interpretation before implementation. This envisages the following:

1. Identify the mandates within the citations of each authority document.
2. Map mandates to *like* mandates (to eliminate duplication).
3. Create an audit methodology to prove you have implemented mandates.

OPTIONS FOR BUILDING A GRC FRAMEWORK

Organizations can choose to pick up an existing standard or a suite of standards like the ISO standards, an audit standard like COBIT, a national standard like those the NIST 800–53 standard, or even something made up (like Secure Controls Framework) as the cornerstone and interpret every mandate according to that cornerstone.

We can define compliance frameworks as a methodology for compiling multiple authority documents into a cohesive whole. The primary goal of any compliance framework is to reduce the burden of following multiple guidelines by finding commonality between mandates. Once mandates have been identified and extracted from citations, the compliance framework must provide a suite of rules and methods for ascertaining commonality.

COMPONENTS OF GRC FRAMEWORK

A GRC framework includes three components, each of which interacts with various elements of the organization and must also coordinate with the other components. Further, each GRC element must interact and respond to internal and external factors, such as laws, regulations, audit reports, risks and threats. As part of overall governance structure, the integrated GRC program must possess the following (Figure 5.5).

Policy Management: Streamline process of policy creation, review, approval and attestation. It has to minimize redundancies, be crisp and should contain self-contained tables to show version history and name of authorized signatories for approval and renewal. Generally, organizations host policies on their policy portal or intranet.

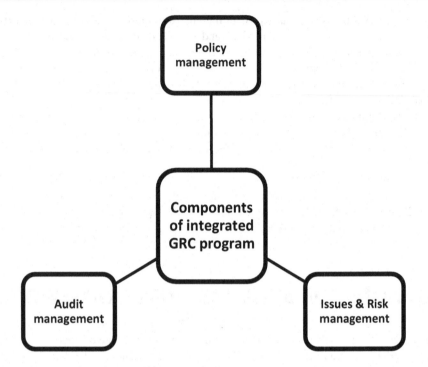

FIGURE 5.5   Components of integrated GRC program components.

Adopt a risk-based approach to compliance: Identifying complex risk areas and issues and monitoring areas of concern and prioritizing compliance risks considering risks across processes and across enterprise boundaries. Some of the issues may include-

i. Lack of accountability
ii. Gap between business units and IT
iii. Lack of information related to risks
iv. Importance not accorded for risk approach

Audit Management: monitoring often incorporates audit requirements, whether external or internal, as part of the regulatory or industry standard. These audits, based on tested reviews, then help ensure the Board of Directors through the audit committee remains informed of the organization's compliance stance.

Reporting: GRC should be supported by dynamic reports based on analysis, scheduling periodically and integrating results for managerial review and also to maintain an audit trail (Figure 5.6).

Dashboards time tracing and analyzing regulatory changes. Aligning with technology framework, customized alerts can be enabled linking them to respective SMEs to take timely and appropriate action.

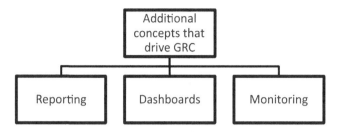

FIGURE 5.6 Additional GRC concepts.

The key responsibilities of the compliance function:

- Advice
- Guidance and education
- Identification, measurement and assessment of compliance risk
- Monitoring, testing and reporting
- Statutory responsibilities and liaison

GRC programs regularly examine how an organization is operating in the context of various metrics. GRC teams interview employees to understand how they operate in order to analyze how various GRC factors apply to their activities. For example, a manufacturing operation will need to follow established operating procedures and practices (governance), identify situations that could disrupt their activities (risk) and ensure regulations associated with their activities are being followed (compliance). Alignment with GRC activities is essential to ensure an organization is performing its work as per highest standards.

SOME EXISTING GRC STRUCTURES

At this stage, it would be interesting to benchmark with some existing GRC structures-

The Three Lines of Defense Model for Management Oversight

The First Line of Defense (Functions that Own and Manage Risks)

The first line of defense consists of internal controls and managerial controls. Most compliance programs incorporate ongoing monitoring, auditing, and testing of controls. Referred to as governance, compliance, and risk (GRC), the continued review enables parties to the compliance effort to ensure no gaps exist. Monitoring must go beyond reviewing policies and procedures. It also requires organizations to test continually for assurance and to respond to weaknesses (Figure 5.7).

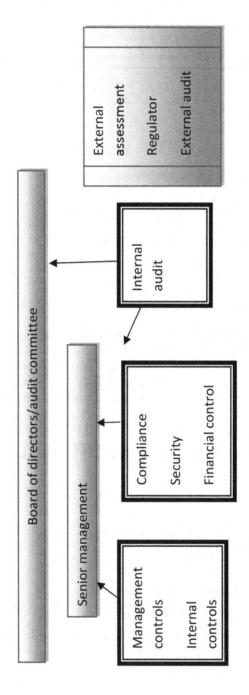

FIGURE 5.7   Three Lines of Defense.

This layer comprises people responsible for identifying and managing risk as part of their accountability for achieving objectives. They must possess the necessary knowledge, skills, information, and authority to operate the relevant policies and procedures of risk control and subsequently of compliance. They must have an understanding of the organization, its objectives, the environment and risks faced by the organization.

The Second Line of Defense (Stands for Functions that Specialize in the Compliance and/or Management of Risk)

This provides the policies, frameworks, tools, techniques and support to enable risk and compliance with, be managed in the first line. It conducts monitoring to judge how effectively they are doing it, and helps ensure consistency of definitions and measurement of risk.

The Third Line of Defense (Independent Assurance)

Internal audit sits outside the risk and compliance process of the first two lines of defense; its main role is to oversee that the first two lines are operating effectively and advise on how to improve the GRC program further. It is reporting to the board/audit committee, it uses a risk-based approach to audit and reports on the effectiveness of governance, risk management, and internal controls within the organization. It also serves to give some level of assurance to the regulators or the external auditors that appropriate controls and processes are in place and are operating effectively.

Integrated Cybersecurity Governance Model

The ICGM utilizes a PDCA (*Plan, Do, Check,* and *Act*) approach to design a governance structure (Figure 5.8):

- **Plan**. The overall GRC/IRM process begins with planning. This planning will define the policies, standards and controls for the organization. It will also directly influence the tools and services that an organization purchases, since technology purchases should address needs that are defined by policies and standards.
- **Do**. This is the most important section for cybersecurity and privacy practitioners. Controls are the baseline for securing processes, applications, systems and services. Procedures (also referred to as control activities) are the processes how the controls are actually implemented and performed. Identifying key controls is a prerequisite for building a secure framework.
- **Check**. A system of checks/balances and setting the right metrics and reporting and reviewing the results of audits/assessments.
- **Act**. This is essentially risk management, which is an encompassing area that deals with addressing two main concepts: (1) real deficiencies that currently exist and (2) possible threats to the organization.

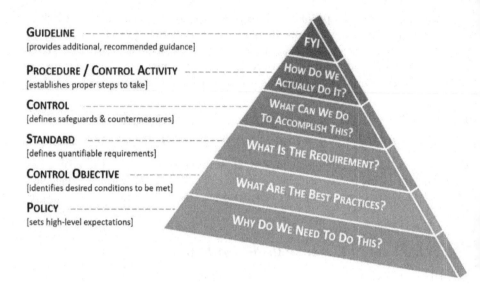

FIGURE 5.8   PDCA model by ISO.

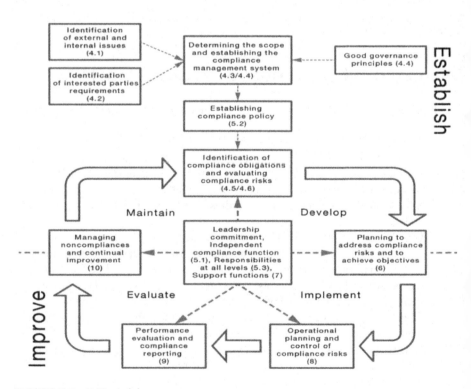

FIGURE 5.9   IMS model.

Integrated Management System (or IMS)

This model can benefit the organization through increased efficiency and effectiveness, and cost reductions while minimizing the disruption caused by several external audits. Increased commitment to increased performance, employee and customer satisfaction, and continuous improvement can be interwoven into a combined framework of controls (Figure 5.9).

This International Standard has adopted a high-level structure to improve alignment to other ISO Standards. It also gives guidance on compliance management system, by providing a Framework to help organizations implement specific compliance specific requirements of the organization.

HOW TO DEFINE A COMPLIANCE FRAMEWORK FOR THE ORGANIZATION

A compliance framework can be defined as well-structured, documented guidelines to support and reinforce diverse and intricate structures of a system for it to expand, develop, and harmonize multiple applications which interrelate into something useful for the organization.

A compliance management framework is a critical part of the structure of every company. It can be defined as a set of procedures for organizations to follow to conduct their businesses within the laws, regulations, and specifications. It consists of tools, processes, functions, controls that are written down by the top management and directors of each organization.

Therefore, it is essential for every organization to have a compliance management framework for the overall growth of the business. When choosing a compliance management framework, one must consider the features of the compliances and select the one that best fits the organization.

DETERMINING COSTS OF COMPLIANCE

The costs of implementing the standards have also to be considered for making a business case to convince the management and to get the approvals for the same.

KEY CAPABILITIES OF A GRC FRAMEWORK

In order to articulate what makes a solution a GRC solution, we must first lay out a GRC solution framework. This framework identifies a comprehensive set of capabilities of a

GRC solution and provides a benchmark to evaluate any solution against it and assess if it is a GRC solution or a point solution. The chief capabilities of a GRC solution include:

1. **Governance activities** that include enterprise risk management, policy compliance documentation and communication; ethics and mission, results of performance measurements such as balanced scorecards, risk scorecards, operational controls dashboards, etc. Documentation of compliance programs is critical to its success:
   - All compliance policies, plans and other documents that describe the organizational approach to managing its compliance program must be meticulously documented
   - Periodic self-assessments (minimum once a year) should be performed and results thereof must be documented
   - All operational functions that interface with the compliance program must be mentioned and the nature of interaction to be documented
   - Compliance committee meeting agenda, minutes, and related board resolutions must be documented
   - Compliance training records, attendance sheets, feedback forms to be maintained as evidence of training in compliance
   - Communication initiatives in compliance, hotline information, logs and follow-up activities in respect of compliance have to be maintained
   - Details of compliance auditing/monitoring reports, trends, and corrective action plans have to be documented
   - Details on incidents including self-reporting, disclosures, evidence of recurring issues that have to be analyzed, and corrective actions to be traced

2. **Risk management** processes that consist of:
   - Risk policy and methodology; risk identification from surveys and workshops/events and their classification
   - Documentation of all risks in a central repository through integrated document management
   - Risk assessment and calculation
   - Risk analysis and prioritization using heat maps
   - Root cause analysis of issues and mitigation measures
   - Risk analytics and trend analysis

Risks are interdependent and controls are shared, leading to gross inefficiency, duplication of efforts, and a silo view of the world. GRC systems should serve as enablers to coordinate and integrate enterprise initiatives and address risk-related issues.

COMPLIANCE CAPABILITIES DESIRED BY ORGANIZATIONS

Compliance process includes assessment, audit, analysis, and flexible controls hierarchy. Advantage of integration should be achieved by the enterprise. GRC framework must possess the ability to support multiple regulations (SOX, risk management, ethics, policy compliance, etc.) as well as operational compliance (such as ISO 9000, ISO 27001, GDPR, and SSAE 18)

Industry framework supports multi-regulatory compliance capabilities: ISO 27001, COBIT, SOX, FDA, ISO 9000, HACCP, FERC, etc. Key compliance capabilities desired include-

- Support for multiple compliance frameworks such as COSO and COBIT
- Ability to create a comprehensive risk-based controls framework
- Comprehensive scheduling and conducting of controls testing capabilities such as inspections, audits, manual and automated assessments

PURPOSE OF A COMPLIANCE PROGRAM

Prevention, Detection, and Correction are three main heads under which the purpose of compliance programs can be displayed (refer to Figure 5.10).

1. Prevention
   i. **Written policies/code of conduct:**
      Written policies should outline compliance program objectives. They are usually embedded in a code of conduct/code of ethics that is broadly applicable to all individuals who are employed by, interact with or serve on the Board

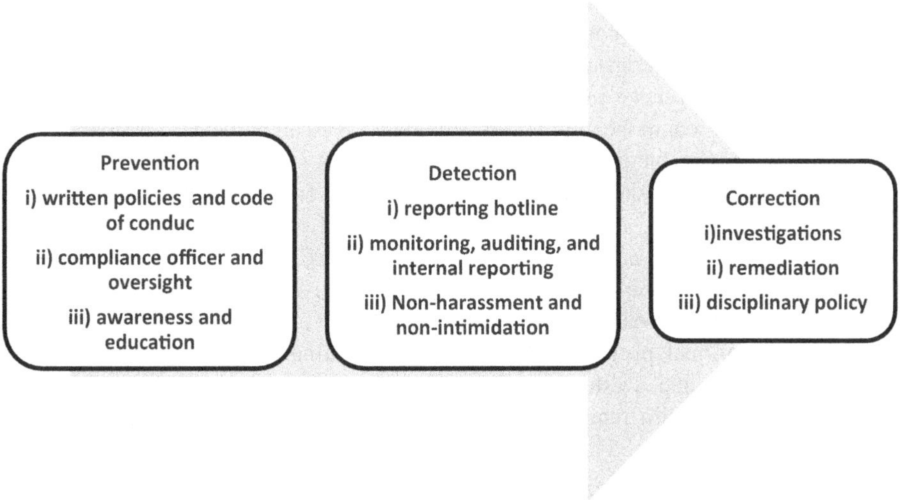

Prevention	Detection	Correction
i) written policies and code of conduc	i) reporting hotline	i)investigations
ii) compliance officer and oversight	ii) monitoring, auditing, and internal reporting	ii) remediation
iii) awareness and education	iii) Non-harassment and non-intimidation	iii) disciplinary policy

FIGURE 5.10   Purpose of GRC compliance.

A second document may exist that details the governance structure and processes for dealing with compliance issues. Some organizations choose to address governance and structure across multiple documents. But for the purpose of auditability, it is preferred to have a single document. It also facilitates an annual review of policies and procedures and helps ensure that compliance programs are evaluated and updated regularly. Policies and procedures should be reviewed and revised each year, with past versions archived.

Communication of policies and procedures to employees is important. It can be posted on the enterprise website or intranet. At minimum, the compliance program and code of conduct should be posted on an external website, as well as on an Intranet

ii. **Compliance officer and oversight:**

Compliance officer should have the requisite skill set to handle the combined compliance requirements of the organization. The best practice is for the compliance officer to report directly to the CEO or the board of directors. He or she should not report to operations or finance, where there could be perceived conflicts of interest. The role of the compliance officer should be reviewed annually and the job description to be updated to reflect added responsibilities. In case the organization has decided to outsource the compliance function, they have to set the rationale for that decision – and define how they will maintain active oversight of the compliance officer role.

In addition, the compliance officer should be supported by a compliance committee. The committee should be multidisciplinary and have a charter that details set responsibilities. Compliance committees should meet at least twice a year and ensure that all members are actively involved and accountable. The compliance committee should keep minutes as evidence of its activities.

Directors are entitled to rely on their officers, employees and consultants but have a duty to make reasonable inquiries when facts warrant gathering further information. The role of the board is general oversight over the compliance program activities. This can be delegated to a subcommittee, but the ultimate responsibility lies with the Board

The board should receive regular updates from the chief compliance officer (CCO), annually assess compliance effectiveness, receive reports on audits and investigations, discuss corrective actions, and approve any changes to compliance programs.

iii. **Training/education:**

Educational programs should include training in general compliance issues; fraud, waste and abuse; as well as inappropriate gifts and relationships with referral sources that could put the company at risk for noncompliance. The training should be documented, including pre-tests and post-tests. To create a culture of compliance, training should be part of the onboarding process and held periodically and be supported with monthly email notifications, road shows that reinforce best practices and in any other way such that compliance training is not just a check box activity.

2. Detection

i. **Reporting hotline:**

It is critical to have a hotline that enables confidential and truly anonymous reporting of compliance issues. The organization may publicize reporting options, such as email, toll-free numbers and mailbox addresses, including information on the kinds of issues to report. To help publicize the hotline, the number can be placed on the email signature lines of employees, external-facing websites, and posters in lunchrooms.

ii. **Monitoring/auditing and internal reporting:**

It is important to perform an organization-wide risk assessment. It should incorporate interviews with key staff to identify each organization's particular risks, as well as look at any compliance challenges over the past 12 months and consider internal controls and accountability. Results should be presented to senior leadership and the board, with a strategy developed to determine how findings fit with other risk assessments and enterprise-wide approaches. The annual risk assessment should be continuously revisited throughout the year to ensure it remains accurate in light of changes facing the organization.

The results and findings from the risk assessment can be leveraged to create an annual monitoring and auditing internal reporting program. The assessment can be used to identify trends, support quality reviews and other operational activities, determine where expertise is lacking and third parties should be engaged, evaluate vendors, and track compliance hotline calls.

Like the risk assessment, the derived work plan is a living document and may change over the year. Any changes or updates should be documented and justified.

iii. **Non-intimidation/non-harassment:**

Non-retaliation and non-intimidation are crucial elements of effective compliance programs. People will not participate if they fear they will lose their jobs for reporting potential issues. The compliance officer should partner with human resources to ensure the policies on non-retaliation and non-intimidation are strictly enforced.

3. **Corrective Action:** Remediation measures can be undertaken as under-

i. **Investigations/remediation:**

It is critical to respond quickly and thoroughly to compliance issues, because the clock starts ticking the day an organization acknowledges an issue. Investigations should be performed by qualified individuals and scoped to determine the 'who, what, when and how' of the issue. It is critical that investigations identify root causes, as well as uncover and correct any areas of system vulnerability to ensure there is no further risk of recurrence.

ii. Disciplinary policies:
Clear disciplinary policies must be in place for anyone indulging in unlawful or unethical actions. The policies should apply consistently across all levels and positions, including employees, board members, and vendors. Strict disciplinary action which may include dismissal from post should be enforced if any misconduct has been identified.

Pain points: Following multiple frameworks as individual entities requires great effort and is seldom effective. Too many competing priorities and timelines tend to result in an inability to achieve any form of effective compliance.

It is critical that a GRC solution can support a large number of Governance and Risk management initiatives within a company. A wrong choice would force the organization to revert to having to support multiple point solutions.

Combination of frameworks: An organization may have three different frameworks running simultaneously:

1. Cybersecurity framework
2. Risk framework
3. Regulatory framework
4. Others mandated by regulatory provisions

1. **A cybersecurity compliance framework** typically centers on risk management and data security. The level of risk appetite for the organization has to be defined in order to make risk-aware decisions. In addition to meeting regulatory compliance requirements, an integrated compliance framework(s) can enhance security, improve business processes, and realize other business objectives, such as providing a secure environment for carrying out business and selling their products/services.

   Components of the cybersecurity framework like access control, encryption authentication, monitoring, incident response, perimeter general controls, and risk management can be used for getting a model of best fit for compliance with standards and regulations. Compliance framework and a cybersecurity framework provide a common language that individuals in all areas of an organization can use to encourage more secure and efficient business practices.

2. **Risk** is all pervasive and covers business operations, IT, third-party transactions, business resilience, and a baseline for every GRC standard whether it endeavors to safeguard assets, critical processes, access, data interception, and compromise of privacy rights or any other compliance requirement of the organization. Managing cyber risk is the core mandate of information security teams in today's business climate. Frameworks are the foundation of the risk management activities that every organization practices. Organizations want to integrate frameworks based on outcomes and comprehensively drive the cyber program and supports business growth.

3. Investors and prospective customers can use **regulatory compliance frameworks** to evaluate the risk they might face if they partner with certain companies and also determine the profitability of those organizations. Meeting regulatory compliance requirements is an ongoing process. That's because a company's business environment is constantly changing. As such, one or more of its internal controls may not operate as effectively as in the past. Each framework contains guidance on the exact meaning of 'regular monitoring'.

4. There are some **external frameworks** that the security team can adopt to meet regulatory requirements. The Payment Card Industry Data Security Standard (PCI DSS) applies to all entities involved in payment card processing, including merchants, processors, acquirers, issuers, and service providers. The PCI DSS offers guidance on securing payment card data and includes a compliance framework of specifications, measurements, tools, and support resources to enable companies to safely handle cardholder information.

Organizations have to provide for capacity management to accommodate new controls, standards and regulations. A compliant organization needs to adopt an effective approach to verify conformance to internal and external requirements. A compliance framework, also known as a compliance program, is a structured set of guidelines and best practices that details a company's processes for meeting regulatory requirements.

HOW TO BUILD AN INTEGRATED FRAMEWORK FOR COMPLIANCE

With an integrated management system, each framework and functions within each of them can be matched, coupled together to form common goals and alignment for timely governance and compliance goals. It will help reduce silos and is more effective. An integrated system will provide a clear, uniform image of the entire organization, how they impact each other, and the associated risks. Efficiency and economy are gained from less duplication, and it becomes easier to adapt to changes in legal and regulatory or other business environments.

CONSIDERATIONS AT THE TIME OF INITIATING AN INTEGRATED COMPLIANCE PROGRAM

1. Identify all stakeholders
2. Establish a joint committee for implementation (Steering committee)

3. Map skill sets in team
4. Delineate the role of IT in integration
5. Benchmark with best practices prevalent in the industry
6. Prepare to conduct a complete gap analysis
7. Calculate the cost/benefit for the integration project.

KEY ASSUMPTIONS IN IMPLEMENTING AN EFFECTIVE GRC PROGRAM CONSISTS OF

1. The vision and ongoing support of Board and executive management in terms of resource allocation and direction
2. Adequate identification and updating of risks and controls and appropriately allocating the ownership and performance of these risks and controls across the lines of defense. Any unintended risks and gaps in controls may be avoided, and unnecessary duplication of work should be avoided by removing layers of redundant controls;
3. Potential conflicts of interest or incompatible responsibilities to be identified and challenged with those risks then they must be either removed or mitigated;
4. Improved reporting to the Board and executive management through removal of duplication and provision of irrelevant information to the management.
5. Alignment of technology controls with business objectives and processes. This is because in the event of a technological control failure, the impact could be catastrophic in terms of finance, legal, compliance, as well as reputation of the company.

HOW TO STITCH MULTIPLE CONTROLS TOGETHER FOR OVERLAPPING CONTROLS

Controls have to be evaluated and mapped so as to fit them according to business imperatives and objectives. Depending on the business objectivity and functions, organizations have to comply with two or more security compliance frameworks to support various business modules. Multiple controls come into play for every domain, and when these overlap, they have to be stitched together to function as one.

This is a manual process where common controls are studied extensively to find overlapping controls, to neutralize them by understanding which controls, as well as to find why do these controls better fit the business module.

CONTROL SHEETS FOR VARIOUS STANDARDS

After taking stock of the applicable standards and regulations, it will be a good practice to prepare control sheets per compliance standard. Identify control domains and put up all controls under each domain. This will help to combine total controls per unique domain identified and make a comprehensive list of domains and related controls applicable to the organization (Table 5.1). It will be observed that amid different requirements of different standards, there will be-

    i. Common domains (e.g., Business continuity, resilience, risk)
   ii. Same controls with different names (helpdesk, issues management)
  iii. Separate domains (SSAE 18 on third-party controls)

Reducing all the applicable compliances to the least common multiple (LCM), we get a sum total of all controls that go into the integrated compliance framework. All common requirements must be combined and all redundant processes must be eliminated. New controls have to be interwoven into the organizational processes so as to ensure compliance.

Ad hoc implementation of controls leads to unnecessary controls being implemented, resulting in an ineffective IT governance system that does not address each key strategic risk area. It is necessary to develop an integrated best practices framework, which will provide guidance to senior management in how to effectively and efficiently address IT governance principles by taking a business' unique strategic objectives into account.

TABLE 5.1 Illustration

STANDARDS/ DOMAINS	ISO 27001	PCI DSS	ISO 22301	SSAE18	SOX	GDPR	ISO 31000
Access control	Review of access rights				Review of access rights		
Data security							
Incident management	Policy						
System development controls							
HR related controls	Pre-hire checks						
Business continuity	BIA report						
Cryptographic controls	Policy						

However, they are quickly finding that as the multiple risk and compliance initiatives become more intertwined from regulatory and organizational perspectives, multiple systems cause confusion due to duplicative and contradictory processes and documentation. In addition, the redundancy of work, as well as sheer expense of maintaining multiple point software solutions causes the cost of compliance with spiral out of control.

IMPLEMENTING AN INTEGRATION OF TWO OR MORE FRAMEWORKS

1. **Identify required governance frameworks:** The organization must understand which frameworks or framework elements are needed to address, at a minimum, the critical governance and security concerns. When addressing control requirements, including more controls is going to mean greater investment in time, money, and effort.
2. **Choose a base framework** to use. An organization should identify a baseline framework to contain the additional controls. This framework should be as broad as is viable, allowing for only minimal, more specific needs to be addressed.
3. **Break the identified framework elements** down according to functional areas and combine controls into like groups or categories. Different frameworks often contain equivalent controls under different headings or focus areas. By mapping like controls existing controls can be enhanced rather than having to add completely different compliance needs.
4. **Identify critical control objectives** that address the most restrictive requirements. In many situations, there will be control objectives that must be accomplished, intermingled with additional categories that are simply 'good-to-have'. The action items that are required for compliance needs should be categorized as more critical.
5. **Numbering of controls:** Organize control 'numbering system' and nomenclature. For ease of evaluation and tracking, the combined framework elements should be indexed in a way that allows them to be viewed as a system and a formal nomenclature to address concepts across the new framework.
6. **Identify data that will be affected:** It is important to identify and tie up controls in multiple frameworks, likewise it is equally important to identify data affected. It becomes necessary to reverse the process, ensuring that all elements of data that are subject to the collected controls are available and additional data sources, repositories and systems be identified.
7. **Understand data flows.** The data flows of points where information is collected, processed, stored, and transmitted are assessed to determine in-scope systems, applications, and processes that must adhere to the new framework.

8. **Identify Dataflow Patterns:** Formally define scope of data controlled by the frameworks. After identifying the data flow patterns and practices, a consolidated list of servers, systems, applications, processes, and governance items must be created and then reviewed against expected values.

9. **Reduce data scope to the extent possible.** Each data control element is an investment in time, money, and effort. Existing business processes and needs should be used to determine if data is being used or retained in inappropriate or unneeded areas. Where possible, data should be consolidated and purged, reducing the overall scope of control coverage, especially critical control requirements such as those brought on by legal or regulatory provisions.

10. **Classify affected data according to impact.** Some controls will be identified as more critical, and the data elements associated with these will likewise be viewed as more sensitive. These classes of information assets should be classified and labeled to ensure that adequate weightage is given according to impact.

11. **Implement a comprehensive data cycle program:** Once the combined framework controls are in place, the data is identified, scoped, and minimized; and once classification levels have been established, a comprehensive data lifecycle program should be implemented. Through this process, end users can manage data elements, complying with the chosen control framework requirements with considerable ease.

12. **Validate the program:** Review existing infrastructure, policy, and procedure against the consolidated framework and data lifecycle requirements and wherever it has to be changed, changes to be made to support new control systems.

13. **Consolidation of security networks:** Networks, systems, and management tools should be designed to scale or be replaced easily. Consolidated security programs (such as incident response, vulnerability management, and change management) and scheduled requirements (audits, penetration testing, vulnerability assessments, risk assessments, and reports) should be updated to address all required controls resulting in a consistent, singular approach to compliance and readiness.

Frameworks are wonderful tools that can greatly simplify an organization's pursuit of effective information governance and compliance. However, one size rarely fits all, and a well-considered combination of framework elements may be the best option.

By taking an integrated GRC process approach and deploying a single system to manage the multiple GRC initiatives across the organization, it is possible to have a dramatic positive impact on organizational effectiveness by providing a clear, unambiguous process and a single point of reference for the organization.

Integration involves considering all regulatory issues at one glance, avoiding setting contradictory projects within compliance, allowing business to set the nature and extent of compliance with be covered in the integrated compliance framework. Refer to Figure 5.11.

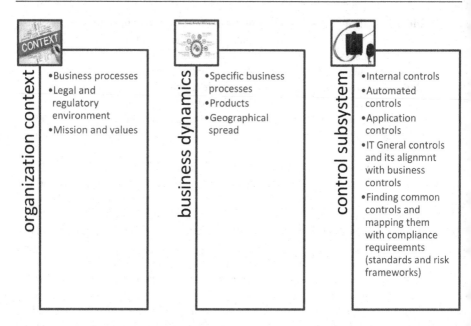

FIGURE 5.11   Process of integration.

METRICS TO BE SET TO MEASURE PERFORMANCE

Performance measurement for the integrated compliance program must be defined at the strategy stage itself and has to be approved by stakeholders. It must be based on objectives and has to accord flexibility and change control. For instance, achievement of milestones on time, lower cost of compliance, no penalties for the period can fairly be good metrics to measure the effectiveness of the compliance program.

Frameworks are, as stated before, typically high level, emphasizing controls to be implemented rather than the processes needed to achieve compliance. The gap between control and execution must be closed in order to address the framework requirements, but the means that organizations use to accomplish this vary greatly. Two like entities that carefully follow identical frameworks to protect the exact same data elements may have significantly different security postures.

REDUCING THE RISK OF NONCOMPLIANCE

Organizations are particular of compliance activities since the cost of noncompliance is high. Other key actions organizations can take to protect themselves include:

- Having a suitable monitoring and oversight into the applicable compliances for the organization
- Hiring qualified professionals to manage compliance function
- Using qualified experts to tackle noncompliance issues
- To supplement internal expertise on compliance, appointing external auditors or reviewers to assess the efficacy of the compliance program.

CRITICAL SUCCESS FACTORS IN IMPLEMENTING AN INTEGRATED COMPLIANCE PROGRAM

The approach to planning, strategizing, and implementing an integrated compliance program can be enhanced by the following:

1. Establish a conducive culture to encourage diligence and good controls.
2. Communication to stakeholders, external regulators, third-party contractors and employees should be proper and timely so that there are no misconceptions.
3. Right type of advisors to be appointed who are SMEs and can guide the implementation process.
4. It should lead to a standardization of processes to facilitate integration.
5. Ensure that management sets the tone.
6. Establish adequate metrics for performance measurement.
7. Use compliance objectives and applicable frameworks to form organizational framework for compliance.
8. Adopt a risk-based approach and ascertain that incident handling procedures are in place.
9. Create incentives for employees to motivate them to participate in compliance activities.

BENEFITS OF A SINGLE INTEGRATED FRAMEWORK FOR COMPLIANCE

- Transparency and accountability
- Prevents breaking the law which may affect the company's reputation and avoid heavy penalties
- Provides guidelines for operations and implementation of the organization
- Assigns responsibilities to different people in a company and holding them accountable
- Facilitate correlation of relevant information for the purpose of preparation of reports. Frameworks assist organizations to set goals, developed and vetted by the community, that define best practices that might be otherwise missed ROI and stakeholder value
- Scope for partnerships and opportunities
- These best practices comply with regulatory and legal requirements for IT controls in privacy and financial reporting areas
- Costs are optimized by using standardized, rather than specifically developed, approaches which make use of experts and this uses scarce IT resources
- There is greater control over the infrastructure, resulting in systems being more reliable, available, and predictable while business managers gain a greater insight into the IT processes, thereby reducing major IT risks, such as the occurrence of project failures, security breaches and failures by service.

INTERNAL AUDIT

Organizations run operations in accordance with government regulations, industry mandates, and corporate governance standards. They are subject to regular audits to ensure compliance. With increasing business complexity and the rising number and types of audits companies need to conduct, audit managers are realizing that it is difficult to manage audit by spreadsheet-based systems.

Challenges being faced include data inconsistency due to varying practices across regions and business units, poor analytics due to lack of visibility and access to information, and productivity loss due to manual processes for information routing and communication. These issues increase the risk of noncompliance as the system does not guide users based on regulatory requirements and cannot enforce a process for audits, corrective actions and investigations. Even if companies are compliant, it is difficult to provide evidence of compliance from an audit standpoint.

Compliance audits are a necessary evil for every business, more so for bigger organizations. When business complexity and boundaries are both expanding, customers need reassurance when it comes to cybersecurity and data-handling. Or, in many cases, auditing may be necessitated by industry norms or for doing business in a particular geographical location.

Auditors and compliance personnel must possess working knowledge about the types of regulatory compliance audits, their periodicity, what they entail, and whether or not they apply to the organization. Some such compliance audits are illustrated as under-

1. **SOC 2 Audit:** This is an audit governed by the American Institute of Certified Public Accountants (AICPA) and applies to any service provider that holds or processes customer data in the cloud. To achieve SOC 2 compliance, most companies prepare themselves for anywhere from six months to a year, including identifying the scope of the audit for their businesses, developing policies and procedures, and putting new security controls in place to reduce risks.

After performing a preparedness exercise, organizations can hire a CPA firm to conduct the audit. The actual process involves scoping, document collection, and an on-site visit. While in your office, the auditor will conduct interviews and review submitted material. The following types of SOC2 audits are carried out-

SOC2 Type 1 Audit: Audit is conducted at a single point in time and is a test of design of controls relating to the standard.

SOC 2 Type II Audit: This type occurs over a period of time, which typically covers six months the first time and a year thereafter.

Assurance provided by SOC 2 helps in the Sales in as much as customers are having more confidence in dealing with the organization and doing business with your organization. Beyond customers and prospects, board members, partners, and insurance companies may find value in an SOC 2 audit, as these audits report on what you're actually doing, the controls that are actually certified by an independent auditor.

2. **ISO 27001 Audit:** Like SOC 2, the standard involves a risk management process that includes people, processes, and technology. Both standards require that an independent auditor assess a company's security controls to ensure its mitigating risks properly. Many organizations seek to achieve an ISO 27001 certification for similar reasons to SOC 2 compliance.

Certification versus Attestation: ISO 27001 is a certification, and SOC 2 is an attestation. An attestation means that an independent auditor has given you an opinion that your security controls meet the guidelines set in SOC 2. In the case of deliverables, with ISO, you receive a certificate, and with SOC 2, you receive an evaluation from your auditor.

3. **General Data Protection Regulation (GDPR):** EU's GDPR is one of the most comprehensive data privacy frameworks implemented to date. GDPR auditing today is mostly self-driven consisting of the following processes:
   i. **Thorough study of the standard requirements** and preparing a step-to-step plan in owning key processes and improvements.
   ii. **Conduct a gap analysis** to identify the areas which are not aligning with GDPR provisions.

iii. **Just like a risk remediation exercise,** the identified gaps need to be remediated so that they fall in compliance with GDPR.

iv. **Perform a control testing** to check the effectiveness of new remediated processes and their compliance with GDPR requirements.

GDPR violations involve heavy fines and penalties up to $20 million or 4% of worldwide annual turnover of previous financial year whichever is higher; hence it is mandatory to comply with GDPR if applicable. If an organization processes personal data of EU citizen irrespective of its geographical location, the applicability of GDPR comes into being.

4. **Sarbanes–Oxley Audit (SOX):** this compliance involves the finance module and an IT module that deals with general IT controls to protect information and processes. A documentation of business processes is mandated by this regulation. It applies to all public companies listed on the NASDAQ. Audit is conducted by a CPA firm.

5. **Other industry-specific compliance audits:**
Many industries like the health and wellness and the banking and insurance are regulated by specific compliances. The following are a few examples of industry-specific compliance audits:

i. **PCI DSS Audit:** It is conducted for examining the 12 requirements of the PCI DSS standard performed by a qualified QSA and applies to the payment card industry (mostly banks and financial institutions).

ii. **HIPAA** (healthcare industry): Audit is carried out to ascertain that patient information and electronic records that contain medical information of patients are not misappropriated, tampered, or exposed publicly.

Compliance audits help organizations to stay updated and current. Alignment of risks with objectives is done, and auditors can test for threats that endanger organizational compliance. Any new risks or new gaps leading to noncompliance can be pointed out, and remediation for the same can be promptly dealt with. It helps organizations to enhance the security profile and supplement the efforts of sales team to close deals. Auditors use risk categorization for scheduling and prioritizing audits.

It will also help to take stock of the costs of noncompliance. Be it loss of goodwill or loss of license in case of regulatory noncompliance, business imperatives have to be achieved by the process of building a customized compliance framework where best practices are adopted and regulations are met.

STANDARDIZING AUDIT QUESTIONS

Most Authority Documents don't write their own audit questions (and neither do most frameworks). The PCI DSS is one of the very few that does. Most audit questions are created by either a working group in a framework committee or (worse) audit management software teams. Only one framework to date has a published standard on methodologies and structures for creating audit questions – the Unified Compliance Framework.

There are two types of auditing methodology that a compliance framework might provide – the simple format and the evidential-based format.

Simple audit questions are often stated as yes or no questions.

- Are vendor-supplied defaults always changed before installing a system on the network?
- Have configuration standards been developed for all system components?
- Evidential-based audit questions provide a methodology to answer the question as well as force the organization being audited to rely on evidence in order to come to the conclusion.
- Test a sample of All Assets to ensure the configuration item of Default configuration settings is 'Account and password settings do not match vendor supplied defaults. Is this configured correctly?'
- Examine the System Security Configuration standard. Does it ensure that it covers all known configuration items and system components?
- Evidential-based audit questions format the question *method* to the *subject* being audited. How do you employ these additional elements of evidence? By formatting the audit question methods into **test**, **observe**, **examine**, and **interview** type questions. Evidential items to support the answers can then be linked to each question.
- **Test** applies to testing systems, testing computations, etc.
- **Observe** applies to watching processes happen.
- **Examine** applies to records or assets that can be scrutinized.
- **Interview** is reserved for speaking to individuals or groups.

A company's internal auditors and other internal stakeholders use the compliance framework to evaluate the organization's internal controls. External auditors can also use the compliance framework to evaluate and verify a company's internal controls.

IT AUDIT AND COMPLIANCE

In most companies, key operational processes are managed by Information Technology (IT) systems. An IT organization, with well-defined internal controls, enables companies to identify and manage their IT related risks. The ability to manage and contain such risks is critical to ensuring compliance with regulations and mandates such as Sarbanes–Oxley Act (SOX), Gramm-Leach Bliley Act (GLBA), and Health Insurance Portability and Accountability Act (HIPAA).

Most organizations regularly test the internal controls within their IT organization to ensure secure and continuous operation of their entire information systems infrastructure. Such controls, typically derived from COBIT control processes, reduce IT-related risks and form the basis for good IT governance. The IT Auditing and Compliance process is inherently complex as it involves multiple internal and external stakeholders. Existing audit infrastructures have evolved from the bottom-up, and organizations need to form an integrated approach to give a top-down visibility and control.

CONCLUSION

Integrated governance needs to move up and down. In order to effectively integrate governance activities, whether to simply increase GRC maturity or working toward an integrated risk management vision, all parts of the organization must be involved. From standardizing processes at all levels of the organization to improving and automating the way that senior technical leadership reports out to the Board and CEO. These changes are only made possible by powerful tools that enable these changes. In order to integrate GRC activities, it requires an integrated solution. Technology can play a significant role in aligning itself to business imperatives and compliance requirements to build an integrated solution. Organizations have begun to determine appropriate structures for themselves taking into account the risk landscape which is ever-increasing and is at the backbone of all compliances. The main goal is risk reduction and safeguarding against noncompliance so as to reduce losses due to noncompliance.

Going ahead we shall take the example of two different industries with different compliances and walk through the development of an integrated compliance management system customized to the industry they belong.

Activities/Phases for Achieving Integrated Compliance

6

Integrated GRC demands that a number of roles – including audit, risk management, and compliance – work together to share information, data, assessments, metrics, risks, and losses. GRC is a discipline that aims at collaboration and synchronization of information and activities. The development of an integrated compliance framework for the organization has manifold merits. In this chapter, we shall take the illustration of two types of industries (hypothetically) and see what activities will be necessary to arrive at an integrated model. We shall deal with this chapter by taking two case studies of two different industries:

ILLUSTRATION I

ABC is a KPO, providing services to the UK, Austria, Canada, and Australia. They have a system of internal controls commensurate with the business, their policies and procedures, and documented standard operating procedures for some business processes. They are subject to:

1. ISO 27001
2. SSAE 18
3. GDPR
4. SOX

The enterprise currently runs the following frameworks to meet its compliance requirements:

1. Cybersecurity framework
2. Risk framework under Chief Risk Officer (CRO)

   3. Data security framework

   4. Third-party security framework

An external firm specializing in Risk Advisory is appointed to draft an integrated compliance framework to the benefit of the enterprise.

The following process was followed:

1. Understand the scope: In a kick-off meeting the scope for the assignment had been discussed with the CRO. The following points had been agreed upon.

  I. The organization shall provide all 'as is' documentation for review of the implementing team. This shall include organization charts, policies and procedures, geographical locations, etc.

  II. In order to understand the context of business and the critical processes, a complete Business Impact Analysis will be conducted. An initial round of divisional interviews with divisional heads will be conducted with coordination of the client team, a set of SPOCs representing each division, to schedule and facilitate such interviews.

  III. A brief communication to the employees on the nature of exercise to be conducted by the team, an introduction to team members, and a sign off on their understanding and acceptance of the project. The onus of such communication will lie with the senior members of the management team.

  IV. Submission of status reports to the managing committee on a fortnightly basis.

2. Set project plan and schedule: Appoint a project team as per Table 6.1. It is imperative that the right people with the necessary skill sets perform the work and hence skills mapping can be a useful exercise.

After listing down proposed resources, it will be important to lay down the time estimate. Refer to Table 6.2.

TABLE 6.1 Project Team

NAME OF MEMBER	DESIGNATION	SKILL SETS
Mr. John	Team Leader	CISA, CISM, ISO 27001 LI
Ms. Badri	Team member	Six sigma experts
Mr. Hussain	Team member	ISO 9000, ISO 31000
Ms. Lucy	Team member	Prince 2 professional for project management

TABLE 6.2 Proposed Time Estimate

PHASE	PROPOSED TIME FOR COMPLETION
Business impact analysis	3 weeks
Analysis and mapping of controls	2 weeks
Final proposed framework for management review	3 weeks

3. Initiating the integration:

The next step is to select the extent of coverage to be done. The following divisions were assessed-

    i. Division A (US)
    ii. Division B (US)
    iii. Division C (Australia)
    iv. Division D (Canada)
    v. Division E (Austria)

4. Conduct a Business Impact Analysis:

A Business Impact Analysis (BIA) measures the potential impacts to a business function if it was unable to operate following a disruption. This measurement establishes a 'prioritization' of business functions and application recovery requirements which are then used as a baseline to develop business continuity and disaster recovery plans and strategies

BIA helps identify business process criticality and the different types of impacts that disruptions can have on the continuous functioning of the business that can bring disrepute and loss of business and customer dissatisfaction. An adequate mapping of resources for all functions can be possible by the successful completion of the BIA exercise (refer to Figures 6.1 and 6.2).

BIA enables the integration team with a complete insight into the business processes and their priority in the organization.

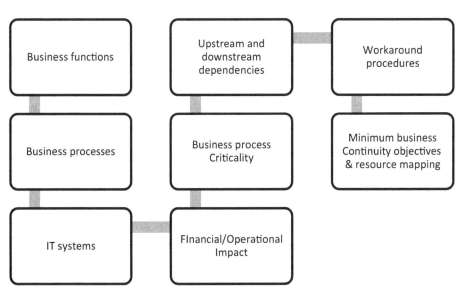

FIGURE 6.1 BIA process.

FIGURE 6.2   Purpose of BIA.

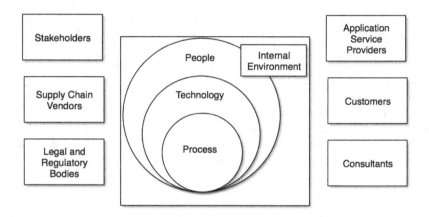

FIGURE 6.3   Extended Enterprise.

Business-specific information and nature of services rendered by each division as also its interfaces and relationships with the external parties were assessed.

It is important to know the existing structure, products, and services. Figure 6.3 shows the interrelationships between internal processes and external relationships. Integration involves viewing the enterprise in its extended version.

Evaluate existing support processes and role of IT in enabling compliance in the existing structure. To analyze information and existing frameworks and develop an integrated framework whereby:

    i. redundant processes are eliminated; and
    ii. cost economy results.

5. Ascertain the legal, regulatory, and other voluntary and mandatory compliances to which the organization is subject to. A compliance stack for the organization can be developed as shown in Figure 6.4.

6. Table of comparative analysis of compliances and provisions or controls necessary for compliance

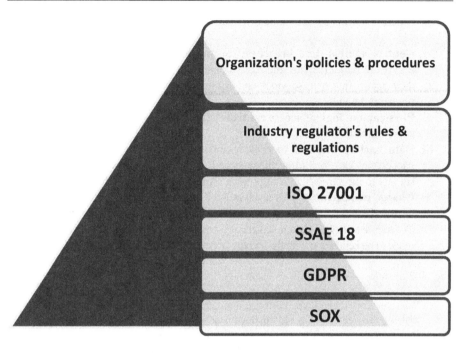

FIGURE 6.4 Compliance stack for ABC Corporation.

The enterprise has a set of policies and procedures which serves as a first line of defense that guides the business processes. Some of the business processes have documented SOPs which were reviewed by the team. Let us briefly see the regulatory compliances to which the enterprise is bound:

i. Sarbanes–Oxley Act (SOX):

SOX main sections are 302, 404 and 409; they provide for the monitoring, logging, and audit of the following parameters/controls.

    a. Internal controls
    b. User Login (success/failure)
    c. Account activity
    d. User activity
    e. Information access
    f. Network activity
    g. Database activity

SOX is an attest function and is covered by annual audit. SOX provides that audit of internal controls can be done using a common control framework. Hence building an integrated controls framework for the enterprise is all the more justified. An audit trail is to be maintained for all access and activity to sensitive business information.

IT general controls covered under SOX include:

i. **Control against data breaches:** Ensure that proper controls are in place to prevent data breaches and have tools ready to remediate incidents should they occur. Invest in services and equipment that will monitor and protect financial database.

ii. **Physical and logical access controls** to prevent unauthorized access to sensitive financial information

iii. **Data backup controls** to protect sensitive data. Data centers containing backed-up data, including those stored off-site or by a third-party are also subject to the same SOX compliance requirements as those hosted on-site.

iv. **Change management**: This involves the IT department process for adding new users and computers, updating and installing new software, and making any changes to databases or other data infrastructure components. An audit trail of changes is made to be kept along with the identity of persons who made the changes.

Sec. 802(a) states:

> Whoever knowingly alters, destroys, mutilates, conceals, covers up, falsifies, or makes a false entry in any record, document, or tangible object with the intent to impede, obstruct, or influence the investigation or proper administration of any matter within the jurisdiction of any department or agency of the United States or any case filed under title 11, or in relation to or contemplation of any such matter or case, shall be fined under this title, imprisoned not more than 20 years, or both.

SOX Compliance Steps

- Determination of Objectives
- Gap analysis
- Lay down control objectives, design and documentation.
- Conduct readiness assessment (refer to Figure 6.5).

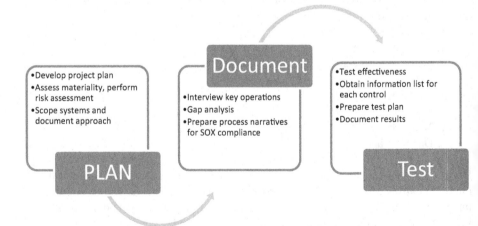

FIGURE 6.5 SOX assessment.

ii. General Data Protection Regulation

Article 3 of the GDPR provides applicability if an organization that processes, holds or somehow controls or monitors the personal data of individuals in the EU, regardless of location or where the processing takes place. The GDPR applies to the processing of personal data that is:

* wholly or partly by automated means; or
* the processing other than by automated means of personal data which forms part of, or is intended to form part of, a filing system.

It provides the data subjects (whose personal details are stored) with rights as under:

* Right to information (Articles 12, 13, 14)
* Right of rectification (Articles 12, 16)
* Right of access (Articles 12, 15)
* Right of erasure (Articles 12, 17)
* Right of data portability (Articles 12, 20)
* Profiling and automated decisions
* Right to objection (Articles 12, 21)
* Right to restriction of processing

The first step would be to understand the location, volume, and risk of personal data that exists throughout the organization. It involves identification of information sources and the processing infrastructure.

GDPR-specific requirement is performance of a 'privacy impact assessment' that identifies security risks and legal loopholes. This phase helps in identifying risk areas in the context of GDPR compliance.

Another GDPR term 'Pseudonymization' means the processing takes place in a manner that personal data can no longer be attributed to a specific data subject without the use of additional information, provided that such additional information is kept separately. Article 23 calls for controllers to hold and process only the data absolutely necessary for the completion of its duties (data minimization), as well as limiting the access to personal data to those needing to act out the processing.

Some Salient Requirements of GDPR:

* Create a central personal data register
* Update policies and privacy notices
* Conduct awareness training for personal data handlers
* Have standard operating procedures documented for GDPR compliance
* Validate and record trans-border transfer of data
* Notify breaches and manage incidents

iii. Statement for standards attestation engagements (SSAE 18):

SSAE stands for Statement for standards attestation engagements. One of the first steps to SOC 1 compliance is having a risk assessment. SOC 2 focuses on risk matrix. SSAE focuses more on organization's overall vendor risk profile.

Vendor management is becoming complex with more service providers and sub-service providers to manage and organize information are used for the organization.

Organizations to maintain evidence of the controls review performed. Organizations can improve compliance by:

1. Review and reconciliation of reports including financial reports and external communications
2. Good communication link with subservice organizations
3. Regular site visits to validate vendor controls
4. Internal audit
5. Review SOC 1 and SOC 2 reports submitted by vendor organizations especially cloud service providers
6. Monitor external communication received, like complaints about services

Need for SSAE 18 Reporting

- The SSAE 18 audit report allows the service organization to provide its customers with independent third-party verification about the state of the internal controls governing the integrity, reliability, effectiveness, and security of the processing services provided to user organizations.
- The SSAE 18 Attestation Report can be used by user organization's financial statement auditors as a substitute for those parties performing their own firsthand audit procedures.

A SSAE 18 audit can improve or sustain business relations between service providers and user organizations. It may also be viable to pass the costs of fees paid for the SSAE 18 attestation to the user organization.

- Serves as a selling point for the services of the organization since customers shall have more confidence.
- Allows the service organization to meet contractual obligations.
- Provide additional comfort on risk, systems, and controls to clients and business partners.
- Provide assurance on the internal controls and meeting objectives in case of adverse situations.

iv. ISO 27001:

The ISO 27001 standard focuses on information security (CIA) that provides a framework for the Information Security Management System (ISMS). It helps the organization to protect their data in a systematic way and maintain the confidentiality, integrity, and availability of information assets to stakeholders. The standard defines a complete set of management objectives for security run through Clause 4 to Clause 10. It helps discover process gaps and assess the readiness of the organization for the ISO 27001 certification. Table 6.3 depicts the management clauses of ISO 27001 standard.

ISO 27001 is a security management system which covers all aspects of the organization, including operations, access, HR, incident management, change control, system development, business continuity management, and a total of 14 different sections in Annexure A that cover the control objectives. ISO 27001 is a good basis to compare with other regulatory and GRC standards in the process of forming an integrated model or framework which would be proprietary for the organization.

The next step was to map the applicable standards with ISO 27001 controls in order to achieve a baseline of control for the integrated framework (refer to Table 6.4).

TABLE 6.4   Table for Mapping and Comparing Applicable Standards

TABLE 6.3   Management Clauses of ISO 27001

CLAUSE	CONTROL OBJECTIVES
Clause 4 Context of organization	4.1 Understanding the organization and its context 4.2 Understanding the needs and expectations of interested parties 4.3 Determining the scope of the information security management system 4.4 Information security management system
Clause 5 Leadership	5.1 Leadership and commitment 5.2 Policy 5.3 Organizational roles, responsibilities, and authorities
Clause 6 Planning	6.1 Actions to address risks and opportunities 6.2 Information security objectives and plans to achieve them.
Clause 7 Support	7.1 Resources 7.2 Competence 7.3 Awareness 7.4 Communication 7.5 Documented information
Clause 8 Operations	8.1 Operational planning and control 8.2 Information security risk assessment 8.3 Information security risk treatment
Clause 9	9.1 Monitoring, measurement, analysis, and evaluation 9.2 Internal audit 9.3 Management review
Clause 10	10.1 Nonconformity and corrective action 10.2 Continual improvement

DOMAIN	ISO 27001	GDPR	SSAE 18	SOX
Policy	5.1.1	Article 5 Article 32 Articles 40, 37, 41, 42, 38	CC 5.3, CC1.4	404, 302
Review of policy	5.1.2	Art. 32, 5, 11, 10, 7, 36, 35, 39, 17, 18, 19, 20, 21, 22	CC1.3, CC5.1, CC6.3	404
Organization of information security	6.1.1		CC1.3, CC1.4, CC1.5	
Segregation of duties	6.1.2		CC1.3, CC5.1, CC6.3	

(Continued)

TABLE 6.4 (Continued)

DOMAIN	ISO 27001	GDPR	SSAE 18	SOX
Contact with authorities	6.1.3		CC 1.3	
Special interest groups	6.1.4		CC1.3	
Information security in project management Control: Information security shall be addressed in project management, regardless of the type of the project	6.1.5			
Mobile devices and teleworking				
Mobile device policy Control: A policy and supporting security measures shall be adapted to manage the risks introduced by using mobile devices	6.2.1		CC 6.7	404
Teleworking Control: A policy and supporting security measures shall be implemented to protect information accessed, processed or stored at teleworking sites	6.2.2			404
Whether teleworking activity is authorized and controlled by management, and does it ensure that suitable arrangements are in place for this way of working?				
Whether such facilities are reviewed/audited/monitored regularly for securing the information used by teleworking facilities? How is it ensured?				
Prior to employment				
Screening Control: Background verification checks on all candidates for employment shall be carried out in accordance with relevant laws, regulations, and ethics and shall be proportional to the business requirements, the classification of the information to be accessed, and the perceived risks	7.1.1	Article 10	CC 1.4	404
Whether a background verification check is part of the recruitment process of the organization?	7.1.2		CC 1.4	404

DOMAIN	ISO 27001	GDPR	SSAE 18	SOX
Whether background verification checks for contractors, and third-party users were carried out in accordance to the relevant regulations or whether it is a condition in the agreement with them?				
Terms And Condition of Employment	7.1.2		CC2.2, CC2.3	404
Control: The contractual agreements with employees and contractors shall state their and the organization's responsibilities for information security				
Whether this agreement covers the information security responsibility of the organization and the employee, third-party users, and contractors?	7.1.2		CC	404
During employment	7.2, 4.2			
Management responsibilities	7.2.1		CC1.1, CC1.2	302
Control: Management shall require employees and contractors to apply information security in accordance with established policies and procedures of the organization				
Whether employees and contractors are briefed on their roles and responsibilities related to information security before giving access to sensitive information or information systems?			CC 1.3	
Whether appropriate conditions are ensured at agreement/PO level to ensure CIA				
Information security awareness, education, and training	7.2.2		CC.1.1, CC1.4, CC 2.2, CC5.3	
Control: All employees of the organization and, where relevant, contractors shall receive appropriate awareness education and training and regular updates in organizational policies and procedures as relevant for their job function				

(Continued)

TABLE 6.4   (Continued)

DOMAIN	ISO 27001	GDPR	SSAE 18	SOX
Disciplinary process Control: There shall be a formal and communicated disciplinary process in place to take action against employees who have committed an information security breach Whether there is a formal disciplinary process for the employees who have committed a security breach?	7.2.3		CC1.1, CC1.5	
Termination and change of employment	7.3.1			
Termination or change of employment responsibilities Control: Information security responsibilities and duties that remain valid after termination or change of employment shall be defined, communicated to the employee or contractor, and enforced Whether responsibilities for employment termination or change of employment are clearly defined or assigned?	7.3.1		CC 2.2	
Whether removal of access rights and return of all equipment's are carried out during termination or change of employment?	7.5	Article 30		
Inventory of assets	8.1.1		CC6.1	
Ownership of assets	8.1.2		CC6.1	
Return of assets	8.1.4		CC6.4, CC6.5	
Classification of information	8.2.1		CC 2.1, CC 3.2, PII.1, P6.7	
Labeling	8.2.2 8.2.3		CC2.1, PII.1	
Whether procedures exist for management of removable media, such as tapes, disks, cassettes, memory cards, pen drives, and reports?	8.3.1		CC6.4, CC6.5, CC6.7	

DOMAIN	ISO 27001	GDPR	SSAE 18	SOX
Disposal of Media Control: Media shall be disposed of securely when no longer required using formal procedures Whether the media that are no longer required are disposed of securely and safely as per formal procedures? Are all media containing sensitive information stored and disposed securely and safely?	8.3.2		CC 6.1	
Physical media transfer Control: Media containing information shall be protected against unauthorized access, misuse, or corruption during transportation Whether media CC6.7 containing information is protected against unauthorized access, misuse, or corruption during transportation beyond the organization's physical boundary?	8.3.3		CC 6.7	
Access control policy Control: An access control policy should be established, documented and reviewed based on business and information security requirements Whether an access control policy is developed and reviewed based on the business and security requirements?	9.1.1	Articles 5, 28, 16, 17		
Access to networks and network services Control: Users shall only be provided with access to the network and network services that they have been specifically authorized to CCuse. Whether networks and network services access policy is in place for the organization? Whether access to network services and networks is provided to the users on need-to-know basis?	9.1.2		CC 6.1	

(Continued)

TABLE 6.4   (Continued)

DOMAIN	ISO 27001	GDPR	SSAE 18	SOX
Whether proper requisition and approvals are in place for users who have been provided access to network and network services?				
Whether access to the network services is removed once the purpose has been served?				
Whether all external connections have proper management and security approvals?				
Whether Perimeter and Internal Firewalls are distinctly installed in the organization?				
User access management				
User registration and de-registration	9.2.1		CC 6.2	
Control: A formal user registration and de-registration process shall be implemented to enable assignment of access rights				
Whether there is any formal user registration procedure for granting access to all information systems and services?				
Whether there exists a process to review user access rights at regular intervals?				
E.g., Special privilege review every three months, normal privileges every six months for application, OS, network, and database				
Is there any method to check the level of access granted is appropriate to the business purpose and is consistent with the security policy and requirement of business/need to know principle, and is it reviewed?				
Whether there is a formal method in place to ensure that accesses are not granted before authorization process is completed?				

DOMAIN	ISO 27001	GDPR	SSAE 18	SOX
User access provisioning Control: A formal user access provisioning process shall be implemented to assign or revoke access rights for all user types to all systems and services Whether a formal process is in place for access provisioning to assign and revoke access rights? Whether access granted are disabled or removed for users who changed roles or jobs or left the organization? Whether user reconciliation is carried out?	9.2.2		CC6.1, CC6.2, CC6.3, CC6.4	
Management of privilege access rights Control: The allocation and use of privileged access rights shall be restricted and controlled Whether allocation and use of any privilege in information system environment is restricted and controlled? Whether privileges are allocated on need-to-have/know basis and after formal authorization process?	9.2.3		CC 6.1, CC 6.2	404
Management of secret authentication information of users Control: The allocation of secret authentication information shall be controlled through a formal management process Whether suitable authentication technique is chosen to substantiate the claimed identity of user?	9.2.4			
Review of user access rights Control: Asset owners shall review user access rights at regular intervals Whether review of user rights at regular intervals, including privileged users, is done by asset owners?	9.2.5		CC6.2, CC 6.3, CC6.4	404

(Continued)

TABLE 6.4   (Continued)

DOMAIN	ISO 27001	GDPR	SSAE 18	SOX
Removal or adjustment of access rights	9.2.6		CC 6.1, CC6.2, CC6.3, CC6.4	404
Control: The access rights of all employees and external-party users to information and information processing facilities shall be removed upon termination of their employment, contract or agreement, or adjusted upon change				
Are access rights to information disabled or removed when employee gets terminated or transferred?				
Are the passwords being changed when the employee leaves the organization?			CC 6.1, CC 6.3	404
Whether dormant accounts/users not logged for say 10 days or more are reviewed periodically and appropriate action taken, recorded, and reported to applicable management representative?				
Whether all logical and physical access granted to the contractor/ third party is being removed immediately at the end of contract or when the third-party organization leaves organization				404
9.3				
User Responsibilities			CC	
Objective: To make users accountable for safeguarding their authentication information				
Use of secret authentication information	9.4.1	Art. 5	CC 6.1	
Control: Users shall be required to follow the organization's practices in the use of secret authentication information				
Are users advised to keep their passwords confidential and change their passwords at regular intervals?				

DOMAIN	ISO 27001	GDPR	SSAE 18	SOX
Whether passwords are stored in computers in a protected manner?				
System and application access control				
Information access restriction Control: Access to information and application system functions shall be restricted in accordance with the access control policy	9.4.1	Article 5	CC 6.1	
Does access policy accord access privileges like read, write, based on business requirements?				
Whether unique identifier (user ID) is provided to every user such as operators, system administrators, and all other staff including technical?				
Whether generic user accounts are supplied only under exceptional circumstances? Whether such generic Ids are reviewed for their requirements?				404
Whether access control matrix is in place?				
Whether review of access control matrix is done regularly and updated suitably based on principles of need to know/ business retirements?				
Secure log-on procedures Control: Where required by the access control policy, access to systems and applications shall be controlled by a secure log-on procedure	9.4.2		CC6.1, P5.1	404
Whether access to operating system, database applications are controlled by secure log-on procedures?				
Whether unsuccessful log-on attempts are configured at OS, database and application level?				

(Continued)

TABLE 6.4   (Continued)

DOMAIN	ISO 27001	GDPR	SSAE 18	SOX
Password management system Control: Password management systems shall be interactive and shall ensure quality passwords Whether there exists a password management system that enforces various password controls such as first log-in, store passwords in encrypted form, not displaying passwords on screen, etc.?	9.4.3		CC 6.1	Sec 404
Use of privileged utility programs Control: The use of utility programs that might be capable of overriding system and application controls shall be restricted and tightly controlled Whether the utility programs capable of overriding system are restricted?	9.4.4			
Policy on the use of cryptographic controls Control: A policy on the use of cryptographic controls for protection of information shall be developed and implemented Whether the policy is implemented? Whether the cryptographic policy considers the management approach toward the use of cryptographic controls, risk assessment results to identify required level of protection, key management methods and various standards for effective implementation?	10.1.1	Articles 5, 20	CC6.1, CC6.7	404
Key Management Control: A policy on the use, protection and lifetime of cryptographic keys shall be developed and implemented through their whole lifecycle Whether key management is in place to support the organization's use of cryptotechniques?	10.1.2			404

DOMAIN	ISO 27001	GDPR	SSAE 18	SOX
Whether cryptographic keys are protected against modification, loss, and destruction?	6.1.2		CC 6.1, CC 6.7	
Whether secret keys and private keys are protected against unauthorized disclosure?	6.1.1, 6.1.2			
Whether equipment used to generate and store keys is physically protected?	6.1.1, 6.1.2			
Whether the key management system is based on an agreed set of standards, procedures, and secure methods?	6.1.1			
Whether the key management system is based on an agreed set of standards, procedures and secure methods?	6.1.1			
Guards at entry point Whether perimeter/boundary of areas that contain sensitive information assets have been defined?	11.1.1		CC6.4, CC6.5	
Whether perimeter is secured by high walls/nondisclosure boards?	11.1.1			
Is the information processing facility physically separated from other areas?				
Surveillance: Whether CCTV cameras are installed at appropriate locations?				
Are all external doors at perimeter physically protected against unauthorized access (alarms, locks etc.)?				
Physical entry controls Control: Secure areas shall be protected by appropriate entry controls to ensure that only authorized personnel are allowed access Whether entry controls are in place to allow only authorized personnel into various areas within the organization?	11.1.2		CC6.4, CC6.5	

(Continued)

TABLE 6.4   (Continued)

DOMAIN	ISO 27001	GDPR	SSAE 18	SOX
Are all personnel entering the information processing facility forced to enter through a controlled entry point that is monitored by a receptionist?	11.1.3		CC6.4, CC6.5	
Is the video surveillance recorded and retained for possible future playback?	11.1.1			
Are access rights to secure areas monitored and reviewed regularly?	11.1.1			
Are all network equipment, servers, etc. secured in a locked, physically secured facility?	11.1.3			
Before gaining access, are visitors required to provide some method of verification of identification, i.e., escorted by employee, business card, vendor identification tag, driver's license, PAN card, etc.?	11.1.1			
Are special service contract personnel, such as cleaning staff and off-site storage services, escorted to information proceeding facility centers?	11.1.1			
Are all visitors required to sign a visitor's log indicating their name, company represented, reason for visiting, and person to see?	11.1.1			
Securing offices, rooms, and facilities Control: Physical security for offices, rooms, and facilities shall be designed and applied	11.1.3		CC6.4, CC6.5	
How access to the information processing facility is controlled? Are there any pin/biometric systems in place for the server farm?	11.1.1			
Whether such access logs review is carried out regularly?	11.1.1			
Protecting against external and environmental threats Control: Physical protection against natural disasters, malicious attack, or accidents shall be designed and applied	11.1.4, 8.3		CC 6.6, A1.2	

DOMAIN	ISO 27001	GDPR	SSAE 18	SOX
Whether the physical protection against damage from fire, flood, or earthquake should be designed and applied? Whether there is any potential threat from neighboring premises?	11.1.1			
Are there fire detection and suppression systems in the office?	11.1.2			
OEM agreements for temperature Lighting arrester Whether temperature/humidity recording is carried out? Are such records maintained?	11.1.4			
Are fire extinguishers tagged for inspection and then inspected annually?	11.1.3			
Is there a fire suppression system in place to automatically activate immediately after detection of highly heat typically generated by fire?	11.1.4			
Are periodic fire and emergency evacuation drills conducted?	11.1.4			
Whether smoke detectors are installed at the information processing facilities?	11.1.4			
Water leakage detection system and rodent repellent system	11.1.4			
Working in secure areas Control: Procedures for working in secure areas shall be designed and applied Whether secure guidelines for secure areas have been defined?	11.1.5	-		
Delivery and loading areas Control: Access points such as delivery and loading areas and other points where unauthorized persons could enter the premises shall be controlled and if possible isolated from information processing facilities to avoid unauthorized access Whether the delivery area and information processing area are isolated from each other to avoid unauthorized access?	11.1.6		CC6.4, CC6.5	

(Continued)

TABLE 6.4   (Continued)

DOMAIN	ISO 27001	GDPR	SSAE 18	SOX
Equipment	11.2		CC6.4, CC6.5	
Equipment siting and protection Control: Equipment shall be sited and protected to reduce the risks from environmental threats and hazards and opportunities for unauthorized access Whether the equipment is protected to reduce the risks from environment threats and hazards and unauthorized access?	11.2.1	-	CC 6.4, CC 6.5	
Supporting utilities Control: Equipment shall be protected from power failures and other disruptions caused by failures in supporting utilities Are equipment protected against power failures and other electrical breakdowns?	11.2.2	-	CC6.4, CC 6.5	
Cabling security Control: Power and telecommunications cabling carrying data or supporting information services shall be protected from interception, interference, or damage Whether the power/telecom cable carrying data to supporting information services are protected from interception or damage?	11.2.3			
Are the power cables segregated from communications cables to prevent interference?	11.2.3			
Equipment maintenance Control: Equipment should be correctly maintained to ensure its continued availability and integrity Whether the equipment is maintained/upgraded as per the supplier's recommended service intervals and specifications?	11.2.4		A 1.2	

DOMAIN	ISO 27001	GDPR	SSAE 18	SOX
Whether maintenance contracts and warranties are available for critical equipment?	11.2.4			
Whether logs are maintained with all suspected or actual faults and all preventive and corrective measures?	11.2.4			
Removal of assets Control: Equipment, information, or software should not be taken off-site without prior authorization Whether any controls are in place so that equipment information and software are not taken off-site without prior authorization?	11.2.5		CC6.5, CC6.4	
Security of equipment off-premises Control: Security shall be applied to off-site assets taking into account the different risks of working outside the organization's premises Whether risks were assessed with regard to any equipment usage outside an organization premises and mitigation controls implemented? Whether security mechanisms implemented on such equipment's e.g., Encryption	11.2.6		CC6.5, CC6.7	
Secure disposal or reuse of equipment Control: All items of equipment containing storage media should be verified to ensure that any sensitive data and licensed software have been removed or securely overwritten prior to disposal or reuse Whether secure disposal policy is in place for sensitive information?	11.2.7		CC6.5, CC6.7	

(Continued)

TABLE 6.4   (Continued)

DOMAIN	ISO 27001	GDPR	SSAE 18	SOX
Unattended equipment control users shall ensure that unattended equipment have appropriate protection Whether the users and contractors are made aware of the security requirements and procedures for protecting unattended equipment? E.g., Log off when session is finished or set up auto log off, terminate sessions when finished, etc. Are idle session timeout/screensaver with password protection enabled?	11.2.8			
Locking screensavers Clear desk and clear screen policy Control: A clear desk policy for papers and removable storage media and a clear screen policy for information processing facilities shall be adopted Whether the organization has adopted a clear desk policy, whether paper docs are stored in fireproof cabinets?	11.2.9		CC6.4	
Whether the operating procedure is documented, maintained, and available to all users who need it (e.g., user manual, baseline, backup management, change management, incident management.) SOPs	12.1.1		CC2.2	
Whether escalation matrix is available for technical support?	12.1.2			
Whether regular health check-up/ housekeeping of server is defined and carried out?	12.6.1			
Change management Control: Changes to the organization, business processes, information processing facilities and systems that affect information security shall be controlled Whether changes to information processing facilities and systems are controlled?	12.1.2		CC8.1, CC2.2, CC2.4, CC6.8	

DOMAIN	ISO 27001	GDPR	SSAE 18	SOX
Whether documented change management policy and procedure is available?				
How are change requests, for minor enhancements, major projects, or operational issues in the production system, submitted and captured by the organization? (e.g., change management tool, paper forms, email, intranet)				
Does an impact analysis process exist in which key IT and business owners review proposed changes to assess impacts?				
Are formalized, documented approvals obtained for change requests?				
Are separate environments utilized for implementing system changes? (e.g., development, test, user acceptance test, stage)				
Are changes regularly tested prior to implementation into the production environment?				
Are test plans used to facilitate the testing of changes? (e.g., test procedures, expected results, scenario/test data, actual test results, pass/fail)				
Does the organization have a separate process for implementing emergency changes?				
Does the organization have rollback procedures for use in the event that a change implementation is not successful?				
Whether the process of regular update to management/review by management for the changes during the period is in place?				

(Continued)

TABLE 6.4   (Continued)

DOMAIN	ISO 27001	GDPR	SSAE 18	SOX
Capacity management Control: The use of resources shall be monitored, tuned, and projections made of future capacity requirements to ensure the required system performance Whether capacity demands are monitored and projections of future capacity requirements made to ensure that adequate processing power and storage are available (monitoring hard disk space, RAM, and CPU on critical servers)?	12.1.3		A 1.1	
Separation of development, test, and operational facilities Control: Development, test, and operational facilities should be separated to reduce the risks of unauthorized access or changes to the operational system Are development, testing, operational facilities separated from each other?	12.1.4			
Whether sensitive data of production is not used in testing environment?				
Protection from malware	12.2		CC 6.8	
Controls against malware Control: Detection, prevention, and recovery controls to protect against malware shall be implemented, combined with appropriate user awareness Has any mechanism to detect malicious codes such as viruses, worms, and Trojans been installed?	12.2.1		CC6.8	
Has any policy to prohibit the use of unauthorized software been installed?	12.5.1			
Has any policy to protect against file/software's been received from either via external networks or any other medium?	12.5.1			

DOMAIN	ISO 27001	GDPR	SSAE 18	SOX
Scanning to detect malicious code installed?	12.2.1			
Scanner to check email attachments?	12.2.1			
Any control to check web pages for malicious codes used?	12.2.1			
Is automatic update and scanning configured?	12.2.1			
Backup	12.3			
Backup copies of information, software and system images shall be taken and tested regularly in accordance with an agreed backup policy	12.3.1	Articles 16, 17, 18, 21	A1.2, A1.3, PII 5, P4.2	
Whether backup of information and software is taken and tested regularly in accordance with the agreed backup policy?				
Whether the backup media are stored at off-site location?				
Whether the backup media are regularly tested for restoration within the time frame allotted in the operational procedure for recovery?				
Whether a comprehensive back-up schedule of essential business applications has been defined?				
Whether backup logs/backup register is maintained to record the backup taken and reviewed?				
Logging and monitoring	12.4			
Event Logging: Control: Event logs recoding user activities, exceptions, faults, and information security events shall be produced, kept, and regularly reviewed	12.4.1		CC 7.2	
Whether system is configured to log exceptions faults and information security events in the system?				
Whether such logs are reviewed regularly?				

(Continued)

TABLE 6.4   (Continued)

DOMAIN	ISO 27001	GDPR	SSAE 18	SOX
Whether centralized syslog server storage is in place?				
If no (syslog), what controls are in place to preserved and monitor logs?				
Whether audit logs recording user activities, exceptions, and information security events are produced and kept for an agreed period to assist in future investigations and access control monitoring?				
Protection of log information	12.4.2			
Control: Logging facilities and log information shall be protected against tampering and unauthorized access				
Whether logging facility and log information are well protected against tampering and unauthorized access?				
Whether logs are archived to central server?				
Administrator and operator logs	12.4.3			CC7.2
Control: System administrator and system operator activities shall be logged and the logs protected and regularly reviewed				
Whether system admin and operator activities are logged?				
Whether the logged activities are reviewed on regular basis?				
Clock synchronization	12.4.4			
Control: The clocks of all relevant information processing systems within an organization or security domain shall be synchronized to a single reference time source				
Whether system clocks of all information processing system within the organization or security domain is synchronized with an agreed accurate time source. It is critical for accuracy of audit logs				

DOMAIN	ISO 27001	GDPR	SSAE 18	SOX
Control of operational software	12.5			
Installation of software on operational systems Control: Procedures shall be implemented to control the installation of software on operational systems. Whether there are any procedures in place to control installation of software on operational systems. This is to minimize the risk of corruption of operational systems	12.5.1		CC8.1	
Technical vulnerability management	12.6			
Management of technical vulnerabilities Control: Information about technical vulnerabilities of information systems being used shall be obtained in a timely fashion, the organization's exposure to such vulnerabilities evaluated and appropriate measures taken to address the associated risk Whether timely information about technical vulnerabilities of information systems being used is obtained? Whether the organization's exposure to such vulnerabilities evaluated and appropriate measures taken to mitigate the associated risk? Does the organization periodically conduct network architecture security assessments in order to identify threats and vulnerabilities?	12.6.1		CC 7.1	
Restrictions on software installations Control: Rules governing the installation of software by users shall be established and implemented Whether policy restricting installation of software is in place?	12.6.2		CC 6.8	

(Continued)

TABLE 6.4   (Continued)

DOMAIN	ISO 27001	GDPR	SSAE 18	SOX
Information system audit considerations	12.7			
Information system audit controls Control: Audit requirements and activities involving verification of operational systems shall be carefully planned and agreed to minimize disruptions to business processes Whether audit requirements and activities involving checks on operational systems are carefully planned and agreed to minimize the risk of disruptions to business process?	12.7.1			
Network Controls Control: Networks shall be managed and controlled to protect information in systems and applications Whether there exists a SOP that addresses concerns relating to networks and network services?	13.1.1	Article 20	CC 6.6	
Which network monitoring tool is used by the organization for monitoring of networks and continuously monitored for its availability and performance?	13.1.3			
Whether the organization maintains a updated and approved network diagram?				
Whether inventory of network devices is maintained and updated with details such as configuration details, IP address, hostname AMC/warranty details?				
Are intrusion detection/prevention systems in place to detect attacks and provide identification of unauthorized intrusion?				
Whether base lines (Base line Security Configurations) are defined for network/network device configurations?				
Whether asset movement register and breakdown register is maintained?				

DOMAIN	ISO 27001	GDPR	SSAE 18	SOX
Whether daily activity checklist is in place and followed and reviewed regularly?				
Whether log monitoring/reviews in place?				
Is there a formal change management process in operation?				
Whether patch management is in place for network devices like routers, switches, firewall, servers?				
Whether there exists any authentication mechanism for challenging external connections. E.g.: cryptography-based technique, hardware tokens, software tokens, challenge/response protocol				
Security of network services Control: Security mechanisms, service levels and management requirements of all network services shall be identified and included in network services agreement, whether these services are provided in-house or outsourced	13.1.2	Article 5	CC 6.6	
Whether security features, service levels, and management requirements of all network services are identified and included in any network services agreement?				
Whether the ability of the network service provider to manage agreed services in a secure way is determined and regularly monitored, and the right to audit is agreed upon?				
Whether firewall rules review is done regularly?				
Whether security incident management (SIEM) tools are used for correlating events/incidents from different devices and identifying any security incidents?				

(Continued)

TABLE 6.4   (Continued)

DOMAIN	ISO 27001	GDPR	SSAE 18	SOX
Is quarterly VAPT carried out?				
Segregation in networks	13.1.3		CC 6.6	
Control: Groups of information services, users, and information systems shall be segregated on networks				
Whether the network (where business partner's and/or third parties need access to information system) is segregated using perimeter security mechanisms such as firewalls?				
Whether VLANs are configured with in network to ensure segregation of network?				
Whether consideration is made to segregation of wireless networks from internal and private networks?				
Information transfer	13.2			
Restriction on email reforwarding Webflash, circulars, email bulletins, IVR messages	13.2.1	Articles 15, 26	CC 6.7	404
Information transfer policies and procedures				
Control: Formal transfer policies, procedures, and controls shall be in place to protect the transfer of information through the use of all types of communication facilities				
Procedure for the use of cryptographic techniques to protect confidentiality, integrity and authenticity of information				
Information transfer policies and procedures				
Agreements on information transfer	13.2.2	Article 9	CC 6.7	404
Control: Agreements shall address the secure transfer of business information between the organization and external parties				
Whether process is in place to ensure secure transfer of business information between the organization and external parties.				

DOMAIN	ISO 27001	GDPR	SSAE 18	SOX
Labeling system for sensitive or critical information while exchanging				
Whether protocols are defined for exchange information?				
Electronic messaging Control: Information involved in electronic messaging shall be appropriately protected. Whether the information involved in electronic messaging is well protected. (Electronic messaging includes but is not restricted to Email, Electronic Data Interchange, Instant Messaging)	13.2.3			
Whether Naming convention is in place?				
Whether restriction in Attachment?				
Whether email attachments are scanned before downloading?				
Confidentiality or NDAs Control: Requirements for confidentiality or NDAs reflecting the organizations needs for the protection of information shall be identified, regularly reviewed and documented. Whether the organization's need for confidentiality or NDA for protection of information is clearly defined and regularly reviewed?	13.2.4	Article 7	CC2.3, CC8.1, CC9.2, P1.1, P2.1, P6.1, P6.4	
Whether security requirements for new information systems and enhancement to existing information system are specified during requirement specification phase?	14.1.1	Articles 5, 14, 15, 13, 12, 11, 7, 9, 16, 17, 18, 19, 20, 21, 22	CC 8.1	
Whether system requirements for information security and processes for implementing security is integrated in the early stages of information system projects.				

(Continued)

TABLE 6.4   (Continued)

DOMAIN	ISO 27001	GDPR	SSAE 18	SOX
Securing application services on public networks Control: Information involved in application services passing over public networks shall be protected from fraudulent activity, contract dispute and unauthorized disclosure and modification. what are the controls implemented to ensure protection from unauthorized information disclosure, fraudulent activity and contract dispute?	14.1.2		CC 6.7	
Whether data confidentiality during transit is ensured by using protocol such as HTTPS etc.				
Are risks identified and corrective measures are implemented (e.g., 1. Secure log on process such as SSL, Two factor authentication etc. 2. Session timeout				
Whether audit trails/logs are maintained?				
Whether adequate user awareness steps are taken?				
Whether Vulnerability assessment as per OWASP top 10 is carried out and vulnerability is addressed?				
Whether information such as card no. CVV no., etc. are ensured not to be stored, displayed during transit and storage if used.				
Protecting application services transactions Control: Information involved in application service transactions shall be protected to prevent incomplete transmission, mis-routing, unauthorized message alteration, unauthorized disclosure, unauthorized message duplication or replay. Whether secure protocols are used?	14.1.3		CC 6.7	

DOMAIN	ISO 27001	GDPR	SSAE 18	SOX
Whether cryptographic controls such as digital signatures are in place?				
Whether adequate authentication (e.g., two factor) is in place?				
Whether transactions details are stored in such a way that they are not directly exposed to the internet?				
Security in development and support	14.2			
Secure development policy Control: Rules for the development of software and systems shall be established and applied to developments within the organization. Whether the production and test environments are separated?	14.2.1	–	CC 8.1	
Whether secure coding guidelines are present?				
Whether security requirements are carried out in design phase.				
Whether source code versions are maintained?				
System change control procedures Control: Changes to systems within the development lifecycle shall be controlled by the use of formal change control procedures.	14.2.2		CC 8.1	
Is there formal change control procedure in place to restrict maintenance and copying of program source libraries				
Is there a procedure in place for change control and has it been documented, approved, implemented				
Is there a process of documentation, specification, testing, quality control and managed implementation for new systems and major changes to existing systems				

(Continued)

TABLE 6.4   (Continued)

DOMAIN	ISO 27001	GDPR	SSAE 18	SOX
Is risk assessment/impact analysis conducted while introduction of new systems or major changes to existing systems				
Does the change procedures addresses the following: 1. Ensures that changes are submitted by authorized users 2. Record of agreed authorization levels for change 3. Ensure a review mechanism on change controls and integrity procedures 4. version control of software updates				
Technical review of application after operating system changes Control: When operating platforms are changed, business critical applications shall be reviewed and tested to ensure there is no adverse impact on organizational operations or security Whether there is process or procedure in place to review and test business critical applications for adverse impact on organizational operations or security after the change to Operating Systems, application platform change? Whether periodic upgrades are carried out regularly – operating system, i.e., to install service packs, patches, hot fixes etc.,	14.2.3		CC 8.1	
Restrictions on changes to software packages Control: Modifications to software packages should be discouraged, limited to necessary changes and all changes should be strictly controlled Whether modifications to software package is discouraged and/ or limited only to necessary changes.	14.2.4		CC8.1	

DOMAIN	ISO 27001	GDPR	SSAE 18	SOX
Secure system engineering principles	*14.2.5*		*CC8.1*	
Control: Principles for engineering secure systems shall be established, documented, maintained and applied to any information system implementation efforts.				
Whether security is designed into all architectures layers (e.g., data, application, platforms, implementation, data transmission, data at rest)				
Whether periodical review is conducted to ensure secure process in view of new technology and new threats?				
Whether security processes are ensured with outsourced parties through contract and binding agreements?				
Whether techniques such as user authentication, secure session control, data validation, sanitization and elimination of debugging codes are considered?				
Secure development environment	*14.2.6*		*CC6.8, CC8.1*	
Control: Organizations shall establish and appropriately protect secure development environments for system development and integration efforts that cover the entire system development lifecycle.				
Whether development is outsourced?				
Whether access to development environment is controlled?				
Whether regular backups are in place in the development environment				
Whether sensitivity of data stored, transmitted and processed is ensured in the development environment?				

(Continued)

TABLE 6.4   (Continued)

DOMAIN	ISO 27001	GDPR	SSAE 18	SOX
Whether it is ensured that sensitive production data not used in development/testing environment?				
Outsourced development Control: The organization shall supervise and monitor the activity of out-sourced system development. Whether the outsourced software development is supervised and monitored by the organization. Whether points such as Licensing arrangements, escrow arrangements, contractual requirement for quality assurance, testing before installation to detect Trojan code are considered.	14.2.7		CC8.1	
System security testing Control: Testing of security functionality shall be carried out during development. Whether test templates are designed to include test inputs and expected output with schedule?	14.2.8		CC8.1	
Whether independent acceptance test is carried out?				
Whether testing is carried out by team different from development?				
Testing of patches in secured environment				
System acceptance testing Control: Acceptance testing programs and related criteria shall be established for new information systems, upgrades and new versions. Whether system acceptance criteria are established for new information systems, upgrades and new versions.	14.2.9		CC8.1	
Test Data	14.3			

DOMAIN	ISO 27001	GDPR	SSAE 18	SOX
Protection of test data Control: Test data shall be selected carefully and protected and controlled. Whether system test data is protected and controlled.	14.3.1		CC8.1	
is 'live'/operational database used for test purposes				
Is sensitive/confidential data of production being used for test purposes				
Information security policy for supplier relationships Control: Information security requirements for mitigating the risks associated with suppliers access to the organizations assets shall be agreed with the supplier and documented.	15.1.1		CC3.2, CC9.2	
1. Whether policy/procedures are in place for identifying the types of suppliers (vendors) and the controls required to safeguard the organization information is in place?				
2. Whether outsource policy as per regulator guidelines is in place?				
Whether SLAs are identified? Whether such SLA monitored Regularly?				
Addressing security within suppliers agreements Control: All relevant information security requirement shall be established and agreed with each supplier that may access, process, store, communicate, or provide IT infrastructure components for the organizations information.	15.1.2		CC3.2, CC9.2, P6.5	
1. Whether confidentiality clause is included in the agreement?				
Documented Procedure for third-party management is in place?				

(Continued)

TABLE 6.4   (Continued)

DOMAIN	ISO 27001	GDPR	SSAE 18	SOX
Any ways to monitor performance criteria of the third-party vendors defined in the agreement and followed?				
Information and communication technology supply chain Control: Agreements with suppliers shall include requirements to address the information security risks associated with information and communications technology services and product supply chain.	15.1.3		CC2.3, CC 9.2	
1. Whether agreement is dated and signed by relevant authorities?				
2. Whether term of the agreement is defined?				
3. Whether extensions of information security requirements are ensured in the agreements in case of supplier sub-contract? (e.g., Background checking of sub-contractors/ Supply chain, NDA)				
4. Whether communication protocols and escalations are defined?				
5. Whether right to audit clause is incorporated in the agreement?				
Whether appropriate clause is included in the clauses where supply chain is involved?				
Supplier service delivery management	15.2			
Monitoring and review of supplier services Control: Organizations shall regularly monitor, review and audit supplier service delivery. Whether SLAs are monitored to verify adherence to the agreements?	15.2.1		CC4.2, CC9.2	
Whether Service reports are reviewed and regular progress meetings are conducted?				

DOMAIN	ISO 27001	GDPR	SSAE 18	SOX
Whether review of records of information security events, operational problems, failures, tracing of faults and disruptions related to the service are carried out?				
Managing changes to supplier services	15.2.2		CC 9.2	
Control: Changes to the provision of services by suppliers, including maintaining and improving existing information security policies, procedures and controls, shall be managed, taking account of the criticality of business information, systems and processes involved and re-assessment of risks.				
Is change management process is applied to suppliers? (example. to include in Renewal of agreements, the enhancement to the services, developments to new application, use of new technologies, change of networks, new development tool, change of physical location, change of supplier/ sub-contracting)				
Responsibilities and procedures	16.1.1		CC7.3, CC7.4	
Control: Management responsibilities and procedures should be established to ensure a quick, effective and orderly response to information security incidents Whether Incident Management Policy and Procedure is in place?				
Whether Incident Management Policy and Procedure is in place?				
Does policy covers reporting procedures				
Whether emergency actions taken are documented in detail?				

(Continued)

TABLE 6.4   (Continued)

DOMAIN	ISO 27001	GDPR	SSAE 18	SOX
Reporting information security events Control: Information security events shall be reported through appropriate management channels as quickly as possible Whether information security events are reported through appropriate management channels as quickly as possible?	16.1.2		CC 2.2, CC 7.2, CC7.3, CC7.4, P6.5, P6.6	
Whether proper incident/problem escalation procedures exist to ensure that identified incidents, errors and problems are solved in the most efficient way on a timely basis?				
Whether formal information security event reporting procedure, Incident response and escalation procedure is developed and implemented?				
Whether suitable feedback processes to ensure that those reporting incidents /events are notified of results after the issue is closed				
Whether any automated tools used for recording of incidents and analysis?				
Is there any process to report Information Security Incident to the Management?				
Reporting information security weaknesses Control: Employees and contractors using the organizations information systems and services shall be required to note and report any observed or suspected information security weaknesses in systems or services Whether there exists a procedure that ensures all employees of information systems and services are required to note and report any observed or suspected security weakness in the system or services.	16.1.3		CC2.2, CC4.2, CC7.2, CC7.3	

DOMAIN	ISO 27001	GDPR	SSAE 18	SOX
Whether there is system to ensure that all non-standard operational events (incidents, errors and problems) are identified, recorded, analyzed and resolved.				
How employees/Contractors reports information security weakness.				
Is the reporting mechanism easy, accessible and available				
Whether end users are intimated after resolution of Information Security Weaknesses?				
Assessment of and decision on information security events Control: Information security events shall be assessed and it shall be decided if they are to be classified as information security incidents. Whether appropriate definition of security incident is documented to clearly define what incidents are required to be addressed immediately or escalated to the correct service support level.	16.1.4		CC7.3, CC7.4,	
Response to information security incidents Control: Information security incidents shall be responded to in accordance with the documented procedure. Whether Incidents have been recorded and resolved as per documented procedure?	16.1.5		CC2.2, CC7.3, CC7.4, CC7.5	
Whether there is a mechanism in place to identify and quantify the type, volume and costs of information security incidents. Whether the knowledge/ solutions are recorded as knowledge base?	16.1.6		CC7.5, CC2.2	

(Continued)

TABLE 6.4   (Continued)

DOMAIN	ISO 27001	GDPR	SSAE 18	SOX
Collection of evidence Control: The organization shall define and apply procedures for the identification, collection, acquisition and preservation of information, which can serve as evidence. Whether evidence relating to the incident are collected, retained and presented to conform to the rules for evidence laid down in the relevant jurisdiction(s).	16.1.7	Article 16		
Planning information security continuity Control: The organization shall determine its requirements for information security and the continuity of information security management in adverse situations. E.g., during a crisis or disaster. Whether requirements of business continuity related to CIA are identified and documented? Whether there is a managed process in place that addresses the information security requirements for developing and maintaining business continuity throughout the organization. Does the organization have a defined business impact analysis (BIA), which identifies all business processes critical to the organization and the resources that support those processes? Whether RTO and RPO as per Business Impact Analysis are defined and documented? Whether Critical processes are documented that management decides are so significant to the mission of the business that the business cannot afford to operate without them after a given period of time.	17.1.1		CC7.6, A1.2	

DOMAIN	ISO 27001	GDPR	SSAE 18	SOX
Whether Risk assessment methodology is in place and various threats considered for Risk Assessment				
Whether various scenarios of contingency are covered and BCP defined for these scenarios?				
Whether the organization have a documented, tested business continuity management (BCM) process				
Implementing information security continuity	17.1.2		CC7.5, A1.2	
Control: The organization shall establish, document, implement and maintain processes, procedures and controls to ensure the required level of continuity for information security during an adverse situations.				
1. Whether plans were developed to maintain and restore business operations, ensure availability of information within the required level in the required time frame following an interruption or failure to business processes?				
2. Whether plan considers redundancy of resources?				
3. Whether BCP test is in place regularly?				
Whether Disaster Recovery site is identified for BCP? If so whether DR site is in place?				
Whether DR site is replica of Data Centre?				
Whether the decisions of DR site are justified by a BIA?				
Whether the plan considers identification and agreement of responsibilities, identification of acceptable loss, implementation of recovery and restoration procedure, documentation of procedure and regular testing.				

(Continued)

TABLE 6.4   (Continued)

DOMAIN	ISO 27001	GDPR	SSAE 18	SOX
Whether communication plans been established to notify appropriate personnel of a disaster, and the initiation of the BCP?				
Whether business continuity roles and responsibilities been assigned to appropriate personnel?				
Verify, review and evaluate information security continuity Control: The organization shall verify the established and implemented information security continuity controls at regular intervals in order to ensure that they are valid and effective during adverse situations. Whether Business continuity plans are tested regularly to ensure that they are up to date and effective?	*17.1.3*		*A 1.3*	
Are they evaluated and updated on review?				
Whether business continuity plan tests ensure that all members of the recovery team and other relevant staff are aware of the plans and their responsibility for business continuity and information security and know their role when plan is evoked.				
Is there any test schedule for testing business continuity plans?				
Whether results of tests are recorded and reported to Sr. management? Whether BCP is updated based on the test observations?				
Whether actions are taken to improve the plans?				
A formal change control process is in place to ensure regular review and distribution of updated plans including changes in network diagram, redundancies, testing plans, etc.?				

DOMAIN	ISO 27001	GDPR	SSAE 18	SOX
Whether the plans are updated in the event of changes or acquisition of new facility?				
Redundancies	17.2			
Availability of information Processing Facilities – Redundancy Control: Information processing facilities shall be implemented with redundancy sufficient to meet availability requirements. Whether the organization have an redundant facility to recover operations in the event that main offices, production locations or distribution centers are inaccessible and single point failure is avoided?	17.2.1		A 1.2	
Whether redundancy in servers is available.				
Whether redundancy in network is available.	18.1	Articles 28, 27		
Identification of applicable legislation and contractual requirements Control: All relevant legislative, statutory, regulatory, contractual requirements and the organization's approach to meet these requirements shall be explicitly identified, documented and kept up to date for each information system and the organization. Whether all relevant statutory, regulatory and contractual requirements are identified and defined? (especially in relation to the design, operation, use and management of information systems?) example: 1. Whether Regulatory guidelines are identified, recorded and implemented? 2. Whether IT Act 2000 /2008 requirements of digital signature, electronic record as legal evidences are identified and handled?	18.1.1	Articles 28, 27	CC3.1, CC 1.1	

(Continued)

TABLE 6.4   (Continued)

DOMAIN	ISO 27001	GDPR	SSAE 18	SOX
3. Whether electronic record retention policy is in place? 4. Whether private keys of PKI if any are secured, renewed, and record maintained?				
Intellectual property rights (IPR) Control: Appropriate procedures shall be implemented to ensure compliance with legislative, regulatory, and contractual requirements related to IPR and use of proprietary software products. Whether the organization has published an IPR compliance policy? (defining legal use of software and information products, design rights, trademarks, patents)	18.1.2		Cc 3.1	
Whether acquisition of software's is from only through known and reputable sources?				
Whether the organization ensures awareness of the policies to protect IPRs?				
Whether the organization has conveyed to staff that copyright infringement can lead to legal action, which may involve criminal proceedings?				
Whether the organization maintains appropriate asset register identifying all the assets relevant to the protection of IPR?				
Protection of records Control: Records shall be protected from loss, destruction, falsification, unauthorized access and unauthorized release in accordance with legislators, statutory, regulatory, contractual, and business requirements. Whether organization categorized records into various types, e.g., accounting records, database records, designs, transaction logs, audit logs, operational procedures?	18.1.3	Articles 7, 20	CC 1.1	

DOMAIN	ISO 27001	GDPR	SSAE 18	SOX
Whether organization has identified retention period for each of these categories?				
Whether organization issued guidelines on retention, storage, handling and disposal of records and information?				
Whether organization has identified types of storage media, e.g., paper, microfilm, magnetic, optical, for these records?				
Privacy and Protection of personally identifiable information	18.1.4	Articles 1, 3, 91, 90, 38, 39 37, 33, 34	CC8.1, P1.6, P2.1, P3.1, P3.2, P4.1, P4.2, P5.1, P5.2	
Control: Privacy and protection of personally identifiable information shall be ensured as required in relevant legislation and regulation where applicable.				
Is any data protection legislation or regulation of any country applicable to organization?				
Whether organizations have documented data protection and privacy policy?				
Whether DLP (data leakage prevention) tools are used to prevent sensitive information leakage?				
Whether data leakage through USB, email, etc. is prevented? How?				
Regulation of cryptographic controls	18.1.5		CC 6.1	
Control: Cryptographic controls shall be used in compliance with all relevant agreements, legislations, and regulations. Whether legal restriction on export and import of computer hardware and software for performing cryptographic function is put in place in law of land.				
Whether any restriction on the usage of encryption is put in place by the law.				

(Continued)

TABLE 6.4   (Continued)

DOMAIN	ISO 27001	GDPR	SSAE 18	SOX
Whether digital signature is being used for any authentication/ non-repudiation mechanism? If so how are the private keys secured? Whether any list of such keys is maintained along with the expiry details? Whether such expiry is renewed?				
Information Security Reviews (annually or when there is change)	A.18.2			
	18.21.			
Independent review of information security	18.2.1		CC4.1, CC 4.2, P8.1	
Control: The organization approach to managing information security and its implementation (i.e., control objectives, controls, policies, processes, procedures for information security) shall be reviewed independently at planned intervals or when significant changes occur				
How often these policies being reviewed? Check for the supporting document				
Who reviewed this? Independent individual/internal audit team/ management committee or independent third-party auditors?				
Compliance with security policies and standards	18.2.2		CC4.1, CC4.2, CC8.2, P8.1	
Control: Managers shall regularly review the compliance of information processing and procedures within their area of responsibility with the appropriate security policies, standards, and any other security requirements. Do the managers regularly review compliance of information processing within area of their responsibility?				
ISMS policy lays down punitive measures for breach of ISMS policy				

Forming a Comprehensive Baseline of Controls

When we tabulate the results of mapping applicable standards, we come across the following situations:

The baseline must be representative of the control infrastructure as required to operate the business of the organization and after complying with legal and regulatory specifications. It must be a sum total of controls as under-

A+B+C=BL

As like LCM of all available controls per domain as prescribed by A or B or C must be included depending on the criticality rating. Defining domains and controls attached to each domain is crucial (refer to Table 6.5).

1. Let us take, for instance, ISMS security policy. Provision of policy control is described in Articles 5, 32, 40, 37, 41 42, and 38 of the GDPR as also CC 5.3, CC 1.4 of the SSAE 18 and under sec. 404 and 302 of SOX. So this control will go under A before common controls.
2. Similarly, employees prior to employment appear for all four standards and hence will be listed under A.
3. Classification of information and labeling of information comes under 8.21, 8.2.2 of ISO 27001 and CC 2.1, CC 3.2, PI 1.1, P6.7, CC 2.1, PII 1.1 of SSAE 18
4. Controls for removable media common to ISO 27001 8.3.1 and SSAE 18, CC 6.5, 6.7
5. Access control and policies around access to be complied even under general policies of the organization. SOX IT controls also cover access policy and access controls.
6. Information security in project management is under 6.1.5 of ISO 27001, but other standards do not have related control. Yet it has to be included in criteria B here.

TABLE 6.5   Inclusions in Baseline Controls

SN	SITUATION	INCLUDE IN BASELINE CONTROLS?
A	Organizational policies and procedures	Yes
B	Controls common for all compliances	Yes
C	Controls specific to individual compliance	Yes

FIGURE 6.6   Monitoring the baseline.

For a complete mapping between compliance standards on the compliance stack, refer to Table 6.4. There will be controls that overlap each other; some of the common domains are:

    i. Logical access
   ii. Physical access
  iii. System change management
  iv. Incident management
   v. Protection against Malware

On the other hand, certain controls specific to the respective standards are unique. For instance, *privacy impact assessment as per GDPR*:

A *Privacy Impact Assessment (PIA)* is a process which assists organizations in identifying and managing the privacy risks arising from new projects, initiatives, systems, processes, strategies, policies, business relationships, etc. Privacy impact assessment (PIA) or data protection impact assessment (DPIA) was introduced with the General Data Protection Regulation (Art. 35 of the GDPR). This refers to the obligation of the controller to conduct an impact assessment and to document it before starting the intended data processing. One can bundle the assessment for several processing procedures.

A PIA should always be conducted when the processing could result in a high risk to the rights and freedoms of natural persons. A privacy impact assessment is not absolutely necessary if a processing operation only fulfills one of these criteria. However, if several criteria are met, the risk for the data subjects is expected to be high and a data protection impact assessment is always required. If there is doubt and it is difficult to determine a high risk, a DPIA should nevertheless be conducted. This process must be repeated at least every three years.

The national supervisory authorities have to establish and publish a list of processing operations which always require a data protection impact assessment in their jurisdiction (Blacklist). They are also free to publish a list of processing activities which specifically do not require a privacy impact assessment (Whitelist). If a company has appointed a DPO, his advice must be taken into account when conducting a DPIA.

Compliance with GDPR is necessary keeping in view the penalties attached to noncompliance. Chief Risk Officer (CRO) also serves as Chief Privacy Officer and he has to form a compliance team to handle and safeguard baseline controls as also the specific controls attached to standards that prescribe a special compliance like PIA.

The risk framework coupled with the cybersecurity framework, which already existed in bits and pieces before integration, must be formalized, and each risk and control ideally should have a unique identifier. Allocating risk owners and responsibilities for risk and other compliances should rest with the risk owners. Accountability for lapses needs to be set.

Document management system in respect of each of the compliances should be defined and maintained. ISO 27001 lays down the following mandatory documentation, which can be examined during audit.

1. Scope of the ISMS (clause 4.3)
2. Information security policy and objectives (clauses 5.2 and 6.2)
3. Risk assessment and risk treatment methodology (clause 6.1.2)
4. Statement of Applicability (clause 6.1.3 d)
5. Risk treatment plan (clauses 6.1.3 e and 6.2)
6. Risk assessment report (clause 8.2)
7. Definition of security roles and responsibilities (clauses A.7.1.2 and A.13.2.4)
8. Inventory of assets (clause A.8.1.1)
9. Acceptable use of assets (clause A.8.1.3)
10. Access control policy (clause A.9.1.1)
11. Operating procedures for IT management (clause A.12.1.1)
12. Secure system engineering principles (clause A.14.2.5)
13. Supplier security policy (clause A.15.1.1)
14. Incident management procedure (clause A.16.1.5)
15. Business continuity procedures (clause A.17.1.2)
16. Statutory, regulatory, and contractual requirements (clause A.18.1.1)
17. Records of training, skills, experience and qualifications (clause 7.2)
18. Monitoring and measurement results (clause 9.1)
19. Internal audit program (clause 9.2)
20. Results of internal audits (clause 9.2)
21. Results of the management review (clause 9.3)
22. Results of corrective actions (clause 10.1)
23. Logs of user activities, exceptions, and security events (clauses A.12.4.1 and A.12.4.3)

In this list, the list of specific documentation such as process narratives, review documents, stipulated under SOX and PIA reports, consent forms under GDPR, controls relating to CIA principles as per SSAE 18, all important and mandatory documentation is critical. To build a database of policies and documentation and making them readily accessible for authorized persons will facilitate the integrated objective for compliance. Building a common technology infrastructure to support storage and management of all compliance-related documentation was necessary here. IT contributed in building the requisite dashboards and reporting formats to monitor controls, compliance, and updating of information of the data relating to compliance. Many redundant processes could be eliminated, and controls were mapped to the consortium of applicable standards and monitored by management for compliance.

ILLUSTRATION 2

Let us take one more example – say an organization is a life insurance business and their compliance stack. Like the previous exercise, building the compliance stack of applicable regulations and standards for the business would be the first step. Refer to Figure 6.7.

Methodology to initiate an integrated compliance framework would be similar:

1. Conduct a BIA.
2. Obtain context of business.
3. Study standards PCI DSS and ISO 31000 to obtain inventory of control.
4. Determine what sub-controls would be necessary to meet the 12 requirements of PCI DSS and controls for ISO 31000. This helps in building the baseline of controls on the A+B+C concept as explained earlier.
5. Baseline ideally represents a sum total of all controls that go to achieve organizational compliance with *all controls chosen to be relevant by the compliance team as endorsed by the managerial team.*

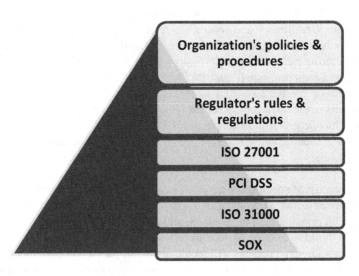

FIGURE 6.7　Case 2 Compliance Stack.

6. Point to note is that anything less than defined baseline is leading to noncompliance and anything above the baseline signifies levy of more controls than prescribed by the baseline, and hence it leads to a more secure compliance framework.

7. Different standards may be managed by different departments. Accordingly, ownership to risks and performance renders clarity and accountability on the part of the asset and risk owners to safeguard their controls – no matter if they may be reflected in a common pool called the baseline.

8. As shown in Figure 6.6, a process of gap analysis should be periodically conducted to identify control deficiencies and remediation of gaps should be ongoing. This is in line with the management's role in monitoring and performance measurement. Revalidation and updating of controls and documentation are extremely important.

9. Finally, employing a technology solution would serve to enhance the compliance model since the multitude of controls, multiplicity of documents, is a challenge to manage manually.

10. At the stage where team is final, mapping of controls is done, ownership of risks and controls is done, baseline is developed, IT can serve as an enabler in developing the monitoring and measurement module, and dashboards are developed to reflect state of compliance according to the customized requirements of the organization. Refer to the table in Annexure A for mapping of controls for the compliances in Illustration II.

This opens the doors for integration and performing compliance through collaboration, mapping, and a common baseline. Systematic planning and design of appropriate controls to meet requirements of the various compliance standards and laws specific to the industry are convenient, time-saving, and manageable.

CONCLUSION

In this chapter we saw how we could combine our requirements for regulatory and legal compliance in different standards applicable to the organization how to perform mapping of controls and go on to build a baseline. In the next chapter we shall see some operating models for different businesses to get the flavor of integrated compliance.

Annexure A
(Control Mapping
for Illustration II)

The next step was to map the applicable standards with ISO 27001 controls in order to achieve a baseline of control for the integrated framework.

Refer to the following table of mapping.

ILLUSTRATION II   Table for Mapping and Comparing Applicable Standards

DOMAIN	ISO 27001	PCI DSS	ISO 31000	SOX
Management Clauses of ISO 27001 (4–10)				
Clause 4 Context of organization				
• Understanding the organization and its context	4.1		5.4.1	
• Understanding the needs and expectations of interested parties	4.2		5.4.1	
• Determining the scope of the information security management system	4.3		5.4.1	
Information security management system				
Clause 5 Leadership	5.1	Requirement 12.1	Clauses 5.2, 5.4.5	
• Leadership and commitment	5.2	Requirement 12.1.3	Clause 6.2	
• Policy	5.3	Requirement 1.1.4, 12.5	Clause 5.2	
Organizational roles, responsibilities, and authorities				

(Continued)

201

DOMAIN	ISO 27001	PCI DSS	ISO 31000	SOX
Clause 6 Planning	6.1			
• Actions to address risks and opportunities	6.2	12.1.2	Clause 6.2 Clause 6.2	
Information security objectives and plans to achieve them.				
Clause 7 Support			Clause 4	
• Resources	7.1			
• Competence	7.2			
• Awareness	7.3			
• Communication	7.4			
• Documented information	7.5			
Clause 8 Operations				
• Operational planning and control	8.1	Requirement 6.4, 12.3.1	Clauses 6.2, 6.5.2, 6.4.1,	
• Information security risk assessment	8.2 8.3	Requirement 12.1.2, 12.8.3	6.4.2, 6.4.3 6.5.2, 6.5.3	
Information security risk treatment				
Clause 9				
Monitoring, measurement, analysis, and evaluation	9.1 9.2	12.1.3	5.6, Clause 6.6	
• Internal audit	9.3		Clause 6.6	
Management review			Clause 6.7	
Clause 10				
Nonconformity and corrective action	10.1		Clause 5.7	
Continual improvement	10.2		Clause 5.7	
Annexure A Controls (A5–A18)				
Policy	5.1.1	Requirement 12.1, 12.3.5		404, 302
Review of policy	5.1.2	Requirement 12.1.3	Clause 5.2	
Organization of information security	6.1.1	Requirement 1.1.4, 12.5, 6.1.1, 6.2	Clause 5.4.3	
Segregation of duties	6.1.2	12.5, 12.9.1, 12.9.3,		
Contact with authorities	6.1.3	Requirement 6.2	Clause 5.2	
Special interest groups	6.1.4	Requirement 6.4, 12.3.1	Clause 5.2	
Information Security in project management Control: Information security shall be addressed in project management, regardless of the type of the project.	6.1.5	6.2		

DOMAIN	ISO 27001	PCI DSS	ISO 31000	SOX
Mobile device policy Control: A policy and supporting security measures shall be adapted to manage the risks introduced by using mobile devices.	6.2.1	Requirement 12.8.3		404
Teleworking Control: A policy and supporting security measures shall be implemented to protect information accessed, processed or stored at teleworking sites.	6.2.2			404
Whether teleworking activity is authorized and controlled by management and does it ensure that suitable arrangements are in place for this way of working.				
Whether such facilities are reviewed/audited/monitored regularly for securing the information used by teleworking facilities? How is it ensured?		Requirement 11		
Prior to employment				
Screening Control: Background verification checks on all candidates for employment shall be carried out in accordance with relevant laws, regulations and ethics and shall be proportional to the business requirements, the classification of the information to be accessed and the perceived risks.	7.1.1	Requirement 12.7, 12.3.3		404
Terms and Condition of Employment Control: The contractual agreements with employees and contractors shall state their and the organization's responsibilities for information security.	7.1.2	Requirement 12.5, 12.6.2, 12.9.1, 12.9.3		404

(Continued)

DOMAIN	ISO 27001	PCI DSS	ISO 31000	SOX
Whether this agreement covers the information security responsibility of the organization and the employee, third-party users and contractors.				
During employment	7.2, 4.2			
Management responsibilities Control: Management shall require employees and contractors to apply information security in accordance with established policies and procedures of the organization	7.2.1		Clause 5.4.1	302
Whether employees, contactors are briefed on their roles and responsibilities related to information security before giving access to sensitive information or information systems?				
Whether appropriate conditions are ensured at agreement/PO level to ensure CIA				
Information security awareness, education and training Control: All employees of the organization and where relevant, contractors shall receive appropriate awareness education and training and regular updates in organizational policies and procedures as relevant for their job function.	7.2.2	Requirement 9.7.1, 12.6, 12.6.1, 12.9.1		
Disciplinary process Control: There shall be a formal and communicated disciplinary process in place to take action against employees who have committed an information security breach. Whether there is a formal disciplinary process for the employees who have committed a security breach?	7.2.3			

DOMAIN	ISO 27001	PCI DSS	ISO 31000	SOX
Termination and change of employment	7.3.1			
Termination or change of employment responsibilities Control: Information security responsibilities and duties that remain valid after termination or change of employment shall be defined, communicated to the employee or contractor and enforced. Whether responsibilities for employment termination or change of employment are clearly defined/assigned?	7.3.1			
Whether removal of access rights and return of all equipment's are carried out while termination or change of employment	7.5	Requirement 12.3.5, 8.5.4, 9.2a		
Inventory of assets	8.1.1	Requirement 12.3.3, 12.9.1, 12.9.3		
Ownership of assets	8.1.2	Requirement 12.3.4		
Return of assets	8.1.4	Requirement 12.4, 12.6.2		
Classification of information	8.2.1	Requirement 9.7.1		
Labeling	8.2.2	Requirement 9.7.1		
	8.2.3			
Whether procedures exist for management of removable media, such as tapes, disks, cassettes, memory cards, pen drives, and reports.	8.3.1	Requirement 9.5, 6.7, 8.9		
Disposal of Media Control: Media shall be disposed of securely when no longer requires, using formal procedures. Whether the media that are no longer required are disposed of securely and safely as per formal procedures.	8.3.2	Requirement 9.10		

(Continued)

DOMAIN	ISO 27001	PCI DSS	ISO 31000	SOX
Physical media transfer Control: Media containing information shall be protected against unauthorized access, misuse or corruption during transportation	8.3.3	Requirement 8.5.4, 9.2.1, 9.7.2		
Access control policy Control: An access control policy should be established, documented and reviewed based on business and information security requirements. Whether an access control policy is developed and reviewed based on the business and security requirements.	9.1.1	Requirement 9.2, 9.3, 9.4 Requirement 7.1, 7.2		
Access to networks and network services Control: Users shall only be provided with access to the network and network services that they have been specifically authorized to access. Whether networks and network services access policy is in place for the organization.	9.1.2	Requirement 9.1, 12.8.2 Requirement 1.1, 7.1, 7.2		
Whether access to network services and networks is provided to the users on need-to-know basis	9.1.3	Requirement 9.1		
Whether proper requisition and approvals are in place for users who have been provided access to network and network services				
Whether access to the network services is removed once the purpose is been served.				
Whether all external connections have proper Management and Security approvals				
Whether Perimeter and Internal Firewalls are distinctly installed in the organization				
User access management				

DOMAIN	ISO 27001	PCI DSS	ISO 31000	SOX
User registration and de-registration Control: A formal user registration and de-registration process shall be implemented to enable assignment of access rights. Whether there is any formal user registration procedure for granting access to all information systems and services	9.2.1	Requirement 7.1, 7.2, 8.1, 8.2, 8.3, 8.5.4, 8.5.5, 12.3.1, 12.3.4		
Whether there exists a process to review user access rights at regular intervals. E.g., Special privilege review every 3 months, normal privileges every 6 months for application, OS, network and database?				
Is there any method to check the level of access granted is appropriate to the business purpose and is consistent with the security policy and requirement of business/need to know principle and is it reviewed?				
Whether formal method in place to ensure that accesses are not granted before authorization process is completed				
User access provisioning Control: A formal user access provisioning process shall be implemented to assign or revoke access rights for all user types to all systems and services. Whether a formal process is in place for access provisioning to assign and revoke access rights	9.2.2			404
Whether access granted are disabled or removed for users who changed roles or jobs or left the organization? Whether user reconciliation is carried out?				

(Continued)

DOMAIN	ISO 27001	PCI DSS	ISO 31000	SOX
Management of privilege access rights Control: The allocation and use of privileged access rights shall be restricted and controlled Whether allocation and use of any privilege in information system environment is restricted and controlled. Whether privileges are allocated on need-to-have/know basis and after formal authorization process	9.2.3	Requirement 2.2.2, 2.2.4, 7.1, 7.2		404
Management of secret authentication information of users Control: The allocation of secret authentication information shall be controlled through a formal management process Whether suitable authentication technique is chosen to substantiate the claimed identity of user.	9.2.4			
Review of user access rights Control: Asset owners shall review user access rights at regular intervals Whether review of user rights at regular intervals including privileged users is done by asset owners?	9.2.5	Requirement 8.5.1, 8.5.5, 12.3.3, 9.7.2, 9.9		404
Removal or adjustment of access rights Control: The access rights of all employees and external party users to information and information processing facilities shall be removed upon termination of their employment, contract or agreement, or adjusted upon change. Is access rights to information disabled or removed when employee gets terminated/transferred?	9.2.6	Requirement 10		404

DOMAIN	ISO 27001	PCI DSS	ISO 31000	SOX
Are the passwords being changed when the employee leaves the organization?	9.2.7	Requirement 9.8		404
Whether dormant accounts/users not logged for say 10 days or more are reviewed periodically and appropriate action taken, recorded and reported to applicable management representative?				
Whether all logical and physical access granted to the contractor/third party is being removed immediately at end of contract or when the third-party organization leaves organization				
9.3				
User Responsibilities				
Objective: To make users accountable and responsible for safeguarding their authentication information.				
Use of secret authentication information	9.3.1			
Control: Users shall be required to follow the organization's practices in the use of secret authentication information.				
Are users advised to keep their passwords confidential and change their passwords at regular intervals?				
Whether passwords are stored in computers in protected manner?				
System and application access control				
Information access restriction	9.4.1	Requirement 8.1, 2.3, 12.3.2, 10.1, 16		
Control: Access to information and application system functions shall be restricted in accordance with the access control policy.				
Does access policy accord access privileges like read, write, based on business requirements?				

(Continued)

DOMAIN	ISO 27001	PCI DSS	ISO 31000	SOX
Whether unique identifier (user ID) is provided to every user such as operators, system administrators and all other staff including technical.				
Whether generic user accounts are supplied only under exceptional circumstances? Whether such generic Ids are reviewed for their requirements?				
Whether Access Control Matrix is in place?				
Whether review of access control matrix is done regularly and updated suitably based on principles of need to know/ business retirements?				
Secure log-on procedures Control: Where required by the access control policy, access to systems and applications shall be controlled by a secure log-on procedure.	9.4.2	Requirement 6.3.1, 8.5.13, 8.5.14		
Whether unsuccessful log-on attempts are configured at OS, Database and Application level				
Password management system Control: Password management systems shall be interactive and shall ensure quality passwords. Whether there exists a password management system that enforces various password controls such as first log-in, store passwords in encrypted form, not displaying passwords on screen, etc.	9.4.3	Requirement 8.5		
Use of privileged utility programs Control: The use of utility programs that might be capable of overriding system and application controls shall be restricted and tightly controlled Whether the utility programs capable of overriding system are restricted?	9.4.4			

DOMAIN	ISO 27001	PCI DSS	ISO 31000	SOX
Policy on the use of cryptographic controls Control: A policy on the use of cryptographic controls for protection of information shall be developed and implemented. Whether the cryptographic policy consider the management approach toward the use of cryptographic controls, risk assessment results to identify required level of protection, key management methods and various standards for effective implementation	10.1.1	Requirement 2.1.1, 2.2.2, 2.3, 3.4, 3.5, 3.6, 4.1, 4.2, 6.3.1, 6.5.3, 6.5.9, 8.4		
Key Management Control: A policy on the use, protection and lifetime of cryptographic keys shall be developed and implemented through their whole lifecycle. Whether key management is in place to support the organization's use of cryptotechniques. Whether secret keys and private keys are protected against unauthorized disclosure. Whether equipment's used to generate, store keys are physically protected. Whether the Key management system is based on agreed set of standards, procedures and secure methods. Whether key management system is based on agreed set of standards, procedures and secure methods.	10.1.2	Requirement 3.5, 3.6, 6.3.1, 6.5.8		
Guards at entry point Whether perimeter/boundary of areas that contain sensitive information assets have been defined? Whether perimeter is secured by high walls/nondisclosure boards	11.1.1	Requirement 7.1, 7.2		

(Continued)

DOMAIN	ISO 27001	PCI DSS	ISO 31000	SOX
Is information processing facility is physically separated from other areas				
Surveillance: Whether CCTV cameras are installed at appropriate locations.				
Physical entry controls Control: Secure areas shall be protected by appropriate entry controls to ensure that only authorized personnel are allowed access. Whether entry controls are in place to allow only authorized personnel into various areas within the organization?	11.1.2	Requirement 9		
Are all personnel entering the information processing facility forced to enter through a controlled entry point that is monitored by a receptionists.	11.1.3	Requirement 7		
Is the video surveillance recorded and retained for possible future playback				
Are access rights to secure areas monitored and reviewed regularly?		Requirement 9		
Are all network equipment, servers, etc. physically secured in a locked, physically secured facility?				
Before gaining access are visitors required to provide some method of verification of identification, i.e., escorted by employee, business card, vendor identification tag, driver's license, pan card, etc.?				
Are special service contract personnel, such as cleaning staff and off-site storage services, escorted to information proceeding facility center?				

DOMAIN	ISO 27001	PCI DSS	ISO 31000	SOX
Are all visitors required to sign a visitor's log indicating their name, company represented, reason for visiting, and person to see?				
Securing offices, rooms, and facilities Control: Physical security for offices, room and facilities shall be designed and applied.	11.1.3	9.5, 9.7.2, 9.9		
How access to the Information Processing Facility is controlled? Are there any pin/biometric systems are in place for the server room?		Requirement 9.2, 9.3, 9.4		
Whether such access logs review is carried out regularly.				
Protecting against external and environmental threats Control: Physical protection against natural disasters, malicious attack or accidents shall be designed and applied.	11.1.4, 8.3			
Whether there is any potential threat from neighboring premises.				
Are there fire detection and suppression systems in the office?				
Whether temperature/Humidity recording is carried out? Are such records maintained?				
Are fire extinguisher tagged for inspection and then inspected annually.				
Is there a fire suppression system in place to automatically activate immediately after detection of highly heat typically generated by fire?				
Are periodic fire and emergency evacuation drills conducted?				
Whether Smoke detectors are installed at the Information Processing Facilities				

(Continued)

DOMAIN	ISO 27001	PCI DSS	ISO 31000	SOX
Working in secure areas Control: Procedures for working in secure areas shall be designed and applied. Whether secure guidelines for secure areas have been defined?	11.1.5			
Delivery and loading areas Control: Access points such as delivery and loading areas and other points where unauthorized persons could enter the premises shall be controlled and if possible isolated from information processing facilities to avoid unauthorized access.	11.1.6			
Equipment	11.2			
Equipment siting and protection Control: Equipment shall be sited and protected to reduce the risks from environmental threats and hazards and opportunities for unauthorized access.	11.2.1	Requirement 9.1.1,		
Supporting utilities Control: Equipment shall be protected from power failures and other disruptions caused by failures in supporting utilities	11.2.2	Requirement 2.2.2, 8.1, 2.2.4, 7.2, 8.5.1		
Cabling security Control: Power and telecommunications cabling carrying data or supporting information services shall be protected from interception, interference or damage. Are the Power cables segregated from communications cables to prevent interference?	11.2.3	Requirement 2.1, 8.1, 8.2.3, 4.5		
Equipment maintenance Control: Equipment should be correctly maintained to ensure its continued availability and integrity.				
Whether the equipment is maintained/upgraded as per the supplier's recommended services intervals and specifications?	11.2.4	9.1.1		

DOMAIN	ISO 27001	PCI DSS	ISO 31000	SOX
Whether maintenance contracts and warranties available for critical equipment.				
Whether logs are maintained with all suspected or actual faults and all preventive and corrective measures?				
Removal of assets Control: Equipment, information or software should not be taken off-site without prior authorization.	11.2.5	9.8		
Security of equipment off-premises Control: Security shall be applied to off-site assets taking into account the different risks of working outside the organization's premises	11.2.6			
Whether Security mechanisms implemented on such equipment's e.g., Encryption				
Secure disposal or re-use of equipment Control: All items of equipment containing storage media should be verified to ensure that any sensitive data and licensed software has been removed or securely overwritten prior to disposal or re-use.	11.2.7	9.10		
Whether secure disposal policy is in place for sensitive information?				
Unattended equipment control-users shall ensure that unattended equipment have appropriate protection.	11.2.8			
Are Idle session timeout/ screensaver with password protection enabled				
Locking Screensavers	11.2.9			
Clear desk and clear screen policy Control: A clear desk policy for papers and removable storage media and a clear screen policy for information processing facilities shall be adopted.				

(Continued)

DOMAIN	ISO 27001	PCI DSS	ISO 31000	SOX
Whether the operating procedure is documented, maintained and available to all users who need it (e.g., User manual, baseline, backup management, change management, Incident management) SOPs	12.1.1	Requirement 2.2, 6.3, 6.4, 6.5, 12.3.7		
Whether Escalation matrix available for technical support				
Whether regular health check-up/ housekeeping of server is defined and carried out?				
Change management Control: Changes to the organization, business processes, information processing facilities and systems that affect information security shall be controlled. Whether changes to information processing facilities and systems are controlled?	12.1.2	Requirement 6.4, Requirement 6.3.3, Requirement 2, Requirement 3		
Whether documented change management policy and procedure is available.		12.1.2, 12.5.1		
Are formalized, documented approvals obtained for change requests?				
Are separate environments utilized for implementing system changes? (e.g., Development, Test, User Acceptance Test, Stage)		6.3.2		
Are changes regularly tested prior to implementation into the production environment?				
Are test plans used to facilitate the testing of changes? (E.g., Test Procedures, Expected Results, Scenario/Test Data, Actual Test Results, Pass/Fail)				
Does the organization have a separate process for implementing emergency changes?				

DOMAIN	ISO 27001	PCI DSS	ISO 31000	SOX
Does the organization have rollback procedures for use in the event that a change implementation is not successful?				
Whether the process of regular update to management/Review by Management for the changes during the period is in place?				
Capacity management	12.1.3			
Control: The use of resources shall be monitored, tuned and projections made of future capacity requirements to ensure the required system performance.				
Whether capacity demands are monitored and projections of future capacity requirements are made to ensure that adequate processing power and storage are available (monitoring hard disk space, RAM, and CPU on critical servers)				
Separation of development, test and operational facilities	12.1.4	6.3.2		
Control: Development, test and operational facilities should be separated to reduce the risks of unauthorized access or changes to the operational system				
Are development, testing, operational facilities separated from each other?				
Whether sensitive data of production is not used in testing environment?				
Protection from malware	12.2			
Controls against malware	12.2.1	Requirement 6.3		
Control: Detection, prevention and recovery controls to protect against malware shall be implemented, combined with appropriate user awareness.				
Any mechanism to detect malicious codes such as viruses, worms, Trojans are installed?				

(Continued)

DOMAIN	ISO 27001	PCI DSS	ISO 31000	SOX
Any policy to prohibit the use of unauthorized software installation	12.2.2	Requirement 6.3, 6.5, 8.5.16,		
Any policy to protect against file/ software's received from via either external networks or any other medium				
Scanning to detect malicious code installed				
Scanner to check email attachments				
Any control to check web pages for malicious codes				
Is automatic update and scanning configured				
Backup	12.3			
Backup copies of information, software and system images shall be taken and tested regularly in accordance with an agreed backup policy.	12.3.1	Requirement 2.1.1, 2.2.2, 2.3, 3.4, 3.5, 3.6, 4.1, 4.2, 6.3.9, 6.5.8, 5.9.8		
Whether back-ups of information and software is taken and tested regularly in accordance with the agreed backup policy.				
Whether the backup media are stored at off-site location				
Whether the backup media are regularly tested for restoration within the time frame allotted in the operational procedure for recovery				
Whether Comprehensive Back-up schedule of essential business applications is defined?				
Whether Backups Logs/Backup Register is maintained to record the backups taken and reviewed?				
Logging and monitoring	12.4			

DOMAIN	ISO 27001	PCI DSS	ISO 31000	SOX
Event Logging: *Control: Events logs recoding user activities, exceptions, faults and information security events shall be produced, kept and regularly reviewed.* *Whether system is configured to log exceptions faults and information security events in the system?* *Whether such logs are reviewed regularly?* *Whether centralized syslog server storage is in place.* *If no. (Sys log) what controls are in place to preserved and monitor logs?*	*12.4.1*	*10.6, 11.4, 11.5, 12.5.5, 9.5*		
Whether audit logs recording user activities, exceptions, and information security events are produced and kept for an agreed period to assist in future investigations and access control monitoring.		*10.1, 10.2, 10.3, 12.5.5*		
Protection of log information *Control: Logging facilities and log information shall be protected against tampering and unauthorized access.* *Whether logging facility and log information are well protected against tampering and unauthorized access?* *Whether Logs are archived to central server?*	*12.4.2*	*Requirement 6.4, 10.5*		
Administrator and operator logs *Control: System administrator and system operator activities shall be logged and the logs protected and regularly reviewed.* *Whether system admin and operator activities are logged?* *Whether the logged activities are reviewed on regular basis.*	*12.4.3*	*Requirement 10.2, 10.3, 12.5.5*		

(Continued)

DOMAIN	ISO 27001	PCI DSS	ISO 31000	SOX
Clock synchronization Control: The clocks of all relevant information processing systems within an organization or security domain shall be synchronized to a single reference time source. Whether system clocks of all information processing system within the organization or security domain is synchronized with an agreed accurate time source. It is critical for accuracy of audit logs.	12.4.4	Requirement 10.4		
Control of operational software	12.5			
Installation of software on operational systems Control: Procedures shall be implemented to control the installation of software on operational systems. Whether there are any procedures in place to control installation of software on operational systems. (This is to minimize the risk of corruption of operational systems	12.5.1 12.5.2 12.5.3 12.5.4 12.5.5	Requirement 6.4 Requirement 6.4, 6.3, Requirement 6.5, 6.6 Requirement 6.4, 6.3, 6.5, 6.6		
Technical vulnerability management	12.6			
Management of technical vulnerabilities Control: Information about technical vulnerabilities of information systems being used shall be obtained in a timely fashion, the organization's exposure to such vulnerabilities evaluated and appropriate measures taken to address the associated risk. Whether timely information about technical vulnerabilities of information systems being used is obtained. Whether the organization's exposure to such vulnerabilities evaluated and appropriate measures taken to mitigate the associated risk.	12.6.1	Requirement 2.2.3, 6.1, 6.2, 11.1, 11.2, 11.3 11.4, 11.5		

DOMAIN	ISO 27001	PCI DSS	ISO 31000	SOX
Does the organization periodically conduct Network Architecture Security assessments in order to identify threats and vulnerabilities?		Requirement 3		
Restrictions on software installations Control: Rules governing the installation of software by users shall be established and implemented. Whether policy restricting installation of software is in place?	12.6.2	Requirement 8		
Information System audit considerations	12.7			
Information systems audit controls Control: Audit requirements and activities involving verification of operational systems shall be carefully planned and agreed to minimize disruptions to business processes. Whether audit requirements and activities involving checks on operational systems are carefully planned and agreed to minimize the risk of disruptions to business process.	12.7.1			
Network Controls Control: Networks shall be managed and controlled to protect information in systems and applications. Whether there exists a SOP that addresses concerns relating to networks and network services.	13.1.1	Requirement 12.9		
Which Network Monitoring tool is used by the organization for monitoring of networks and continuously monitored for its availability and performance?		Requirement 10		
Whether the organization maintains a updated and approved network diagram.				

(Continued)

DOMAIN	ISO 27001	PCI DSS	ISO 31000	SOX
Whether Inventory of Network Devices is maintained and updated with details such as Configuration Details, IP address, hostname AMC/ Warranty Details				
Is Intrusion Detection/Prevention system in place to detect attacks and provide identification of unauthorized intrusion?				
Whether baselines (Baseline Security Configurations) are defined for network/network device configurations?				
Whether Asset Movement Register and breakdown register is maintained?				
Whether Daily Activity Checklist is in place and followed and reviewed regularly				
Whether Log monitoring/ Reviews in place				
Is there a formal change management process in operation?				
Whether Patch Management is in place for Network Devices like Routers, Switches, Firewall, Servers				
Whether there exists any authentication mechanism for challenging external connections. Examples: Cryptography-based technique, hardware tokens, software tokens, challenge/response protocol, etc.				
Security of network services Control: Security mechanisms, service levels and management requirements of all network services shall be identified and included in network services agreement, whether these services are provided in-house or outsourced.	13.1.2			

DOMAIN	ISO 27001	PCI DSS	ISO 31000	SOX
Whether security features, service levels and management requirements of all network services are identified and included in any network services agreement.				
Whether the ability of the network service provider, to manage agreed services in a secure way, is determined and regularly monitored, and the right to audit is agreed upon.				
Whether firewall rules review is done regularly?		Requirement 1		
Whether Security incident management (SIEM) tools are used for correlating events/ incidents from different devices and identifying any security incidents?				
Is quarterly VAPT carried out?		Requirement 3		
Segregation in networks control: Groups of information services, users and information systems shall be segregated on networks.	13.1.3	Requirement 3		
Whether the network (where business partner's and/ or third parties need access to information system) is segregated using perimeter security mechanisms such as firewalls.				
Whether VLANs are configured with in network to ensure segregation of network?				
Whether consideration is made to segregation of wireless networks from internal and private networks.				
Information Transfer	13.2			

(Continued)

DOMAIN	ISO 27001	PCI DSS	ISO 31000	SOX
Information transfer policies and procedures Control: Formal transfer policies, procedures and controls shall be in place to protect the transfer of information through the use of all types of communication facilities. Procedure for the use of cryptographic techniques to protect confidentiality, integrity and authenticity of information	13.2.1	Requirement 12.9.1, Requirement 12.5.3		404
Agreements on information transfer Control: Agreements shall address the secure transfer of business information between the organization and external parties. Whether process is in place to ensure secure transfer of business information between the organization and external parties. Labeling system for sensitive or critical information while exchanging Whether protocols are defined for exchange information	13.2.2	Requirement 12.9.6		404
Electronic messaging Control: Information involved in electronic messaging shall be appropriately protected. Whether the information involved in electronic messaging is well protected. (Electronic messaging includes but is not restricted to Email, Electronic Data Interchange, Instant Messaging) Whether Naming convention is in place? Whether email attachments are scanned before downloading?	13.2.3	Requirement 12.9.1		

DOMAIN	ISO 27001	PCI DSS	ISO 31000	SOX
Confidentiality or nondisclosure agreements Control: Requirements for confidentiality or NDAs reflecting the organizations needs for the protection of information shall be identified, regularly reviewed and documented. Whether the organization's need for confidentiality or NDA for protection of information is clearly defined and regularly reviewed?	13.2.4			
Whether security requirements for new information systems and enhancement to existing information system are specified during the requirement specification phase?	14.1.1	Requirement 12.9.1		
Whether system requirements for information security and processes for implementing security is integrated in the early stages of information system projects.				
Securing application services on public networks Control: Information involved in application services passing over public networks shall be protected from fraudulent activity, contract dispute and unauthorized disclosure and modification. what are the controls implemented to ensure protection from unauthorized information disclosure, fraudulent activity and contract dispute?	14.1.2	Requirement 4, 5, 6, 11		
Whether data confidentiality during transit is ensured by using protocol such as HTTPS				

(Continued)

DOMAIN	ISO 27001	PCI DSS	ISO 31000	SOX
Are risks identified and corrective measures are implemented (e.g., 1. Secure log on process such as SSL, two factor authentication). 2. Session timeout				
Whether audit trails/logs are maintained?				
Whether adequate user awareness steps are taken?				
Whether Vulnerability assessment as per OWASP top 10 is carried out and vulnerability is addressed?				
Protecting application services transactions Control: Information involved in application service transactions shall be protected to prevent incomplete transmission, mis-routing, unauthorized message alteration, unauthorized disclosure, unauthorized message duplication or replay. Whether secure protocols are used?	14.1.3	Requirement 12.9.1		
Whether cryptographic controls such as digital signatures are in place?	14.1.5	Requirement 11.1, 11.2, 11.3, 11.4, 11.5, 12.9.2		
Whether adequate authentication (e.g., two factor) is in place?				
Whether transactions details are stored in such a way that they are not directly exposed to the internet?				
Security in development and support	14.2			
Secure development policy Control: Rules for the development of software and systems shall be established and applied to developments within the organization. Whether dev, production and test environments are separated?	14.2.1			

DOMAIN	ISO 27001	PCI DSS	ISO 31000	SOX
Whether secure coding guidelines are present?				
Whether security requirements are carried out in design phase.				
Whether source code versions are maintained?				
System change control procedures Control: Changes to systems within the development lifecycle shall be controlled by the use of formal change control procedures.	14.2.2			
Is there a procedure in place for change control and has it been documented, approved, implemented				
Is there a process of documentation, specification, testing, quality control and managed implementation for new systems and major changes to existing systems				
Is risk assessment/impact analysis conducted while introduction of new systems or major changes to existing systems				
Does the change procedures addresses the following:				
1. Ensures that changes are submitted by authorized users				
2. Record of agreed authorization levels for change				
3. Ensure a review mechanism on change controls and integrity procedures				
4. Version control of software updates				
Technical review of application after operating system changes Control: When operating platforms are changed, business critical applications shall be reviewed and tested to ensure there is no adverse impact on organizational operations or security	14.2.3			

(Continued)

DOMAIN	ISO 27001	PCI DSS	ISO 31000	SOX
Whether periodic upgrades are carried out regularly – operating system, i.e., to install service packs, patches, hot fixes.				
Restrictions on changes to software packages Control: Modifications to software packages should be discouraged, limited to necessary changes and all changes should be strictly controlled	14.2.4			
Secure system engineering principles Control: Principles for engineering secure systems shall be established, documented, maintained and applied to any information system implementation efforts.	14.2.5			
Whether security is designed into all architectures layers (e.g., data, application, platforms, implementation, data transmission, data at rest)				
Whether periodical reviews are conducted to ensure secure process in view of new technology and new threats?				
Whether security processes are ensured with outsourced parties through contract and binding agreements?				
Whether techniques such as user authentication, secure session control, data validation, sanitization and elimination of debugging codes are considered?				
Secure development environment Control: Organizations shall establish and appropriately protect secure development environments for system development and integration efforts that cover the entire system development lifecycle. Whether development is outsourced?	14.2.6			

DOMAIN	ISO 27001	PCI DSS	ISO 31000	SOX
Whether access to development environment is controlled?				
Whether regular backups are in place in the development environment				
Whether sensitivity of data stored, transmitted and processed is ensured in the development environment?				
Whether it is ensured that sensitive production data not used in development/testing environment?				
Outsourced development Control: The organization shall supervise and monitor the activity of outsourced system development. Whether the outsourced software development is supervised and monitored by the organization.	14.2.7			
Whether points such as licensing arrangements, escrow arrangements, contractual requirement for quality assurance, and testing before installation to detect Trojan code are considered.				
System security testing Control: Testing of security functionality shall be carried out during development. Whether test templates are designed to include test inputs and expected output with schedule?	14.2.8	Requirement 11		
Whether independent acceptance test is carried out?				
Whether testing is carried out by team different from development?				
Testing of patches in secured environment				

(Continued)

DOMAIN	ISO 27001	PCI DSS	ISO 31000	SOX
System acceptance testing Control: Acceptance testing programs and related criteria shall be established for new information systems, upgrades and new versions. Whether system acceptance criteria are established for new information systems, upgrades and new versions.	14.2.9			
Test Data	14.3			
Protection of test data Control: Test data shall be selected carefully and protected and controlled. Whether system test data is protected and controlled. is 'live'/operational database used for test purposes Is sensitive/confidential data of production being used for test purposes	14.3.1			
Information security policy for supplier relationships Control: Information security requirements for mitigating the risks associated with supplier's access to the organizations assets shall be agreed with the supplier and documented.1. Whether policy/procedures are in place for identifying the types of suppliers (vendors) and the controls required to safeguard the organization information is in place? Whether SLAs are identified? Whether such SLA monitored Regularly?	15.1.1	Requirement 3.1, Requirement 12.9.1 Requirement 12.8.3, Requirement 12.8.2		
Addressing security within suppliers agreements Control: All relevant information security requirement shall be established and agreed with each supplier that may access, process, store, communicate, or provide IT infrastructure components for the organizations information. 1. Whether confidentiality clause is included in the agreement?	15.1.2	Requirement 12.8.3, Requirement 12.8.2		

DOMAIN	ISO 27001	PCI DSS	ISO 31000	SOX
Documented Procedure for third-party management is in place?		Requirement 12.8.3, Requirement 12.8.2		
Any ways to monitor performance criteria of the third-party vendors defined in the agreement and followed?		Requirement 12.8.2		
Information and communication technology supply chain Control: Agreements with suppliers shall include requirements to address the information security risks associated with information and communications technology services and product supply chain.	15.1.3	Requirements 3.1, 3.2, 3.3, 3.4, 3.5, 4.1, 9.9, 9.10, 12.3.5		
1. Whether agreement is dated and signed by relevant authorities? 2. Whether term of the agreement is defined? 3. Whether extensions of information security requirements are ensured in the agreements in case of supplier sub-contract? (e.g., Background checking of sub-contractors/ Supply chain, NDA) 4. Whether communication protocols and escalations are defined? 5. Whether right to audit clause is incorporated in the agreement?				
Whether appropriate clause is included in the clauses where supply chains are involved?				
Supplier service delivery management	15.2			
Monitoring and review of supplier services Control: Organizations shall regularly monitor, review and audit supplier service delivery. Whether SLAs are monitored to verify adherence to the agreements?	15.2.1	Requirement 1.1.6, 10.5		

(Continued)

DOMAIN	ISO 27001	PCI DSS	ISO 31000	SOX
Whether Service reports are reviewed and regular progress meetings are conducted?				
Whether review of records of information security events, operational problems, failures, tracing of faults and disruptions related to the service are carried out?				
Managing changes to supplier services	15.2.2 15.2.2	Requirement 11.1,		
Control: Changes to the provision of services by suppliers, including maintaining and improving existing information security policies, procedures and controls, shall be managed, taking account of the criticality of business information, systems and processes involved and re-assessment of risks.		Requirement 11.2, Requirement 11.3 Requirement 11.1, 11.2, 11.3		
Is change management process is applied to suppliers? (example. to include in Renewal of agreements, the enhancement to the services, developments to new application, use of new technologies, change of networks, new development tool, change of physical location, change of supplier/ sub-contracting)				
Responsibilities and procedures Control: Management responsibilities and procedures should be established to ensure a quick, effective and orderly response to information security incidents Whether Incident Management Policy and Procedure is in place?	16.1.1			
Whether Incident Management Policy and Procedure is in place?				
Does policy covers reporting procedures				

DOMAIN	ISO 27001	PCI DSS	ISO 31000	SOX
Whether emergency actions taken are documented in detail?				
Reporting information security events	16.1.2			
Control: Information security events shall be reported through appropriate management channels as quickly as possible				
Whether proper incident/ problem escalation procedures exist to ensure that identified incidents, errors and problems are solved in the most efficient way on a timely basis?				
Whether formal information security event reporting procedure, Incident response and escalation procedure is developed/ implemented?				
Whether suitable feedback processes to ensure that those reporting incidents /events are notified of results after the issue is closed				
Whether any automated tools used for recording of incidents and analysis?				
Is there any process to report Information Security Incident to the Management?				
Reporting information security weaknesses	16.1.3			
Control: Employees and contractors using the organizations information systems and services shall be required to note and report any observed or suspected information security weaknesses in systems or services Whether there exists a procedure that ensures all employees of information systems and services are required to note and report any observed or suspected security weakness in the system or services.				

(Continued)

DOMAIN	ISO 27001	PCI DSS	ISO 31000	SOX
Whether there is system to ensure that all non-standard operational events (incidents, errors and problems) are identified, recorded, analyzed and resolved.				
How employees/Contractors reports information security weakness.				
Is the reporting mechanism easy, accessible and available				
Whether end users are intimated after resolution of Information Security Weaknesses?				
Assessment of and decision on information security events Control: Information security events shall be assessed and it shall be decided if they are to be classified as information security incidents. Whether appropriate definition of security incident is documented to clearly define what incidents are required to be addressed immediately or escalated to the correct service support level.	16.1.4		CC7.3, CC7.4,	
Response to information security incidents Control: Information security incidents shall be responded to in accordance with the documented procedure. Whether Incidents have been recorded and resolved as per documented procedure?	16.1.5			
Whether there is a mechanism in place to identify and quantify the type, volume and costs of information security incidents. Whether the knowledge/ solutions are recorded as knowledge base?	16.1.6			

DOMAIN	ISO 27001	PCI DSS	ISO 31000	SOX
Collection of evidence Control: The organization shall define and apply procedures for the identification, collection, acquisition and preservation of information, which can serve as evidence. Whether evidence relating to the incident are collected, retained and presented to conform to the rules for evidence laid down in the relevant jurisdiction(s).	16.1.7			
Planning information security continuity Control: The organization shall determine its requirements for information security and the continuity of information security management in adverse situations. For example, during a crisis or disaster. Whether requirements of business continuity related to CIA are identified and documented? Whether there is a managed process in place that addresses the information security requirements for developing and maintaining business continuity throughout the organization.	17.1.1			
Does the organization have a defined business impact analysis (BIA), which identifies all business processes critical to the organization and the resources that support those processes?				
Whether RTO and RPO as per Business Impact Analysis are defined and documented?				
Whether Critical processes are documented that management decides are so significant to the mission of the business that the business cannot afford to operate without them after a given period of time.				

(Continued)

DOMAIN	ISO 27001	PCI DSS	ISO 31000	SOX
Whether Risk assessment methodology is in place and various threats considered for Risk Assessment				
Whether various scenarios of contingency are covered and BCP defined for these scenarios?				
Whether the organization have a documented, tested business continuity management (BCM) process				
Implementing information security continuity	17.1.2	Requirement 11.1, 11.2, 11.3, 11.4, 11.5, 12.9.2		
Control: The organization shall establish, document, implement and maintain processes, procedures and controls to ensure the required level of continuity for information security during an adverse situations.				
1. Whether plans were developed to maintain and restore business operations, ensure availability of information within the required level in the required time frame following an interruption or failure to business processes?				
2. Whether plan considers redundancy of resources?				
3. Whether BCP test is in place regularly?				
Whether Disaster Recovery site is identified for BCP? If so whether DR site is in place?				
Whether DR site is replica of Data Centre?				
Whether the decisions of DR site are justified by a BIA?				
Whether the plan considers identification and agreement of responsibilities, identification of acceptable loss, implementation of recovery and restoration procedure, documentation of procedure and regular testing.				

DOMAIN	ISO 27001	PCI DSS	ISO 31000	SOX
Whether communication plans been established to notify appropriate personnel of a disaster, and the initiation of the BCP?				
Whether business continuity roles and responsibilities been assigned to appropriate personnel?				
Verify, review and evaluate information security continuity Control: The organization shall verify the established and implemented information security continuity controls at regular intervals in order to ensure that they are valid and effective during adverse situations. Whether Business continuity plans are tested regularly to ensure that they are up to date and effective?	17.1.3			
Are they evaluated and updated on review?				
Whether business continuity plan tests ensure that all members of the recovery team and other relevant staff are aware of the plans and their responsibility for business continuity and information security and know their role when plan is evoked.				
Is there any test schedule for testing business continuity plans?				
Whether results of tests are recorded and reported to Sr. management? Whether BCP is updated based on the test observations?				
Whether actions are taken to improve the plans?				
A formal change control process is in place to ensure regular review and distribution of updated plans including changes in network diagram, redundancies, testing plans etc.?				

(Continued)

DOMAIN	ISO 27001	PCI DSS	ISO 31000	SOX
Whether the plans are updated in the event of changes or acquisition of new facility?				
Redundancies	17.2			
Availability of information Processing Facilities – Redundancy Control: Information processing facilities shall be implemented with redundancy sufficient to meet availability requirements. Whether the organization have an redundant facility to recover operations in the event that main offices, production locations or distribution centers are inaccessible and single point failure is avoided?	17.2.1			
Whether redundancy in servers is available.				
Whether redundancy in network is available.	18.1			
Identification of applicable legislation and contractual requirements Control: All relevant legislative, statutory, regulatory, contractual requirements and the organization's approach to meet these requirements shall be explicitly identified, documented and kept up to date for each information system and the organization. Whether all relevant statutory, regulatory and contractual requirements are identified and defined? (especially in relation to the design, operation, use and management of information systems?) example:	18.1.1	Requirement 11.1, 11.2, 11.3		
1. Whether Regulatory guidelines are identified, recorded and implemented?				
2. Whether electronic record retention policy is in place?				
3. Whether private keys of PKI if any are secured renewed and record maintained?				

DOMAIN	ISO 27001	PCI DSS	ISO 31000	SOX
Intellectual property rights (IPR) *Control: Appropriate procedures shall be implemented to ensure compliance with legislative, regulatory, and contractual requirements related to IPR and use of proprietary software products. Whether the organization has published an IPR compliance policy? (defining legal use of software and information products, design rights, trademarks, patents)*	*18.1.2*			
Whether acquisition of software is from only known and reputable sources?				
Whether the organization ensures awareness of the policies to protect IPRs?				
Whether the organization has conveyed to staff that copyright infringement can lead to legal action, which may involve criminal proceedings?		*Requirement 3.1, 2.9.1*		
Whether the organization maintains appropriate asset register identifying all the assets relevant to the protection of IPR?				
Protection of records *Control: Records shall be protected from loss, destruction, falsification, unauthorized access and unauthorized release in accordance with legislators, statutory, regulatory, contractual, and business requirements.*	*18.1.3*	*Requirement 9.1, 11.5, 5.1*		
Whether organization categorized records into various types, e.g., accounting records, database records, designs, transaction logs, audit logs, and operational procedures?				

(Continued)

DOMAIN	ISO 27001	PCI DSS	ISO 31000	SOX
Whether organization has identified retention period for each of these categories?				
Whether organization issued guidelines on retention, storage, handling and disposal of records and information?				
Whether organization has identified types of storage media, e.g., paper, microfilm, magnetic, optical etc. for these records?				
Privacy and Protection of personally identifiable information	18.1.4			
Control: Privacy and protection of personally identifiable information shall be ensured as required in relevant legislation and regulation where applicable.				
Whether organization has documented data protection and privacy policy?				
Whether DLP (data leakage prevention) tools are used to prevent sensitive information leakage?				
Whether data leakage through USB, email, etc. is prevented? How?				
Regulation of cryptographic controls	18.1.5			
Control: Cryptographic controls shall be used in compliance with all relevant agreements, legislations, and regulations. Whether legal restriction on export and import of computer hardware and software for performing cryptographic function is put in place in law of land.				
Whether any restriction on the usage of encryption is put in place by the law.				

DOMAIN	ISO 27001	PCI DSS	ISO 31000	SOX
Whether Digital signature is being used for any authentication/non-repudiation mechanism? If so how are the private keys secured? Whether any list of such keys is maintained along with the expiry details? Whether such expiry is renewed?				
Information Security Reviews (annually or when there is change)	A.18.2			
Independent review of information security	18.2.1	Requirement 11		
Control: The organization approach to managing information security and its implementation (i.e., control objectives, controls, policies, processes, procedures for information security) shall be reviewed independently at planned intervals or when significant changes occur. How often these policies being reviewed?				
Who reviewed this? Independent individual/internal audit team/ management committee or independent third-party auditors?				
Compliance with security policies and standards	18.2.2			
Control: Managers shall regularly review the compliance of information processing and procedures within their area of responsibility with the appropriate security policies, standards, and any other security requirements. Do the managers regularly review compliance of information processing within area of their responsibility?				
Whether the ISMS policy lays down punitive measures for breach of ISMS policy?				

It may be noted that the mapping table is indicative of the provisions and is not exhaustive. It is flexible, it can be used to include sector-specific policies, regulator provisions and other standards which are not in our purview, in this chapter. Objective is to build a baseline that will eliminate redundant processes and create a commonality of purpose that will lead to timely compliance and better discipline within the organization.

Designing an Operating Model for Risk and Compliance Aligned with the Business Model

7

We have discussed the different compliances and standards that are mandatory or accepted as commonly accepted industry standards. The CCO of the organization shall be mandated to study the compliance needs of the organization and to propose the customization of the organization's integrated GRC model. It is easy to build a model, but it is challenging to implement the model, especially because of complexities in processes and commonalities in controls.

Steps for Building an Integrated GRC Model

1. Define the GRC requirements and set the parameters for implementing GRC controls. The CFO must understand and analyze the existing processes in the area of governance, risk, and compliance in the organization. This will help him to identify areas where change is required.
2. Assess the legal and regulatory requirements, since they form a significant part of compliance.
3. Develop a phased approach to GRC implementation. It is possible to implement a small area and communicate the results and then proceed to other areas for implementation.
4. GRC model can include digitized tools and technology to improve governance and achieve compliance objectives. Use of advanced analytics facilitates autonomous processing of data using sophisticated tools to discover insights and make recommendations. It improves decision-making process; big companies have started using digital analytics in areas like fraud management and pricing.

DOI: 10.1201/9781003018100-7

The mark of an efficient and effective GRC program is one that defines business requirements adequately as well as uses the right blend of automation and technology to support these requirements. In order to increase the maturity of the GRC program, the following measures should be undertaken that will help build a road map and a business case to create and implement an appropriate GRC model.

1. **Define compliance, business, and IT future-state requirements**
   - Assess functional and technical design across the legal, regulatory compliance landscape and identify the IT scope according to requirements.
   - Prioritize and rank identified requirements to facilitate and differentiate key requirements into good to have and must have and rank them as per priority level.
2. **Perform the automation and technology fit, costing model, and value-return assessments**
   - Identify the GRC technology applications that will meet key requirements based on the current and proposed GRC technologies and functionalities.
   - Ascertain the Return on Investment that accounts for the impact on technology data, people, and processes for the technology and GRC solutions identified.
3. **Prepare a business case and an implementation road map**
   - Create a dynamic business case that can be used as an operational tool to document program operating model and success factors.
   - Identify a road map for building out the target operating model, including project scope, timeline and technology deployment plan.
4. **Test and verify the GRC target operating model**
   - Validate the functionality and performance of the GRC target operating model by working with business and IT organizations.
   - Define and execute the go-live procedures through working with the GRC program stakeholders and deploying the new technologies, data model and processes as required.

GRC as an acronym denotes governance, risk, and compliance – but the full story of GRC is so much more than those three words. The acronym GRC was invented by the OCEG (originally called the 'Open Compliance and Ethics Group') membership as a shorthand reference to the critical capabilities that must work together to achieve compliance.

Performance – the capabilities that integrate the governance, management and assurance of performance, risk, and compliance activities. This includes the work done by departments like internal audit, compliance, risk, legal, finance, IT, HR as well as the lines of business, executive suite, and the board itself. It is important to remember that organizations have been governed, and risk and compliance have been managed, for a long period of time. Actually, GRC doesn't burden the business; it supports and improves it.

GRC DRIVERS

Organizations are facing many risk and compliance issues irrespective of their size and nature of business. Let us view a few GRC models.

OCEG Model

OCEG is a non-profit organization which is dedicated to achieve a model that enables every organization and every person to achieve objectives, address uncertainty, and act with integrity. OCEG developed the GRC (integration of governance, risk management, and compliance) capability model as the means to achieve principled performance that promotes the achievement of objectives, the addressing of uncertainty and maintaining integrity. OCEG is a knowledge vertical that informs and empowers a community of more than 65,000 members' worldwide, helping to advance knowledge of how to integrate and mature governance, risk management, and compliance.

As shown in Figure 7.1, the components of the GRC model are as under:

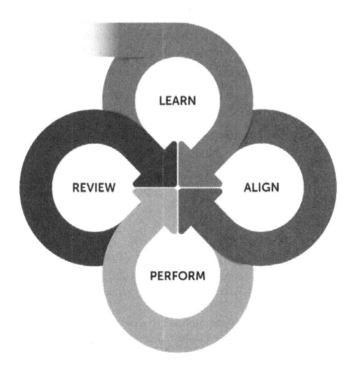

FIGURE 7.1   Components of the GRC capability model.

1. **LEARN** about the organization context, culture, and key stakeholders to inform objectives, strategy, and actions.
2. **ALIGN** strategy with objectives, and actions with strategy, by using effective decision-making that addresses values, opportunities, threats, and requirements.
3. **PERFORM** actions that promote and reward things that are desirable, prevent, and remediate things that are undesirable, and detect when something happens as soon as possible.
4. **REVIEW** the design and operating effectiveness of the strategy and actions, as well as the ongoing appropriateness of objectives to improve the organization.

Chief Drivers of the GRC Function

- Stakeholders: they want transparency and want a high level of performance
- Regulations and enforcement: they are constantly evolving and are unpredictable
- Recent trend toward third-party relationships and risks
- Increasing costs of legal and regulatory compliance
- Threat risk impact that has been identified and treated

OCEG research has found that organizations are faced with problems of disjointed GRC activities. As a result, they form departments such as risk management, compliance, and performance measurement. But such separate departments often operate in silos and prove to be ineffective, leading to drawbacks (refer to Figure 7.2) such as:

- Hike in costs
- Improper mapping of risks
- No earmarked methodology to address third-party risks
- Poor integration
- Lack of effective oversight
- Lack of metrics to measure risk adjusted performance
- Increased complexity
- Lack of integrity
- Duplication

GRC represents a coordinated approach to achieve efficiencies in an organization's activities of corporate governance, risk management, and compliance with regulations.

While 'big data' is being harnessed to free the human mind from number crunching to perform higher-level analysis, GRC is an area that is benefiting from not only the availability of more data but also the ability to assimilate data from different areas of an organization's activities. The OCEG GRC capability model contains eight integrated components, and each embodies a number of related practices.

As can be seen in Figure 7.3, an integrated approach to GRC, beginning with the determination of context whether internal, external, cultural, or of common objectives,

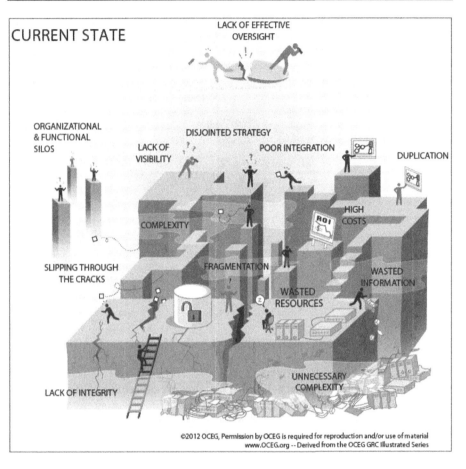

FIGURE 7.2   Drawbacks in GRC Integration.

is recommended. Organizing the organization structure and processes to meet desired outcomes and defining roles and responsibilities to promote responsibility and accountability goes a long way. Where management policies and code of conduct serve as the first line of defense, documentation of procedures, communication with stakeholders and continuous improvement add depth in defense.

Assessment of performance is also necessary to discipline the people and remediate inadequacies detected.

Integrating GRC is optimizing the business processes by making GRC all-pervasive in the organization such that employees are aware of GRC controls and activities, and leveraging technology to monitor and test the effectiveness of the GRC model over a period of time for continuous improvement. It is important that integrity of information and communication within the organization is kept intact so that the right people can get and use the information for the purpose they want and achieve the objectives of

MONITOR & MEASURE
M1 – Context Monitoring
M2 – Performance Monitoring & Evaluation
M3 – Systemic Improvement
M4 – Assurance

CONTEXT & CULTURE
C1 – External Business Context
C2 – Internal Business Context
C3 – Culture
C4 – Values & Objectives

ORGANIZE & OVERSEE
O1 – Outcomes & Commitment
O2 – Roles & Responsibilities
O3 – Approach & Accountability

RESPOND & RESOLVE
R1 – Internal Review & Investigation
R2 – Third-Party Inquiries & Investigations
R3 – Corrective Controls
R4 – Crisis Response & Recovery
R5 – Remediation & Discipline

ASSIGN & ALIGN
A1 – Risk Identification
A2 – Risk Analysis
A3 – Risk Optimization

INFORM & INTEGRATE
I1 – Information Management & Documentation
I2 – Internal & External Communication
I3 – Technology & Infrastructure

DETECT & DISCERN
D1 – Hotline & Notification
D2 – Inquiry & Survey
D3 – Detective Controls

PREVENT & PROMOTE
P1 – Codes of Conduct
P2 – Policies
P3 – Preventive Controls
P4 – Awareness & Education
P5 – Human Capital Incentives
P6 – Stakeholder Relations & Requirements
P7 – Risk Financing/Insurance

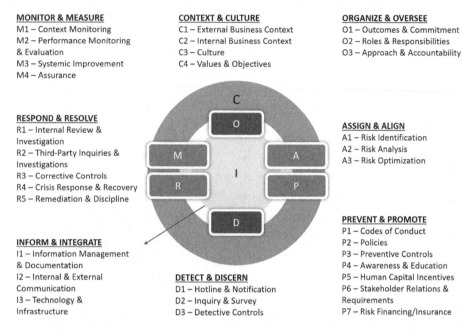

FIGURE 7.3　Components of GRC OCEG model.

risk management and compliance. For this purpose, use of technology tools and software can be made for getting more accuracy and controlling uncertainty.

As seen in Figure 7.4, there are many benefits that can be reaped from a properly implemented and coordinated GRC model:

1. Cost economy
2. Smooth execution of operations without interference from GRC activities
3. Reduced redundancies and timely compliance
4. Accurate and authentic information, relating to GRC activities
5. Inculcating capability to perform repeatable GRC tasks automatically by using appropriate technology tools.

KPMG's GRC Target Operating Model (TOM)

GRC functions are subject to complex risks, stringent regulatory issues and a demanding compliance environment. Organizations continue to work in silos and that is deterrent to GRC requirements of the organization. Some other consequences of silo-based programs could be ad hoc selection of tools for implementing GRC, inadequate scoping of program domain, etc.

The KPMG model aims at integrating compliances and has developed an integrated GRC Target Operating Model. This model is built around two dimensions: first

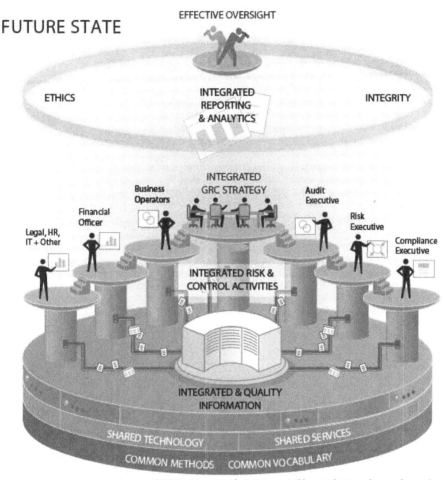

FUTURE STATE

EFFECTIVE OVERSIGHT

ETHICS

INTEGRATED
REPORTING
& ANALYTICS

INTEGRITY

INTEGRATED
GRC STRATEGY

Business
Operators

Financial
Officer

Legal, HR,
IT + Other

Audit
Executive

Risk
Executive

Compliance
Executive

INTEGRATED RISK &
CONTROL ACTIVITIES

INTEGRATED & QUALITY
INFORMATION

SHARED TECHNOLOGY   SHARED SERVICES

COMMON METHODS   COMMON VOCABULARY

©2012 OCEG, Permission by OCEG is required for reproduction and/or use of material
www.OCEG.org -- Derived from the OCEG GRC Illustrated Series

FIGURE 7.4   A well-integrated GRC model.

dimension consists of three components (Figure 7.5); the second dimension includes five Design Layers, which need to be tailored to the risk appetite and strategy for every TOM component of the organization.

The KPMG model has the following benefits:

The process involved in creating TOM envisages the identification and scoping of risk and compliance as has been demonstrated in Chapter 6. Along with this, the strategy for risk appetite and risk treatment has to be determined. Understanding of current state and identifying gaps is also prescribed.

KPMG developed a diagnostic model consisting of eight steps, as can be seen in Figure 7.6, to help organizations design or refresh their GRC TOM.

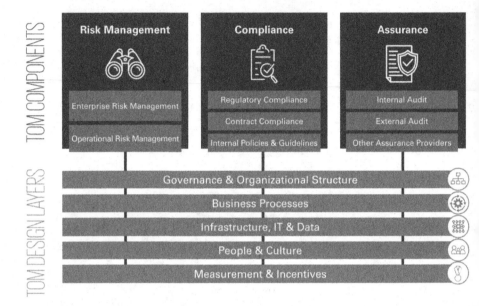

FIGURE 7.5   KPMG's GRC TOM.

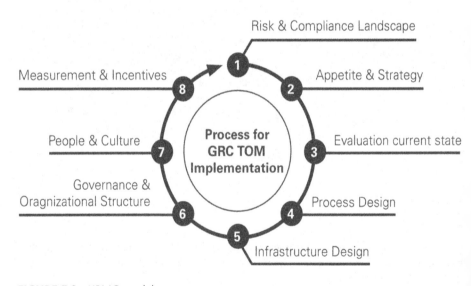

FIGURE 7.6   KPMG model.

1. **Risk** and **Compliance Landscape:** Perform a thorough assessment of organizations' TOM components with regard to the risk and compliance context, the strategy, and the current state. It includes identification and scoping of the risk and compliance requirements which would be the basis for the GRC TOM model.

2. **Determination of the Risk Appetite:** Determine the risk appetite and compliance and risk strategy for each component of the TOM Model. This will lay the foundation for understanding organizational objectives.

3. **Current State Evaluation:** Perform a current state evaluation for each component of the TOM to understand current strengths and weaknesses and identify gaps between the 'as is' and the 'to be' situation.

4. **Design of key processes** that will address the key risk and compliance areas to ensure necessary controls are embedded within the processes.

5. **Deign of the IT infrastructure** that supports the processes and key controls for each of the TOM components to achieve set objectives.

6. **Defining an optimum governance structure** for future risk and compliance functions within the organization. This covers revisiting the organization chart as well as preparing the assurance map for the organization.

7. **People are an important component** in the organization, and care will be taken to ensure that there are right people at the right place and the organization advocates an adequate risk and compliance culture.

8. **Performance measurement** measures shall be introduced with the introduction of proper incentives after identification of risk and compliance indicators so that organizations can ensure and monitor compliance in these areas.

Benefits of Integration of GRC

a. **Fostering a risk-aware culture:** It will result in enhancement of business value augmenting informed decision-making and addressing varied compliance and assurance needs of the organization.

b. **Enhance operational efficiency:** By rationalizing risk management, controls and assurance structures and processes, and through the smart use of IT and data management structures.

c. **Proactive and dynamic approach:** By enabling organizations respond quickly, consistently and efficiently to challenges arising from evolving risk profiles and rapidly changing regulatory requirements.

d. **Align to strategy:** By enabling meeting of compliance objectives and also improving processes in the process, the strategic objectives of business shall also be realized.

The Three Lines Model for GRC

The Three Lines Model as seen in Figure 7.7 clearly delineates roles and responsibilities of the governing body, as well as executive management, and internal audit. These roles are not limited to risk management but focus on the overall governance of the organization. While not a governance model, the increased focus on governance supports both value creation and protection and deals with both the offensive and defensive aspects of managing risk. This addresses one of the principal criticisms of the Three Lines of Defense model, which is its primary focus on defense.

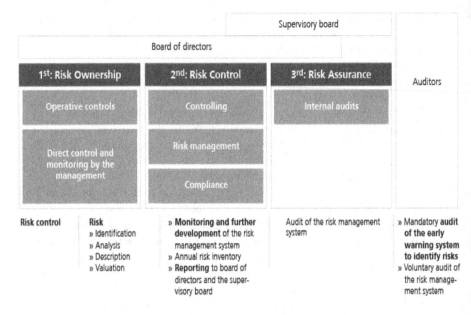

FIGURE 7.7 Three Lines Model for GRC.

The Three Lines is based on the following principles:

1. Existence of adequate structure and processes that ensures accountability, assurance, and security.
2. Governing structure provides for structures and processes for effective governance.
3. Management uses the first two lines of defense to achieve organizational objectives. The first line is directed toward delivery of products and services and support functions for the same. The second line of defense takes care of risk management and risk treatment.
4. In the third line of defense, internal audit plays an important role and provides independent assurance on the adequacy and effectiveness of governance and risk management.
5. It is important to have independence in the internal audit in order to have objectivity, credibility, and authority to their reports.
6. An integrated approach to GRC with alignment with all elements of business with priority to interests of stakeholders will contribute to value addition to the business.

The challenge for all organizations that adopt this model would be to apply and adapt their organization's needs and priorities in accordance with the Three Lines of Defense. Roles and responsibilities in each Line of Defense will vary according to the nature of business and complexity of business and the legal and regulatory provisions that they are subject to.

The model integrates the main roles and responsibilities of the internal control system of the company in a consistent GRC system and helps to demonstrate effective co-ordination and communication in the area of risk management. The IIA recommends systemization of risk management regardless of the size and complexity of the organization and determines that 'Risk management is normally strongest when there are three separate and clearly identified lines of defense.'

The core of the model is the assignment of company functions which serve to control company risks to three levels below the supervisory board and board of directors.

In the first line of defense the operative management is confronted with risks in daily business operations which have to be controlled. This line is responsible for the identification and assessment of these risks as early as possible and the setting up of effective control measures in the value chain to prevent the risks from occurring or to discover and correct these risks in the operational process.

Depending on the business model, the associated frequency or probability, and potential amount of damage from risks, the board of directors sets up functions in the company which primarily monitor the control activities of the first line of defense and which are allocated to the second line of defense. Due to extensive planning and information tasks, in this respect controlling in many companies has an important role to play.

The third line of defense in particular in large companies and complex organizations is the carrying out of internal audits. They ensure extensive security with the reduction of risk based on the highest level of independence and objectivity within the company.

The functions which are assigned to the respective three lines of defense in the model have to be linked to the tasks of the risk management which are regularly described with a standard management control loop as shown in Figure 7.8.

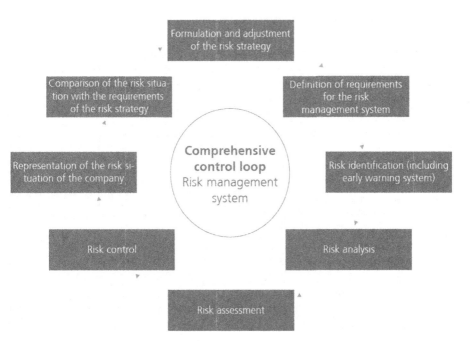

FIGURE 7.8 Comprehensive control loop of the management.

GRC MODEL FOR BANKS

Regulatory compliance has affected banks in a variety of challenging ways, increasing the cost of service and sometimes making the delivery of great customer experiences more difficult. However, as the regulatory environment evolves, we see a major opportunity for the compliance function to get ahead of the curve by implementing targeted changes to its operating model and processes, and thus delivering a better quality of oversight while at the same time increasing its efficiency.

This process is analogous to regulatory review of bank lending. When looking at loan files, examiners do not usually rely exclusively on the review work performed by loan officers and loan review staff, but also look at original financial statements and other documents to verify the loan was properly underwritten and risk graded

Banks that have or are successfully making this shift will enjoy a distinctive source of competitive advantage in the foreseeable future, being able to deliver better service, reduce structural cost, and significantly de-risk their operations. Digital information plays an essential role in supporting organizational business. However, incidents of sensitive information leakage often happen in organization environment. Therefore, risk analysis needs to be performed to recognize the impact of information security threat in organization.

A GRC model has to be developed to meet the ongoing needs for security and confidentiality. A risk analysis is to be regularly performed to map the risks of information security threats. Banks that have successfully developed GRC model enjoy a definitive competitive advantage since they are able to deliver better service, reduce structural cost, and significantly de-risk their operations.

Digital information plays an essential role in supporting organizational business. However, incidents of sensitive information leakage often happen in organization environment. Therefore, risk analysis needs to be performed to recognize the impact of information security threat in organization.

In order to carry out risk analyses, risk model is needed to map risk of information security threat (refer to Figure 7.9). The selection of a proper risk model provides proper result related to risk analysis. The proper risk model must have objectivity and appropriate context.

However, most of the existing risk models focus on the technical approach and use expert judgment as a weighting method. Meanwhile, organizations use business perspectives to determine decisions. Therefore, this study has the objective to fill the needs of organizations by developing a new risk model.

The proposed risk model focuses on business aspects involvement and reducing subjective methods. The proposed risk model also uses three processes to result output, i.e., adaptable classification data, data measurement, and cross-label analysis. Test mining and categorical clustering are involved to handle those three processes.

The IIA recommends systemization of risk management regardless of the size and complexity of the organization and determines that 'Risk management is normally strongest when there are three separate and clearly identified lines of defense.'

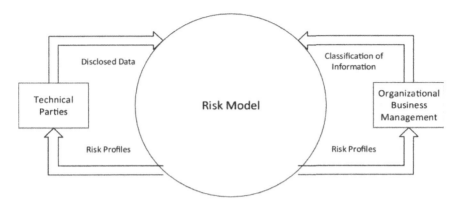

FIGURE 7.9 Risk model.

Risk management is an integral part of this model. But it is difficult for smaller organizations to have enough resources to maintain all processes involved in risk management. In such cases, it is recommended to have a smaller risk management wing but it takes care of all risk functions in the organization. In the context of risk management, the following concepts must be considered:

- Risk ownership involves directly facing risks in the process of the operational management. The risk register must contain names of risk owners.
- Risk control or mitigation involves control and support for the risk control measures through the risk management functions.
- Risk assurance involves the monitoring and checking of the risk management system to enable the supervisory board to base its decisions on independent and reliable information which includes external and internal audit reports.

Let us see how an appropriate methodology can build a good GR model (refer to Figure 7.10).

Most of the existing risk models focus on the technical approach and use expert judgment as a weighting method. Meanwhile, organizations use business perspectives to determine decisions. Therefore, this study has the objective to fill the needs of organizations by developing a new risk model. The proposed risk model focuses on business aspects involvement and reducing subjective methods. The proposed risk model also uses three processes to result output, i.e., adaptable classification data, data measurement and cross-label analysis. Testing of the proposed model is carried out to define ability and limitation of model by involving 30 targets. The result states that the proposed model has advantages in objectivity, context approach and detailed output, while the limited scope of work becomes a weakness of these models.

1. **Define compliance, business, and IT future-state requirements**.

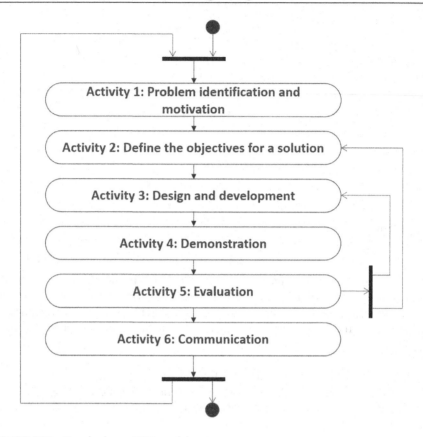

FIGURE 7.10   Developing a GRC model.

Assess functional and technical design across the legal, regulatory compliance land-scape and identify the IT scope according to requirements. Prioritize and rank identified requirements to facilitate and differentiate key requirements into good to have and must have and rank them as per priority level.

2. **Perform the automation and technology fit, costing model, and value-return assessments.**

Identify the GRC technology applications that will meet key requirements based on the current and proposed GRC technologies and functionalities. Ascertain the return on investment that accounts for the impact on technology data, people, and processes for the technology and GRC solutions identified.

3. **Prepare a business case and an implementation road map.**

Create a dynamic business case that can be used as an operational tool to document program operating model and success factors. Identify a road map for building out the target operating model, including project scope, timeline, and technology deployment plan.

4. Test and verify the GRC target operating model.

Validate the functionality and performance of the GRC target operating model by working with business and IT organizations. Define and execute the go-live procedures through working with the GRC program stakeholders and deploying the new technologies, data model, and processes as required.

EVOLUTION OF VIRTUAL BANKING

Information technology has brought significant changes in the banking sector, resulting in a new type of banking called virtual banking. It is based on computer systems with minimum manpower requirements but a lack of requisite infrastructure has brought in two challenges; lack of focus on current models of banking and the other is a lack of integrated approach to GRC. Virtual banking on one hand is influenced by economic crises and on other hand is influenced by benefits from emerging technologies. But GRC stipulations suffered a setback because of less supervision, banks resorted to operating at lesser staff model. The steps for the setting up of an appropriate GRC model for banks include (refer to Figure 7.11).

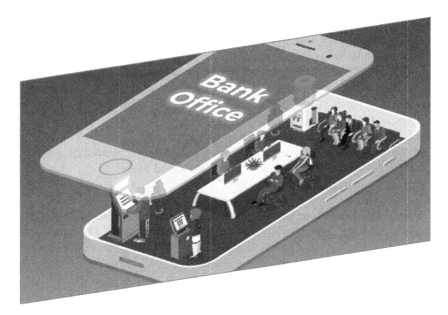

FIGURE 7.11 Virtual bank illustration.

Customers are now smarter and more aware of technology. They are demanding and want instant gratification for services and products offered by the bank. Banks are now adopting data governance models to analyze customer data and predict the behavior of customers. Data privacy assessment is carried out to ensure that customer data is protected and prevent misuse of data. Banks operate in an unforgiving market ecosystem where the slightest lapse or slippage in security can cost them a lot in terms of reputation and image and can lead to loss of business.

Banking industry is the most affected by regulatory compliances. It has become essential to maintain organizational integrity and credibility. Hence risk and compliance functions are well defined in the organization structure in banks. Banks have embraced new emerging technologies for risk and compliance which help them be compliant as well as lead in the race for business.

Disruptive innovations like blockchain, cryptocurrencies, and artificial intelligence are challenging the principle of a trusted intermediary on which the banking system operates. Banks are going to have a tough time evaluating such technologies and fitting them in their GRC frameworks. Use of AI and Analytics are providing reliable data for banks to take weighted decisions. This data is then used to-

(a) Predict emerging and evolving risk trends,
(b) Monitor systemic risk metrics continuously and in real time,
(c) Design forward-looking market scenarios to assess systemic stress, and
(d) Prescribe regulations. In the wake of stringent regulatory compliances and frameworks such as Basel II and Basel III, the GRC model for banks, need to be robust.

Figure 7.12 depicts a typical bank governance structure, with the Basel II and Basel III compliances factored in the model. Scarred by recent financial frauds, misconduct, and other scandals, banks have started adopting global best practices in GRC.

Implementation to ensure that the reputation of financial markets remain unaffected. Many banks still struggle with the fundamental issues of the control environment in the first line of defense such as compliance literacy, accountability, performance incentives, and risk culture.

Finally, compliance activities tend to be isolated, lacking a clear link to the broader risk-management framework, governance, and processes (e.g., operational-risk management, risk-appetite statement, and risk reporting and analytics). As a result, costs of compliance are high, but there is positive difference and impact on the residual risk profile of the bank.

Model documentation: Documentation provides an insight into the working of the model and guides new users as to the operational procedures. GRC models to have appropriate documentation to accomplish the two objectives of ease of use and standard practices. Generally, elements of documentation include:

• A description of model purpose and design.
• Model theory, including the logic behind the model and sensitivity to key drivers and assumptions.

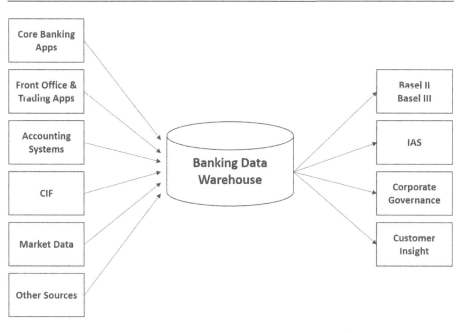

FIGURE 7.12   GRC model for bank.

- Data needs.
- Detailed operating procedures.
- Security and change control procedures.
- Validation plans and findings of validations performed.

MODEL MONITORING AND CONTROL

When examining controls around individual GRC models, regulators review model documentation for:

1. A discussion of model theory, with particular attention to model limitations and potential weaknesses.
2. The operating procedures.
3. Review data reconciliation procedures and business line analysis of model results.
4. Evaluate security and change control procedures.

By conducting a review of model documentation and controls, it is possible to gain a stronger understanding of the model's process flow. This understanding enables examiners to test the findings of the bank's validation and internal audit review against their own observations.

MODEL VALIDATION

Validation procedures focus not only on confirming the appropriateness of model theory and accuracy of program code, but also test the integrity of model inputs, outputs, and reporting. Validation is typically completed before a model is put into use and also on an ongoing basis to ensure the model continues to perform as intended. The frequency of planned validation will depend on the use of the model and its importance to the organization. The need for updated validation could be triggered earlier than planned by substantive changes to the model, to the data, or to the theory supporting model logic.

COMPONENTS OF VALIDATION

- **Developmental evidence:** The review of developmental evidence focuses on the reasonableness of the conceptual approach and quantification techniques of the model itself. This review typically considers the following:
  - I. Documentation and support for the appropriateness of the logic and specific risk quantification techniques used in the model.
  - II. Testing of model sensitivity to key assumptions and data inputs used.
  - III. Support for the reasonableness and validity of model results.
  - IV. Support for the robustness of scenarios used for stress testing, to authenticate test results.
- **Process verification:** Process verification considers data inputs, the workings of the model and model output reporting. It includes an evaluation of controls, the reconciliation of source data systems with model inputs, accuracy of program coding, and the usefulness and accuracy of model outputs and reporting. Such verification also may include benchmarking of model processes against industry practices for similar models.
- **Outcome analysis:** Outcome analysis focuses on model output and reporting to assess the predictive outcome of the model. It may include both qualitative and quantitative techniques:
  - I. Qualitative reasonableness checks consider whether the model is generally producing expected results.
  - II. Back-testing is a direct comparison of predicted results to observe actual results.

III. Benchmarking of model output compares predicted results generated by the model being validated with predicted results from other models or sources.

When reviewing validation, examiners:

- Evaluate the scope of validation work performed;
- Review the report summarizing validation findings and any additional work papers needed to understand findings;
- Evaluate management's response to the report summarizing the findings, including remediation plans and time frames; and
- Assess the qualifications of staff or vendors performing the validation.

Third-party validation: Vendors are sometimes used to meet the need for a high level of independence and expertise. They can bring a broad perspective from their work at other financial institutions, providing a useful source for theory and process benchmarking. It is mandatory on the part of the management to review their GRC model on an ongoing basis. Such review should comprise a review of model governance policies, their adequacy in the organizations' context, and their accuracy and completeness of coverage. The validation and review process should include the alignment of GRC models with the overall policies and procedures set by the management (refer to Figure 7.13).

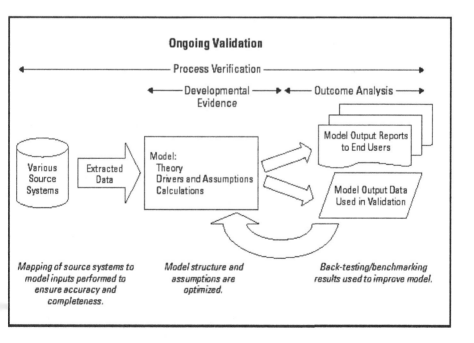

FIGURE 7.13   Validation process for GRC models.

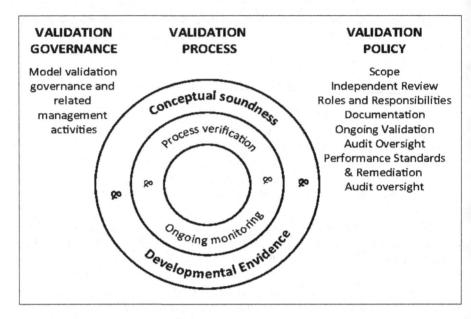

VALIDATION GOVERNANCE	VALIDATION PROCESS	VALIDATION POLICY
Model validation governance and related management activities	Conceptual soundness Process verification Ongoing monitoring Developmental Evidence	Scope Independent Review Roles and Responsibilities Documentation Ongoing Validation Audit Oversight Performance Standards & Remediation Audit oversight

FIGURE 7.14 Validation of GRC models.

Organization must bind organizational GRC policies to a broad single policy approved by the Board, other separate policies can be supplemented to the one central policy that drives the GRC function.

Such policies should adequately define:

i. Standards for validation and the components of the various sub-systems that shall be subject to GRC governance procedures. The standards for model validation based on criticality and complexity of the GRC model must be pre-set.

ii. GRC models to be verified for effectiveness prior to implementation for control procedures and comprehensive coverage of all organizational GRC requirements.

iii. Organization to make adequate allocation of roles and responsibilities in respect of business units, internal audit, IT, and external consultants. And responsibility is to be defined for the development and implementation of the GRC model.

As seen in Figure 7.15, organization exists in a business environment that has opportunities and obstacles in the backdrop of organizational objectives to do business. GRC activities consists of mandatory boundary set by legal, regulatory and industry best practices and the voluntary boundary is set by management policies and procedures.

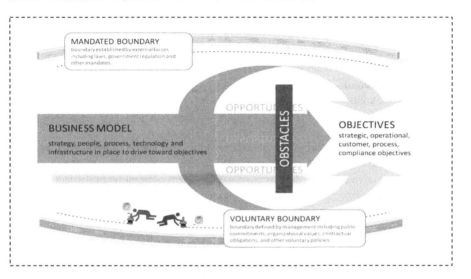

FIGURE 7.15 Setting GRC boundaries.

GRC METRICS AND MEASUREMENTS

Measuring ROI in GRC is an essential part of the GRC solution. OCEG has released the OCEG GRC Metrics and Measurement Guide that will help organizations understand the issues and processes concerning analysis of the performance of an organization's GRC capability.

It is a time-tested adage that what cannot be measured cannot be improved. GRC Metrics and Measurement consists of a GRC measurement strategy, selecting relevant indicators, and addressing challenges. The results may be used to make an improvement in GRC measurement program including the acquisition of technology that can enable the gathering, analyzing and analysis of GRC information.

GRC metrics will provide the tools to evaluate performance and bring programs in-line with strategic business goals to create success for risk, compliance and audit executives and leadership with governance responsibilities. An effective GRC measurement program recognizes critical risks and applies controls where they will have the most significant impact. As seen in Figure 7.16, the efficient use of financial resources and optimum use of people skills for GRC program leads to effective implementation of the program. Design-effectiveness of GRC controls is also a contributor toward its success.

Measures of GRC Program: There are many ways to evaluate the GRC program. Consider the following indicators.

i. Absence of fraud

ii. There is no regulatory change that may invalidate a product line

    iii. Absence of incidents of network breach
    iv. Not encountered any critical system failure

Developing the measurement strategy and program is a distinct project that requires sufficient time and resources allocated to it for success. The development process begins with analyzing three areas: enterprise objectives, maturity objectives, and operational objectives.

    Achieving business agility is one of the indicators of a good GRC approach. Refer to Figure 7.17.

    As can be seen, the formula for business agility is a sum total of sensing of risks, environment and changes, responding proactively to events and adapting to new normal after a disruption. In other words responsiveness to events, adaptation to changes in a controlled way and having flexibility in operations can lead to an agile business environment.

    It is the responsibility of senior management to introduce improvements in the GRC structure. After obtaining buy-in, all efforts to be made to align the business and evaluate organizational capabilities to determine how many of the GRC requirements can be fulfilled using internal resources and which areas need external resources having specific capabilities. Finally, there is the work of actually implementing the model.

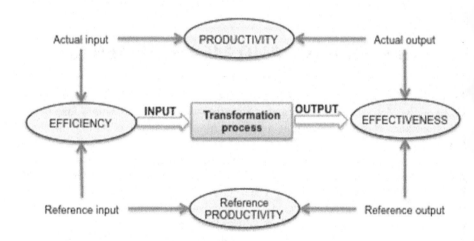

FIGURE 7.16 Assessing performance through metrics.

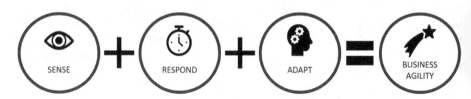

FIGURE 7.17 Business agility.

For this purpose, subject matter expertise from professional firms can be sought to make transition smooth. Transformation is not a siloed effort. The full impact of the GRC model to be implemented should combine operational improvements around customer-facing processes with integrated use of approaches and capabilities.

DATA INTEGRITY

Maintaining data integrity is vital to model performance. Much of the information used in a model is electronically extracted or manually input from source systems; either approach provides opportunity for error. Business line management is responsible for the regular reconciliation of source system information with model data to ensure accuracy and completeness.

Data inputs need to be sufficient to provide the level of data consistency and granularity necessary for the model to function as designed. Data lacking sufficient granularity, such as product- or portfolio-level information, may be inadequate for models that use drivers and assumptions associated with transaction-level data.

Security and change control: GRC models should be subject to the same controls as those used for other controls. Change control helps maintain model functionality and reliability as ongoing enhancements occur. Proper backup procedures should be organized to recover important modeling programs in the event of technological disruption.

MODEL CONTROL PRACTICES

When examining controls around individual models, regulators:

- review model documentation for (1) discussion of model theory, with particular attention to model limitations and potential weaknesses, and (2) operating procedures;
- review data reconciliation procedures and business-line analysis of model results; and
- evaluate security and change control procedures.

By conducting their own review of model documentation and controls, examiners gain a stronger understanding of the model's process flow. This understanding enables examiners to test the findings of the bank's validation and internal audit review against their own observations.

Risk culture has a special place in compliance. Elements of 'strong' risk culture are relatively clear and include timely information sharing, rapid elevation of emerging risks, and willingness to challenge practices; however, they are difficult to measure objectively. Risk-culture surveys can be used to get a better understanding of risk culture within the organization. Effective monitoring and good leadership can promote a conducive risk culture.

There is a constant change in the risk environment and given this evolution, responsibilities of the compliance function should include the following:

1. Developing a GRC perspective toward compliance with laws, rules, and regulations across businesses and processes and how they affect operations is necessary. Creating standards for risk materiality considering materiality of risk, tolerance level and building a risk appetite is absolutely necessary.
2. Setting a process for risk identification and assessment, including comprehensive inventory of risks, objectives for risk-assessment scorecards, and setting risk-measurement methodology has to be done.
3. Developing and enforcing standards for an effective root-cause analysis and performance tracking to ensure that it addresses root causes of compliance issues and does not merely treat symptoms that emerge.
4. Setting up training programs and incentives commensurate to each type of job or work environment.
5. Ensuring that appropriate tools and processes are developed and utilized for compliance.
6. Ensuring that clients' transactions and products are approved on the basis of predefined rules formulated by risk department. For this a periodic assessment of the compliance program shall have to be performed. In short, it will pay to understand the bank's risk culture, its strengths, and also its potential shortcomings.

Scaling a GRC program for the cloud, emerging technologies, and innovation

GRC programs are sometimes looked upon as hindrance in the imposing of cybersecurity work. But a good GRC program establishes the foundation for meeting security and compliance objectives. It can be used proactively to minimize impact from incidents and trigger rapid response to incidents.

Security should be weighed keeping in mind all three components of business; people, processes, and technology. Technology is a preferred solution since it is easy to maneuver. Although automation is a better choice the price of automating a bad process can be disastrous. Governance establishes the strategy and checkpoints for meeting specific requirements that align and support the business. Risk management aligns specific controls to governance subsystem and provides business owners the information they need to prioritize resources and make risk-informed decisions. Compliance is the adherence and monitoring of controls to specific governance requirements. Security architecture, engineering, and operations are built upon the GRC foundation.

Without a GRC program, people tend to solely focus on technology and stove-pipe processes. For example, say a security operations employee is faced with four events to research and mitigate. In the absence of a GRC program, the staffer would have no context about the business risk or compliance impact of the events, which could lead them to prioritize the least important issue (refer to 7.18).

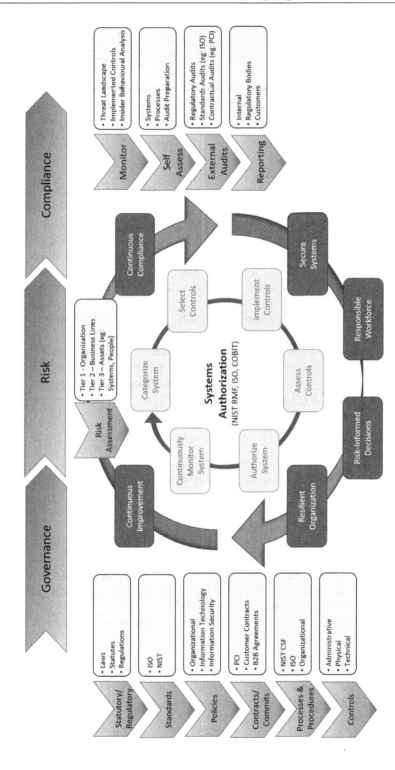

FIGURE 7.18   GRC has a symbiotic relationship.

The breadth and depth of a GRC program vary with each organization. Regardless of its simplicity or complexity, there are opportunities to transform or scale that program for the adoption of cloud services, emerging technologies, and other future innovations.

Here is a checklist of best practices to help GRC efforts. The key takeaways of the checklist are base governance on objectives and capabilities, include risk context in decision-making, and automate monitoring and response.

1. Governance

- Identify the requirements for compliance.
- Identify applicable legal or regulatory frameworks (such as HIPAA or PCI) and other contractual obligations.
- Identify restrictions/limitations if any to emerging technologies or cloud technologies.
- Identify other frameworks or standards that the management has chosen to adopt (e.g., NIST, ISO, COBIT, CSA, CIS).
- Conduct program assessment based on industry best practices or global standards.
- Determine the desired maturity for the GRC program.
- Identify gaps in resources to be candidate for resource allocation.
- If organization uses cloud services, then it shall draft and publish a cloud strategy that will cover procurement, security, and business continuity.
- Publish policies, processes, and procedures based on objectives and desired capabilities that align business.
- Allocate roles and responsibilities and their functions.

2. Risk

- Conduct an organization-wide risk assessment (e.g., market, financial, reputation, legal).
- Review and update a risk assessment for every business line (market, products, and services, financial markets).
- Update the risk process for each category of assets. It is advisable to use threat models since they will simplify the risk assessment process at all stages.
- Update/revise risk plans to mitigate, avoid, transfer, or accept risk at each tier, business line, and asset (e.g., a business continuity plan, a continuity of operations plan, a systems security plan).
- Implement risk plans for specific areas such as supply chain management and insider threat modeling.
- Deploy risk frameworks such as NIST and ISO 31000 to authorize systems and do the monitoring.
- Select suitable security framework to select controls and implement them.
- Adopt a risk-based approach to decision-making. Link system risk to organizational risks faced by business.

- Implement risk-monitoring and status reporting systems to check on risks.
- Identify different levels and classes of risk and factor them in strategic decision-making process.

3.   Compliance

- Monitor compliance with policy, standards, and security controls.
- Where possible automate the monitoring and reporting function for greater efficiency.
- Enforce manual monitoring of non-technical controls such as examination of physical security logs.
- Link compliance monitoring with security information and event management (SIEM) and other tools.
- Perform continuous self-assessment and do security testing and vulnerability scans.
- Responsiveness to events and changes to the risk environment.
- Integrate security operations with the compliance team for proactive management.
- Establish standard operating procedures (SOPs) to standardize processes and guard against unauthorized modification of controls or processes.
- Set reporting thresholds for incidents and a reporting framework for root cause analysis (RCA) for incidents.

In this chapter, we have seen different models adopted across the world from whom organizations may get hint to build their own GRC model as per the nature of business, complexity of processes, applicable laws and regulations and level of people who are going to own the GRC model adopted by the organization. In the final section in the next chapter, we shall discuss the role of technology in building automated models to serve the compliance function.

Next Steps – Through Automation

8

It is easy to have a manual model for GRC with all controls and to work with checklists and audit procedures, set in advance. But in a constantly evolving legal and regulatory environment and dynamic nature of business, change is going to be a constant factor. Hence for managing change and proper governance process, automation is the ultimate step which ensures precision and effectiveness. Compliances applicable to business can be mapped through a baseline which will be associated with questionnaires and checklists related to compliance. If this workflow is automated, it will ease the compliance function, make monitoring more efficient and will save audit time and audit resource necessary to conduct compliance audits. This chapter discusses a model through flowcharts, Venn diagrams, etc., and builds a possible base in the form of dashboards for organizations to follow.

When we plan the GRC function, it is necessary to use a combination of policies, procedures, guidelines, and standards. Before we start planning, it will help to achieve clarity and differentiate between each part. Besides these, legal and regulatory and industry-specific regulatory provisions get added to the stack of our compliance needs.

1. **Policies:** They are formal high-level statements signed by the Board or the highest level of management portraying organization's intent on issue specific or system/security specific objectives. It represents a mandatory pressure on the entire organization to comply with the provisions set and serves as a guide in case of dispute.
2. **Procedures:** They are a description of the steps to be followed to comply with policies and standards. For instance, the Board will come up with the policy to implement security standards and the CISO will develop the procedures to implement a chosen standard like ISO 27001 and lay step-by-step procedures to be followed to achieve adoption, implementation, and maintenance of the standard.
3. **Guidelines:** They are a statement of industry best practices that are good to have, open to interpretation, and not mandatory unless a policy mandates the adoption of such policies.
4. **Standards:** They are setting rules and boundaries and actions to support policies and give directions for implementation.

It is essential to have an organization wide consensus on policies, procedures, and guidelines. To further complicate the compliance function, there are ever-increasing demands on business and increasing requirements from customers and clients including adoption of security standards. Finally, an effective compliance program has to be integrated along with business objectives keeping in mind the risk and compliance function to enable in-built controls to safeguard adherence to the adopted program objectives.

The dynamic nature of business, new domains, and changing environments require that risk evaluation be incorporated in every section of business, IT, operations, etc. There is a maze of disruptive technologies, cyber threats, complex business ecosystems, globalizing markets, and amplified regulatory scrutiny that makes organizations to be extra sensitive to security, governance, and overall compliance while keeping an eye on meeting stakeholder expectations.

Governance, risk management and compliance are three pillars that work together for the purpose of assuring that an organization can meet its objectives. Governance is the combination of processes established and executed by the board of directors of a company that are enabled through the organization's structure and how it is driven toward achieving the objectives. Risk management is a formal process of identifying, assessing, and managing risks that could hinder the organization from achieving its objectives. Compliance ensures that an organization has the processes and internal controls to meet the requirements imposed by governmental bodies, regulators, industry mandates, or internal policies.

The effectiveness of GRC function in ensuring organizations meet its stated objectives in a well-managed and compliant environment can be further enhanced by technology. Let us look at how technology is positively impacting the GRC function and making its contribution more relevant to the business.

1. **Use of specialized software applications:**
   There is an upward trend in automation of the GRC activities in companies using in-house or third-party GRC software applications. The primary purpose of GRC software is to automate work associated with the documentation and reporting of the risk management and compliance activities that are most closely associated with corporate governance and business objectives. The key functions organizations look for in a GRC software are audit management, policy management, compliance management, and risk management. It is an integrated platform solution to integrate multiple aspects of GRC seamlessly, to drive continuous improvement in the program, and also to provide top management real-time update on the compliance posture in the company.

2. **Link GRC with management strategy:**
   As organizations evaluate their current risk information and data needs, executives involved with GRC will find it valuable to work with their CIO and IT functions and consider the organization's information management strategy and capabilities as they make decisions to purchase, enhance, or build GRC support systems. These organizations might also find it beneficial for the GRC program

to actively participate in the overall IT governance process so their needs for risk information can be incorporated into the organization's information management strategy. GRC programs are now focusing on alignment of GRC activities with their strategic planning and goal-setting processes. Future risk applications using this technology can further enhance risk management when integrated with workflow process and business rule logic software. Business rules systems can be pre-programmed to seek out and capture emerging risk data within transaction execution systems.

3. **Using analytics for real-time and accurate GRC decision-making:**
   The supply chain has extended beyond organizational boundary and this makes GRC initiatives even more complex. Companies are leveraging technology driven data analytics for their GRC program to get real-time, relevant and cognitive information useful to make the business decision without diluting the GRC requirements within the operating model. Additionally, Big Data analytics technology is helping organizations to optimally allocate resources to most critical areas as per their GRC requirements.

4. **Integration of GRC requirements into business process automation:**
   Business process automation technologies like robotics and process-specific platforms have enabled organizations to capture, design and build some of their key GRC requirement into the process automation framework. This enables companies to better manage GRC objectives at the micro level, which lends itself well into the overall GRC framework at the organizational level. Multiple process automation vendors have come up who incorporate GRC into their design to enable organizations to meet their GRC obligations.

5. **Greater return on investment (ROI) for the business:**
   An organization's ability to incorporate changes into their GRC practices becomes very important for good governance and risk management. Investments in technology driven risk management and compliance practices have shown to provide improved returns for organization due to ease of scalability and flexibility. As technology has driven business and operating models, technology has also enabled GRC programs to absorb changes in environment and changes in the legal and regulatory landscape and adapt rapidly for keeping the organization well governed, compliant to requirements and proactive to business trends.

GRC is a set of processes and practices that run across departments and functions. While it is beneficiary to deploy a dedicated GRC platform and other tools, it is not compulsory. While organizations generally don't need to maintain a separate GRC department, most organizations have a team in place to manage the GRC platform and tools. GRC helps to avoid the ill effects of silos in the governance, assurance, and management of business attributes.

Many people think of a platform when referring to GRC. But GRC refers to a capability that helps an organization achieve its objectives, with responsibility running right across the organization. GRC domain includes assurance and performance management. In real practice GRC framework now extends to information security management, quality management, ethics and values management, and business continuity management.

Any requirement analysis for a good GRC solution or application can be initiated by first understanding business dimensions. Figure 8.1 brings out the different dimensions of business.

The tenets of business consist of a vision, mission, policies, procedures, an organization structure governed by management intent, people who make the organization achieve their objectives, stakeholders, vendors, and other third-party service providers who function as one enterprise. Business will also have IT and support functions such as finance, HR, administration, legal, marketing, procurement, and audit.

Business attributes include performance management, including goals, targets, outcomes, profitability, and SLAs. Types of risks include financial risk, credit risk, market risk, strategy risk, operational risk, fraud risk, reputational risk, information security risk, technology risk and compliance risk, etc. Compliance solutions have to cover regulatory compliance (SOX, PCI/DSS, GDPR), legal compliance (labor laws), organizational compliance (policies and standards), security (human, physical and information security), quality, ethics, and values.

Controls – to realize value from the business, resources should be utilized efficiently and effectively, and business attributes should optimize. This is only possible

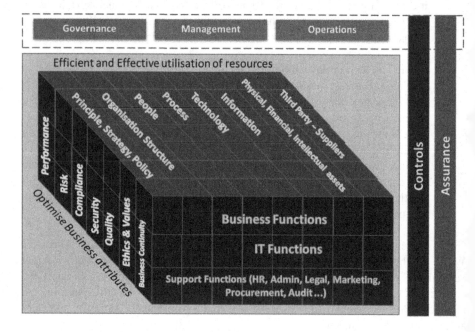

FIGURE 8.1 Mapping of business dimensions.

when appropriate controls are implemented and executed. The controls can be classified as management controls, process controls, technical controls, and physical controls. Controls apply to the resources as well as the attributes.

Assurance – independent assurance is required to ensure that controls are designed and operating effectively, and compliance requirements are met consistently. It is the responsibility of governance to monitor and obtain assurance. Assurance will be primarily through audits. There are several types of audits: Internal and external audits, certification audits, financial audits, IT audits, compliance audits, process audits and security audits, etc.

The scope of GRC solution should be based on defined structures and current trends. Figure 8.2 shows a basic GRC structure that covers governance, management, and assurance; and the GRC activities under each of these headings.

The GRC model revolves around the following features (refer to Figure 8.3).

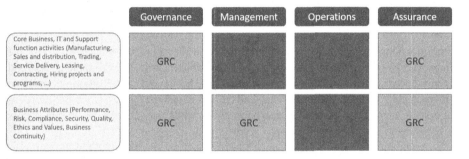

FIGURE 8.2   GRC function over management functions.

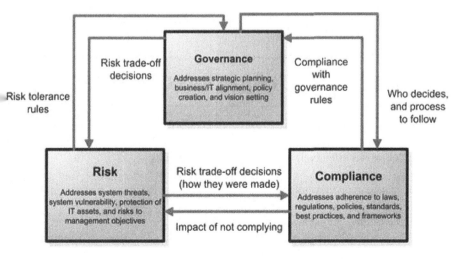

FIGURE 8.3   GRC model.

Organizations aim at reducing risk and improving controls and security profile of the organization. It also addresses organizational silos and redundancies. Compliance activities managed in silos often lead to the inevitable failure of an organization's GRC program.

Compliance today is more than checking boxes on regulatory to-do lists, more than finding and fixing problems. Compliance and governance are evolving from scattered silos to a strategic enterprise pillar. Oversight demands are changing the role of the compliance department to an active, independent program that can manage and monitor compliance risk. The breadth and depth of compliance risk bearing down on companies today requires a robust compliance program operating in the context of integrated enterprise risk management.

NEED FOR AN INTEGRATED GRC PLATFORM

Organizations face risks from many quarters, and they must be managed by business including, third-party risk. GRC solutions can enable organizations to manage risk and compliance. Disparate technologies, taxonomies, frameworks, and processes produce inconsistent conclusions on risk. This leads to stakeholder (executives, the Board, regulators, etc.) confusion on how to compare results when the aggregation of data occurs and results in manifold duplication of efforts.

An integrated GRC solution aims to provide friendly user-interface to store efficiently and seamlessly, mine, and extract risk data from risks various sources, whether those come from systems, external feeds, social media, customer interactions, regulatory changes, functional activities, or the back office. Organizations now prefer a holistic approach to GRC function to optimize the compliance with risks faced by the organization.

PROCESS OF INTEGRATING GRC FUNCTION

The integration of governance, risk, and compliance management initiatives into one combined approach is quite a challenge. However, a well-embedded integrated GRC platform that works effectively gives the following benefits:

1. A transparent view of the risk and control environment that affects the organization.
2. Streamlining of business processes.
3. A better awareness of risk and control environment and increased communication of risks at process and project levels.

4. Developing the ability to collect risk data from multiple sources and define common controls that help remove redundant efforts.
5. A focused approach, leading to risk reduction and containment in the cost of compliance.
6. Ease auditor's efforts by collating risk data in a comprehensible format easy to audit and analyze.
7. It leaves scope for process improvement on a continuous basis and enhanced compliance in all respects.

To benefit from the integration, it is recommended that an organization starts with the development of a GRC strategy including the financial and non-financial (e.g., culture) justification of the investments needed to embed and sustain the program (refer to Figure 8.4). Internal Audit, Risk Management and Compliance departments must work closely together and to agree on whether an existing framework should be used, such as COSO or ISO, or an adaptation given the maturity of the organization's risk management practices. Consensus also must be reached on the risk definitions, library of terms, governance model, as well as the GRC platform to enable the GRC strategy.

Key concerns to be addressed-

i. What should be the methodology to integrate risk management functions related to information technology risks, third-party risks, etc. into the corporate framework?

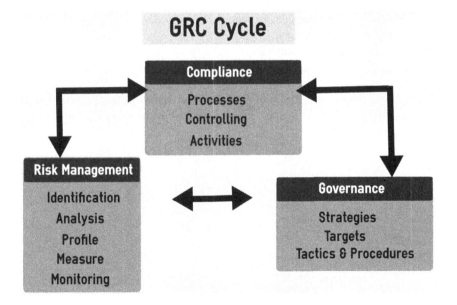

FIGURE 8.4 GRC cycle.

ii. What is the existing business model and ways to procure information and how they relate to the risk and control environment?

iii. Whether the process of GRC transformation can be speeded so as to achieve transparent monitoring of the risk and control segments and be able to ease the decision-making process.

iv. Facilitate the testing of common control together to give one result and avoid duplication.

v. How much costs are involved in rolling out a GRC solution and whether it is possible to achieve savings in cost by eliminating redundancies.

vi. Finally, are all efforts concentrated on integrating different GRC tools into an integrated platform?

WORKING ON A GRC STRATEGY FOR TRANSFORMATION

Many organizations have the misconception that the role of legal and regulatory obligations only rests with the compliance department. ISO 19600 clearly defines that compliance is more expansive and obligations should be included in the standard operating procedures. Key areas to focus on include:

- Compliance with management policies and procedures
- Compliance with contracts
- Legal and regulatory compliance
- Compliance with people policies

GRC compliance is a combination of processes that work together to ensure that an organization meets its objectives. Governance describes the oversight role where the

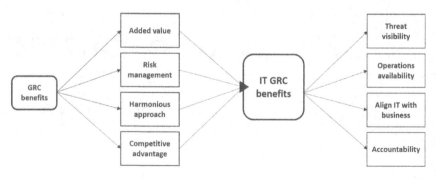

FIGURE 8.5   Benefits from GRC and IT-governed GRC.

senior executives plan, direct and control the whole organization. Risk management helps organizations to identify and evaluate all business and regulatory risks and put in measures to mitigate them effectively. Risks must be managed and treated if organization desires to stay in business. Compliance on the other hand refers to the state of conforming to the requirements. It ensures that an organization puts in place internal controls and processes to meet the stated requirements imposed by various regulatory bodies or internal policies. GRC therefore emphasizes on the ability to achieve the goals of an organization while addressing all uncertainties and working with integrity.

GRC compliance makes a robust environment and leads to an improvement in internal processes. Some of these are listed here:

- It gives comprehensiveness of understanding as far as roles and responsibilities between the management and the persons executing GRC controls.
- Adopting a GRC strategy gives a structure to its activities and helps meet necessary legal and regulatory requirements.
- A proper GRC strategy facilitates proper risk treatment and mitigation and hence reduces losses and enforces proper compliance. Organizations can then make GRC function sustainable on a continuous basis and at an optimal cost.
- Integrating CRC reduces redundant activities, identifies common controls that ease out on testing and save on audit time and resources. Thus, an overlap of tasks and wastage of resources in the organization can be brought under control.

GOOD TO KEEP A SUGGESTION BOX

Sometimes the best suggestions come out of collaboration. It is good practice to have a suggestion box where employees can give their ideas and suggestions. It also gives staff a good feeling on being heard and some of their suggestions in respect of important issues and safety are implemented.

COMMONALITY OF PURPOSE IS IMPORTANT

Making a GRC strategy for the organization where all the elements and people work harmoniously to achieve the goals of governance risk and compliance is very important. Adopting a unified approach brings in a lot of additional benefits to the organization. Compliance personnel have the responsibility to assist management in formulating a good plan that connects management with business to achieve desired results.

Benefits that accrue out of good coordination among personnel include:

i. Goodwill for the organization on account of proper risk management techniques adopted by the organization and leading to brand protection.
ii. Improved processes build customer confidence resulting in more customers and retention of existing customers.
iii. Improved asset management, including monitoring, protection and accounting.
iv. A well informed and educated workforce who understand the concepts of risk and compliance.
v. Enhanced management information systems and effective decision-making on the part of the management.
vi. Revenue enhancement through cost containment.

CREATING A STRATEGIC GRC PLAN

A GRC strategy (GRC) is vital for every company whether big or small. GRC entails ensuring that a company develops a culture of practicing sound governance, managing risks, and complying with regulations. It is also concerned with whether the company effectively communicates its ethics, procedures, and policies to its employees. A company that implements GRC principles should also ensure that its values are known within and without the business and that compliance has a positive impact on its performance, objectives, and strategies.

As a result, the company can have a more receptive board of directors that help its employees think critically and strategically and have oversight on the IT strategy and IT governance. GRC strategy enhances security and safety in the company as well as provides checks and balances necessary for monitoring and coordinating the company's projects to ensure that they are running smoothly. A risk-based approach to GRC minimizes conflicts and disagreements. With all these benefits, it is important to know how you can create a cohesive and productive GRC plan. Here are the simple steps to follow:

1. Study processes identify the different problems, research widely and acquire as much knowledge about GRC requirements and technology. Also evaluate and classify the number of methodologies, processes, frameworks and technologies used in managing risks and enabling compliance throughout the business operations. This is a good starting point in initiating a GRC strategy.
2. Identify the GRC objectives, start by setting goals and formulate a mission and vision statement for the GRC strategy that you intend to implement. A program to structure GRC strategy should include centralized or intentional

but unplanned cooperation. The structure will influence the systematic use of technology.

3. Once the GRC plan is formulated, then a draft of a short-term plan can be made. Indicators of success factors for GRC should be defined. Factors to determine GRC success can be pre-defined.

4. Carry out a thorough risk assessment exercise, conduct a comprehensive risk analysis for your organization and use the findings to understand, control and monitor the risks better.

5. Create a comprehensive and a practical action plan: use the short-term plan as a guiding factor for meeting long term plan of the organization. The final action plan should incorporate all the parts for an effective GRC plan for the long-term implementation in the organization.

GRC is more than a software platform or a set of tools. In fact, GRC is effectively a broad framework that helps with decision-making processes, emergency preparedness, and collaboration across all segments of a business. Any organization, regardless of industry or size, can benefit from a GRC strategy. It will help you optimize performance, stay up to date with all compliance requirements, and be proactive in preventing and addressing all threats to your organization.

To illustrate suppose the organization has a retail business in pharma. Their GRC strategy must provide for secure collection of data, appropriate use of data and meeting other compliance criteria such as HIPAA.

FEATURES OF GRC PLATFORMS

The GRC platforms having mention in the Gartner Magic Quadrant have supported a lot of GRC use cases to align GRC efforts with business functions and risk analysis. Most GRC platforms employ some combination of features in the following areas to accomplish these goals:

- Risk management
- Documentation of controls
- Policy management
- Audit management
- IT risks and risk scoring
- Third-party risk management
- Workflow analysis
- Dashboards and reports
- Customized integration of GRC functions
- Ease for end users to use

CRITERIA FOR CHOICE OF GRC APPLICATION

There are a few factors to be considered in making the right choice of GRC software.

1. It Should Be User-Friendly

A GRC platform should be easy to use. It is better to take a demo and opt for a few days of trial before contemplating to acquire the software. Understanding of all features is essential.

2. Support Mobile Devices

The GRC platform must support mobile devices so that you have a comfort level even when you are moving.

3. Support Cloud Application

SaaS (Software as a Service) products are more popular nowadays. SaaS solutions are more cost-effective, easier to implement, and much more flexible to operate along with the business. Additionally, the SaaS GRC vendor will maintain the GRC platform and make the customer free to focus on bigger priorities.

4. Security

The GRC platform should include security features such as encryption, user access controls, and firewall security. This will lead to prevention of breaches and exposure.

5. Cost

Budget is a major consideration when implementing any kind of technology. The ROI of a GRC platform is a little difficult to calculate. But if we could list out damages if a proper GRC solution is not implemented, it would justify investment in the GRC software.

6. Vendor Support

Getting constant support from vendor on all difficulties in the use of the GRC product is also one of the criteria in the selection of the GRC software. Vendor should provide good documentation and troubleshooting capabilities, and these points prove useful when evaluating a platform's customer support capabilities.

7. Automation

Automation is a norm in today's business world; any technology solution that your business adopts must be able to keep up. A GRC with automation capabilities will be able to send you alerts the second a vulnerability is identified so that the team can jump into action. It can also perform data validation and auditing operations in the background. If manual processes can be eliminated or reduced, information that is supplied from the GRC would be more reliable and freer from human error.

IDENTIFYING A BUSINESS-READY GRC SOLUTION

Although there are several off-the-shelf solutions available for GRC, as per the nature of business, the nature of risks related to that business, the legal and regulatory norms to be complied by the business, and the various audits to be faced by the organization, the GRC application has to be built/molded and adjusted to serve organizational purpose.

Since high-functionality solutions are costly and involve a lot of adjustments to implement, organizations prefer to invest in a base code environment, where they can essentially build their GRC solution within. But GRC requirements are evolving at a rapid pace. Most of the custom-built applications lack the scalability and speed of operation. There is a definitive disconnect between GRC tools and teams. This is caused by the first line of defense, and traditional GRC professionals; both second-line risk and compliance managers as well as audit professionals. This functional barrier in communication exists from the line of business users (bottom-up), as well as reporting to leadership (top-down) for business insights, into the organization's risk posture and performance over time.

MIS REPORTING

One of the important aspects of GRC strategy is data exchange and collaboration. But reporting timely and meaningful insights to leadership is also an essential function for GRC solutions. Template reporting and dynamic dashboards should deliver a meaningful narrative. GRC solutions should provide a baseline KRI and KPI metrics to gauge performance on what matters most based on role or business function.

Defining relevant metrics and collection of context-relevant data from all teams to translate risk into different types and streamlining the reporting system add value to business. Once GRC strategy is in place, implementation can be started. A step-by-step implementation is preferred than a 'big bang' approach. Also defining adequate channels of communication to relate the progress of GRC implementation to interested stakeholders (e.g., executives, audit and risk committees, the business, regulators) provides confidence that capital and time investments are meeting their goals.

The main aim of the GRC software and tools is to manage IT-related operations that need meeting compliance and risk standards. As organizations expand operations and business relationships (e.g., vendors, supply chain, consultants, and staffing), their risk profile grows exponentially. Compliance activities managed in silos often lead to the inevitable failure of an organization's GRC program.

Let us view some of the GRC software available to enterprises.

1. LogicManager

This software has manifold applications across financial services, government, education, healthcare, retail, and IT sectors. It speeds the process of aggregating and mining data, building reports, and managing files. Its features include:

- Enterprise risk management
- IT governance and security
- Compliance management
- Third-party risk management
- Audit management
- Incident management
- Policy management
- Business continuity planning
- Financial reporting compliance

LogicManager has user-friendly features and was named as a challenger in Gartner Magic Quadrant 2020. Forrester has also termed it as a leader under GRC solutions in Q1 2020.

2. SAP's GRC Offering

For large enterprises, SAP's GRC offering is a robust suite of tools that provide real-time visibility and control over business risks and opportunities. These modules include:

- Process control
- Audit management
- Business integrity screening
- Regulation management
- Enterprise threat detection
- Privacy governance and management
- Global trade management
- S/4HANA implementation

SAP's in-memory data access provides big data and predictive analysis capabilities linked to risk management. The bottleneck here is that implementation can take longer time but it can support larger volumes for integration and for customizing. SAP was not recognized in Gartner's 2020 Magic Quadrant for IT risk management, but Forrester did name it a Contender in its Q1 2020 GRC Wave. Additionally, SAP was given the number two spot in the 2020 GRC Emotional Footprint Awards by Software Reviews for delivering outstanding customer service.

3. MetricStream GRC Platform

This platform is best for organizations that have unique requirements for different sets of users, including auditors, IT managers, and business executives. Its features include:

- Enterprise and operational risk management
- Business continuity management
- Policy and compliance management
- Regulatory engagement and change management
- Case and survey management
- Internal audit management
- IT threat and vulnerability management
- Third-party management

MetricStream's GRC platform is centered on three principles risk, stakeholder engagement and agility. Risk is unavoidable but agility and resilience can be powerful antidotes. Both stem from an integrated and forward-looking approach to risk management where all the lines of defense work together to predict, detect, and respond to risks. Better visibility into emerging and evolving risks, as well as risk interconnectedness and trends – all of which help stakeholders make faster, more risk-aware decisions.

Gartner named MetricStream a Leader in its 2020 Magic Quadrant for IT risk management, and Forrester named it a Strong Performer in its Q1 2020 GRC Wave. MetricStream has its focus is on risk and control assessments, risk analytics, compliance tracking, and cybersecurity risk management, is offered via SaaS or as a privately hosted, hybrid or on-premises solution. Its operations are geographically diversified, representing clients in the financial services, healthcare and manufacturing verticals.

Some salient features of the GRC solution include:

- **Market understanding:** MetricStream stands out in the market for its vision to include risk owners from different parts of the organization to voluntarily submit anomalies and observations to be considered for risk assessment or incident analysis. This evidences maturity in understanding the state of ITRM buyers and their challenges in staying on top of all exposures or material information that informs risk decision-making. In sync with some of its competition, the product offers dedicated landing pages for business users and senior management.

- **Use of innovation automation and analytics in the effort to improve** the usability, reliability and security of the platform, while enhancing features within existing use cases. Risk analysis, advanced integrations, digital asset discovery and near-real-time assessments exceed customer expectations.
- **Good feedback on deployment of MetricStream GRC solution:** Customers have indicated reasonable customer satisfaction in previous years. MetricStream has aligned deployment teams geographically with customers, and invested in customer success teams and readiness and maturity methodology to address customer success criteria. It is recommended to confirm output, deliverables and success criteria of implementation services before contract negotiation and deployment.
- **Wide geographic presence and they work** through a robust partner network. However, buyers implementing ITRM in multiple geographies, particularly in EMEA, should confirm a local presence or the availability of local partners.

4. ServiceNow

ServiceNow, as the name implies, provides exactly the insight that organizations need *now*. It uses sophisticated monitoring, automation, and analysis tools to identify risks in real time so you can respond to them as efficiently as possible. Features include:

1. **Policy and compliance management** giving monitoring on actual basis.
2. **Risk management** to do gap analysis, identify risk, and plan mitigation measures.
3. **Business continuity management**. It assists in business impact analysis and to identify and prioritize critical business services to produce recovery time objectives (RTO) and recovery point objectives (RPO).
4. **Vendor risk management**. It helps to institute a standardized and transparent process to manage the lifecycle for risks assessments, due diligence, and risk response with business partners and vendors Idea is to identify risks in real-time.
5. **Operational risk management** and resilience against operational risks.
6. **Continuous authorization and monitoring**. All activities must have the appropriate level of authorization.
7. **Regulatory change** to take care of fine-tuning controls in line with regulatory changes.
8. **Audit management**. Scope and prioritize audit engagements using risk data and profile information to eliminate recurring audit findings, enhance audit assurance, and optimize resources around internal audits.
9. **Performance analytics.** Implementing real-time monitoring ServiceNow, GRC identifies noncompliant controls, monitors high-risk areas, and

manages the key risk indicator (KRI) and key performance indicator (KPI) library with automated data validation and evidence gathering. To complement existing GRC capabilities, we provide out-of-the-box integration with performance analytics (PA) for GRC, which uses PA indicators and thresholds as another means to detect failing critical controls between assessments.

10. **Predictive intelligence** and predictive analysis use historical data to predict future events. Historical data is used to predict future trends. Organizations can use this feature to take necessary steps for achieving optimal outcomes.

ServiceNow simplifies workflow management and tracking for collaboration with internal and external teams and serves as a valuable project management tool in many cases. Its reporting tools leave something to be desired and could use improvement with its data visualization, but overall, it is regarded as a powerful force in the GRC arena. As such, Gartner named it a Leader in its 2020 Magic Quadrant for IT risk management, and Forrester named it a Leader in its Q1 2020 GRC Wave.

ServiceNow GRC helps transform inefficient processes across the extended enterprise into an integrated risk program. Through continuous monitoring and automation, ServiceNow delivers a real-time view of compliance and risk, improves decision-making, and increases performance across your organization and with vendors.

5. The Cura Software GRC Management Platform

Due to increasing demands on GRC compliance, and multiple areas of overlap of GRC domain, a coordinated approach can help an organization maximize results while reducing overall costs. To help its customers institute this coordinated approach, Cura Software developed a powerful and flexible GRC platform that serves as the foundation for a strong GRC management program.

A combination of workflow, surveys, forms, reporting and a whole lot more, the Cura GRC Platform is the underlying technology behind all of Cura's leading GRC management software applications. Because Cura's applications are built on a single platform, they can easily be integrated together to create an enterprise-wide GRC system.

The Cura GRC Platform is installed in hundreds of organizations around the world. Specific benefits include:

- **Manage risk and compliance programs within one flexible, configurable solution:** The Cura GRC Platform is completely configurable to support every organization's unique risk and compliance requirements. It provides the ability to configure custom workflows, calculations, multiple methodologies, a limitless hierarchy, and executive dashboards/reports that match how an organization wants to manage its GRC initiatives.
- **Unite silos of GRC information into a single coordinated system**: The Cura GRC Platform enables organizations to improve insight and oversight of the issues and exposures of the business at a strategic level. All GRC

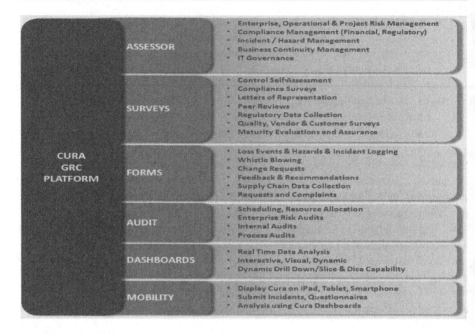

FIGURE 8.6   Cura GRC Platform.

information is represented in a common, normalized scaling, rating and scoring mechanism. Actions, trends and treatment strategies that affect or 'creep' across multiple business disciplines and areas can be identified and treated.

- **Gain better insight into the state of business operations**: While providing a high level of clarity through convergence, the Cura GRC Platform enables each department to track GRC information in their own unique workflows, data parameters, calculations, metrics and libraries. This allows employees and managers to retain responsibility and independence in their business areas, while preserving the bigger picture for executives.

- **Create a single system for all GRC information**: The Cura GRC Platform captures 100 percent of an organization's key GRC data. Cura's dynamic data model easily allows for the addition of data elements an organization needs to capture (processes, risks, controls, tests, incidents, KPIs, etc.), inclusive of associated properties.

- **Improve GRC efficiency while enforcing corporate policies**: Simple-to-use notification-driven web interfaces make Cura applications extremely easy to learn and use. Cura solutions streamline the identification, assessment, review and treatment processes.

- **Enhance decision-making through superior reporting and analysis:** Cura's best-in-class reporting system allows your business users to easily analyze the information captured. Cura applications are delivered with standard report templates for the most common reporting scenarios. Additionally, customers can quickly modify or create new reports and dashboards to support the decisions that improve productivity and performance.

- **Facilitate integration with other enterprise systems**: The Cura GRC Platform is built on a web-based architecture built around web services. It also includes adapters for LDAP, Windows Authentication and other enterprise applications to make authentication management simple. Cura's GRC Platform features powerful dashboard and reporting capabilities that streamline the information-sharing process by removing the time-intensive and error-prone process of manually creating reports.
- Each Cura GRC solution allows users to launch a rich set of reports and executive dashboards directly from their Cura home page within their web browser. Reports range from simple list/table reports to sophisticated interactive dashboards that update live as users change parameters using simple controls. Drill-down functionality enables users to click on problem areas to be automatically redirected to the specific data/issue in question.
- Cura provides both out-of-the-box reports and dashboards, and provides the capability to create custom reports as needed. All Cura reports can be exported to multiple formats (including PDF, Rich Text, Microsoft Word and Microsoft Excel) so information can be shared with individuals that do not have access to the system.

6. OneTrust

OneTrust GRC and Data Guidance products focus on cybersecurity, risk management, and risk intelligence, and they are delivered via multitenant, dedicated SaaS, private cloud and on- premises implementations. Its operations are geographically diversified, representing clients in multiple industries, including government, healthcare, technology, and media.

OneTrust has the following strengths:

i. **Extensive Information Mapping:** OneTrust's primary differentiator in the market is the knowledge capital, product design, and experience the team brings on information-mapping capabilities. Identifying, classifying, and mapping information to policy, stakeholder needs or regulatory obligations is among 'prework' activities for a successful ITRM implementation focused on information risk.

ii. **Risk Assessment Automation:** OneTrust GRC is also differentiated in triggering risk assessment workflows by pre-flagging conditions in risk surveys. There is visibility into the side-by-side scoring of risk values for risk owners and risk and compliance teams aimed at reducing disagreements over risk treatment. Assets are onboarded to recognize their association with processes, initiatives and related assets, such that buyers can prioritize risk according to business importance as opposed to subjective asset importance.

Customer references report privacy compliance as a primary driver for leveraging OneTrust to integrate GRC, privacy and third-party management initiatives in one place. At the time of writing this report, Gartner did not observe non-privacy-compliance-linked ITRM implementations in the market. ITRM buyers seeking a solution for the risk management team should evaluate through a proof of concept. Customers leveraging ITRM capabilities report above-average satisfaction, and recognize attractive pricing, agility and customer support.

SPEED OF DIGITAL TRANSFORMATION

As organizations have become increasingly digitized, interconnectivity between systems and teams is essential. The rate at which an application can process data is what matters most, once the data is collected. Leveraging static assessment technology will no longer suffice as organizations move toward solutions to support adaptive risk decision-making. By leveraging the standardization of some out-of-the-box functionality, businesses can increase time to value and operationalize teams in record time to track, monitor, and analyze risk scenarios.

Digital technologies have raised customer expectations for responsive, seamless online services and information-enriched products. Many companies are struggling to meet those expectations and will continue to struggle unless they embrace enterprise architecture. We define *enterprise architecture* as the holistic design of people, processes, and technology to execute digitally inspired strategic goals. Every negative customer interaction via a company app, website, telephone call, or service provider exposes one's architectural inadequacies. Left unresolved, these issues will destroy formerly great organizations.

Many businesses are designed around product verticals. Those verticals optimize profits and define a customer experience for that specific product independently of the rest of the organization. The digital economy, however, rewards integrated solutions, which require that people work across product lines. To meet these demands, companies must rethink how work gets done and how that work relies on people, processes, and technology.

THREE PRINCIPLES FOR ORGANIZATIONAL REDESIGN

Enterprise architecture provides a road map for organizational redesign. Adopting three enterprise architecture principles – breaking key outcomes into components with designated accountability, empowering cross-functional teams, and allowing business design to influence strategy – can help initiate the function of redesigning architecture.

Principle 1: Breaking of enterprise processes and products into components. Enterprise architecture involves componentizing a company's key outcomes – products, customer experiences, and core enterprise processes – and assigning clear accountability for each component. Organizations steer their architecture by optimizing the people–process–technology in a way that facilitates both operational excellence and adaptability to change. Componentization helps organizations use data more effectively and respond to business opportunities faster. Organizations will stage the development of new components when they know for certain it is clear that they will create value.

Principle 2: Enterprise architecture is operated through cross-functional teams. Employees must be empowered with responsibility for the processes and technology within each component.

The leadership task becomes one of formulating teams and then coaching team members to help clarify their missions, establish meaningful metrics, and design experiments to test innovations. Team members need to understand the component's process and technology requirements, so most teams will need product experts, software developers, and user design specialists.

Principle 3: Enterprise architecture influences strategy. Employee teams respond to customer demands and try to meet these demands through identification of new opportunities guided by digital technologies. As component teams address strategic objectives, they simultaneously reformulate strategy based on continuous learning about what customers want and what digital technologies make possible.

In this context, strategy becomes both a top-down and bottom-up exercise. Leaders create new teams (or pivot existing teams) to seize emerging opportunities. Meanwhile, component teams can restate goals aimed at implementing high-level strategy.

DATA ANALYTICS

In view of various financial crimes becoming more and more common, enterprises are building their compliance programs based on data analytics. A recent survey has found that approximately 47% of the enterprises leverage data analytics and other technology processes to conduct root cause and trend analysis, with 51% of CCOs ranking improving data quality for risk data aggregation and risk reporting as a top compliance objective.

COMPLIANCE ANALYTICS TECHNIQUES

As defined by Deloitte, compliance analytics is a category of information analysis; it involves gathering and storing relevant data and mining it for patterns, discrepancies, and anomalies.

It enables companies to better detect and head off potentially attempts by employees, third parties, or even criminals either to steal or achieve other nefarious objectives. Compliance analytics help companies proactively identify issues, take corrective action, and self-report to regulators on a timely basis. 'That has led more companies to proactively detect noncompliance and fraud, rather than waiting to fall victim to it. It's better if you find an issue, take action, and tell regulators if required, rather than them finding it,' he explains. In compliance analytics, which is part of the larger discipline of enterprise fraud and misuse management (EFM), some of the most frequently used advanced analytics techniques include:

- Rules-based monitoring to identify known fraud and compliance risks
- Anomaly detection to recognize potential new fraud and compliance risks
- Network analysis to identify potentially worrisome collusive activity across entities
- Text analytics to mine and sense written documents for insights
- Visual analytics/dashboards to summarize actionable results for stakeholders.

These techniques can be applied to data captured and stored in an organization's systems, and can process enormous volumes of structured numerical data related to organizational processes and transactions. They can also integrate structured data with other sources of information, including unstructured data that is typically difficult to analyze in bulk. To determine how effective the enterprise's compliance analytics program is, the following questions must be considered:

1. Does the enterprise have a scalable technology to analyze different types of data?
2. What are the types of activities and processes and the roles and responsibilities of the people working in the enterprise?
3. Does the enterprise have structured data or unstructured data, and what are the capabilities of its applications?
4. What is the capacity of the enterprise to process a large volume of transactions?
5. Are there any manual processes to complete tasks?
6. Are there any inadequacies faced in the system or processes?
7. What are the risks involved around the pain areas identified?
8. Does identification of high-risk areas mark the beginning of the enterprise compliance analytics road map to monitor the system and highlight areas of improvement?

Areas where compliance analytics is commonly used:

1. Banks, where there is high risk of money laundering and that are under constant scrutiny of regulators. Analytics help to identify potential risks and respond in a timely manner.

2. Compliance analytics bring value to enterprise risk management by performing transaction monitoring, reviews of customer due diligence, risk indicators, and dashboarding for monitoring.

3. Monitor payment flows to identify countries of origin and destination and institutions initializing such payments.

4. Perform a trend analysis to identify unusual trends over a range of transactions.

In the type of business environment emerging, the use of compliance analytics is going to be more common and useful, especially to the banking and financial sector. It helps organizations that are already struggling with the management of Big Data.

ISO 19600 – A CERTIFICATION FOR GRC

ISO 19600:2014 is based on the principles of good governance, transparency and sustainability, providing guidance for establishing, developing, implementing, evaluating, maintaining, and improving an effective and responsive compliance management system (CMS) within an organization. Although organizations find that their compliance costs are increasing, the effectiveness of the compliance management systems is declining. ISO 19600 brings the discipline of ISO standards and improvises the compliance function.

The different areas covered under the standard are:

- Understanding the scope and context of the compliance management system.
- Examining the role of leadership in compliance.
- Understanding the origin and nature of compliance obligations.
- Using compliance as a tool for mitigating risk.
- Understanding how to meet compliance objectives
- The use of awareness training to embed a strong compliance culture.
- Understanding how to develop effective communication and supporting documentation
- Attributing ownership through management controls of the compliant management system.
- Aiming at continuous improvement of the compliance program.

The structure of ISO 19600 also follows a similar structure to other ISO standards (refer to Figure 8.7).

As seen in Figure 8.8, scoping of compliant system is the commencement of an enterprise's compliance system. Having a compliance policy in place based on good governance principles and the internal/external issues, as well as requirements of stakeholders, is essential for developing a good compliance system. Implementing a

High Level Structure for ISO management system standards		ISO 19600
Clause 4	Context of the organization	• Understanding the organization and its context • Understanding the needs and expectations of interested parties • Principles of good governance • Compliance obligations • Assessment of compliance risks
Clause 5	Leadership	• Leadership and commitment • Establishing the organization's compliance policy • Defining the organizational roles, responsibilities and authorities (including the governing body, top management, employees and compliance officer)
Clause 6	Planning	• Planning of actions to address risks related to compliance • Establishing the compliance objectives
Clause 7	Support	• Determining and providing the necessary resources for the operation of a compliance management system • Competence & training • Awareness (behavior of top management & compliance culture) • Communication (both internal and external) & documentation
Clause 8	Operation	• Operational planning and control • Establishing controls and procedures
Clause 9	Performance evaluation	• Monitoring of compliance • Analysis of information and reporting of results • Internal Audit and Management Review
Clause 10	Improvement	• Actions on noncompliances and nonconformities (including escalation) • Corrective actions • Continual improvement

FIGURE 8.7   Structure of the ISO 19600 standard.

compliance system includes identification of compliance risks and operational planning and control. Performance appraisals, reporting and maintaining the CMS by continuous improvement is the full cycle of development. Implementation, and maintenance of a sustainable CMS which is measurable and can be evaluated against performance or non-performance is important.

But adhering to compliance-related requirements can be difficult due to many diverse laws/regulations, rules, and standards that organizations are subject to on national, international, and industry-wide levels; and failure to comply with some of these matters can result in fiscal, legal, or even criminal penalties. Compliance is a continuous process in an organization and not just a one-time project. ISO 19600 helps organizations address legislative requirements, industry codes, and organizational standards, as well as standards of good corporate governance, best practices, ethics, and community expectations; it offers the opportunity for the establishment

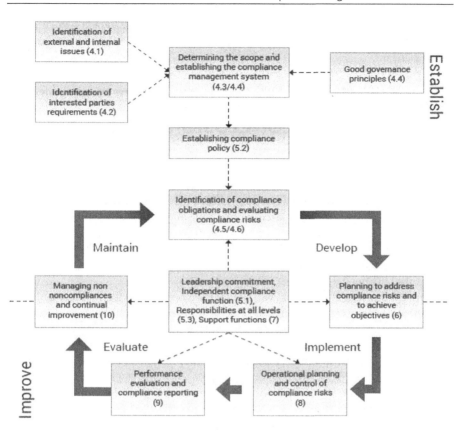

FIGURE 8.8 Implementing ISO 19600.

of a successful and sustainable organization. At the same time, it also emphasizes on leadership and a promotion of a culture of integrity and compliance. It recommends to management to inculcate the core principles of the standard into the core processes of the organization.

GOVERNANCE RISK AND COMPLIANCE CERTIFICATION

In the current landscape of GRC, it has become inevitable that organizations should implement control infrastructure suited to their business, for ease of administration. Obtaining certification in GRC standards is definitely a positive move toward formalizing the compliance process and implementing standard processes that will support the compliance management system within the organization. Certification in GRC is a way to prove that organizations are competent in one or more of the subject areas specified by the standard.

CONCLUSION

In this chapter, we have dealt with the technological transformation of the GRC function – factors that positively impact the GRC function and contribute toward the compliance initiatives of the organization. We saw how GRC can be linked to management strategy and how digital analytics can be used for real-time and accurate decision-making. We have seen how GRC requirements can be interwoven into business process automation and enable to capture, design, and build some GRC requirements into the process automation framework. We also saw the overlap of GRC over management functions. We studied the GRC model and its various components.

Finally, throughout this book, we have stressed on the need for an integrated GRC model that can take organizations out of silos to interact proactively, to build a common compliance structure. There is need to use technology to work across multifarious platforms and extract relevant data for a common purpose and at the same time remove redundancies. We saw different ways in which integration can be made possible and the benefits of integration. We noted the constituents of a strategic GRC plan and the features of GRC platforms. We discussed the criteria for choosing appropriate GRC solution for your enterprise.

We also delved on the option of identifying a business-ready GRC solution; in this context, we discussed some of the off-the-shelf GRC solutions provided by MetricStream, CURA, SAP, OneTrust, etc. Digital transformation is made possible at a rapid pace, and organizations can move toward redesign of their infrastructure/ processes to accommodate the change. With the pressure of different risks and compliances and the Big Data playing a significant role in GRC compliance, compliance analytics is emerging to facilitate GRC endeavors.

Finally, certification for GRC brings discipline in the GRC function. ISO principles of Plan-Do-Check-Act divide confirming to the standard and moving toward a continuous improvement schedule for GRC.

(Please note that the different software listed here are taken from the public domain and are not proprietary to any organization. A number of case studies have been given in Annexure A to highlight the significance of GRC solution and how they benefited different businesses.)

Annexure A
Case Studies

CASE STUDY 1

A large technology company decided to streamline SOX compliance and bring the responsibility for assessment and remediation of controls back to process owners. This led to cost reduction by freeing dedicated resources and consultants. The decision to shift responsibility did not affect the SOX compliance. They expected to take a risk-based approach to rationalize the number of controls being tested and streamline their change management process. The company decided to implement a GRC solution to sustain SOX compliance at lower costs. In addition, their plan was to ensure that when SOX streamlining was completed, they would use the platform to target other compliance initiatives. Their initiative turned out to be successful.

CASE STUDY 2

ABC was a footwear company; they had to be compliant with ISO 9000 in order to qualify for sales to a large customer. After an initial appraisal it was discovered that they were in danger of missing the certification, creating a huge business risk for the company. The executive team decided to put a focused initiative around ISO 9000 compliance. They realized that to maintain compliance on an ongoing basis, the cross-functional teams across their global operations needed to work closely. Hence, they decided to use GRC software as an enabler for the initiative – the solution would ensure all relevant documentation across the company had change control and provide mechanisms for audits, tracking issues, identifying corrective actions, and remediation. Once implemented, they wanted to leverage the GRC solution for their SOX and operational risk management initiative.

CASE STUDY 3

A pharmaceutical company was growing fast and realized that the complexity of their operations would increase the risk of noncompliance with FDA cGMP regulations if they continued to use spreadsheets, paper, and email to manage the manufacturing process. They realized that a GRC solution would give them the ability to provide strict change control on SOP documents, track process deviations and non-conformance across the two plants. In addition, it would identify appropriate corrective actions through a cross-functional team, and ensure that suitable remediation would take place. Once the cGMP implementation was completed, the company wanted to extend the GRC solution to other aspects of their operations, including ensuring that they can systematically reduce their development risks and accelerate New Drug Application (NDA) approval cycles by enabling them to capture and track potential safety issues, assess risks, and implement corrective actions along with identifying potential quality issues by using trending and data analytics. In addition, they wanted to use the GRC solution for automating the pharmacovigilance processes to record, investigate, and report cases as per the adverse event reporting guidelines mandated by the FDA and other international regulatory bodies.

CASE STUDY 4

The board of a large semiconductor company directed the head of internal audit to identify risks in their current stock options program and ensure that there were adequate controls in place to prevent backdating. In addition, the board also wanted to ensure that the newly approved charter of ethics was not violated by any of the operations within the company. The head of internal audit decided to use GRC solution as the system of record to manage the two initiatives. He wanted to make sure that a systematic process was in place to perform risk assessment, as well as test and report on compliance with internal charter of ethics, recommend additional controls, and ensure that such controls were implemented. This is one more instance where GRC solution helped organizations to fulfill the compliance objectives.

CASE STUDY 5

A large manufacturer generated about 25% of their revenue from exports to Europe, Middle East, and Africa. In light of recent political events, increased global terrorism and USA Patriot Act of 2001, the company wanted to protect its brand and ensure that they have a repeatable process for OFAC compliance, so all export orders pass through restricted party screening and end-use screening. In addition, they were concerned about any unknown holes in their customer-facing processes across their global operations that potentially could violate the regulations. As a result, they decided to undertake a risk assessment initiative, identify issues, and then put an annual compliance assessment process in place. The scale and cross-functional scope of this global assessment process ruled out spreadsheets and email as the underlying framework. The company decided to use a GRC solution as the framework for their OFAC risk management and OFAC compliance initiatives.

Index

Printed in the United States
by Baker & Taylor Publisher Services